UNSOLVED MYSTERIES OF THE SEA

Unsolved Mysteries of the Sea

by

Lionel and Patricia Fanthorpe

A HOUNSLOW BOOK
A MEMBER OF THE DUNDURN GROUP
TORONTO

Editorial Director: Anthony Hawke
Copy-Editor: Jennifer Bergeron
Design: Bruna Brunelli, Brunelli Designs
Printer: Friesens

National Library of Canada Cataloguing in Publication Data

Fanthorpe, R. Lionel
    Unsolved mysteries of the sea / Lionel and Patricia Fanthorpe.

Includes bibliographical references.
ISBN 1-55002-498-1

1. Ocean — Popular works. 2. Seas — Popular works. 3. Underwater exploration — Popular works.
I. Fanthorpe, Patricia II. Title.

GC21.F35 2004   551.46   C2004-900458-1

1   2   3   4   5   08   07   06   05   04

We acknowledge the support of the **Canada Council for the Arts** and the **Ontario Arts Council** for our publishing program. We also acknowledge the financial support of the **Government of Canada** through the **Book Publishing Industry Development Program** and **The Association for the Export of Canadian Books**, and the **Government of Ontario** through the **Ontario Book Publishers Tax Credit** program, and the **Ontario Media Development Corporation's Ontario Book Initiative**.

Care has been taken to trace the ownership of copyright material used in this book. The author and the publisher welcome any information enabling them to rectify any references or credit in subsequent editions.
                    J. Kirk Howard, President

Printed and bound in Canada.⊕
Printed on recycled paper.

www.dundurn.com

Dundurn Press	Gazelle Book Services Limited	Dundurn Press
8 Market Street	White Cross Mills	2250 Military Road
Suite 200	Hightown, Lancaster, England	Tonawanda NY
Toronto, Ontario, Canada	LA1 4X5	U.S.A. 14150
M5E 1M6		

This book is dedicated to our friend Chris Roberts, an outstanding master craftsman, watchmaker, and jeweller, with many thanks for his kind help in allowing us to photograph his superb collection of artistic model ships.

Model of the Cutty Sark.

TABLE OF CONTENTS

FOREWORD

by Canon Stanley Mogford, MA

It has been said, "There are no stones in a street without a voice and no house without echoes." Such may or may not be true. If true at all, imaginative people long to capture some of those voices and those echoes. It's human to probe, not altogether out of sheer inquisitiveness, but from a need to get to a truth. How much poorer and less advanced this world of ours would be had we not been blessed with men and women who probed: Edison, Marconi, Jenner, Pasteur — and so many others. Their determination to know about something, not always without cost to themselves, transformed life for millions of us.

The authors of this book are well known for their probing and penetrating researches. Over the years they have presented us with much that is baffling and invited us to consider their interpretations and conclusions.

Lionel has done much of this interpretative work in the full glare of prime-time television with millions of viewers. His programs, including *Fortean T.V.* and *Talking Stones*, have extended over several series. In the first, he introduced us to the paranormal, with many differing aspects of psychic phenomena, and led us into the company of ghosts and hobgoblins and much that goes "bump in the night." In *Talking Stones* he concentrated, in the main, on inscriptions on gravestones, and resurrected for us those men and women long buried there. It became clear some people deserve never to be forgotten.

Lionel and Patricia together have pursued the same theme of search-and-interpret in a series of books. In one, they introduced us to a number of fascinating people with out-of-the-ordinary lives. In the normal way of things, few would know of Bérenger Saunière, of

Rennes-le-Château. He was simply a parish priest, one of many such French priests, poor like all the others before and since, but one who moved somehow from poverty to immense wealth with no one ever knowing, apparently, where his vast fortune originated. Some of his associates were found murdered, but whether they were connected with his rise to riches no one ever knew, or lived to tell the tale. Nor was the secret of Spring-Heeled Jack — Victorian England's version of Jumping Jack Flash — and his out-of-this-world athleticism ever fully understood. If his ability to vault hedges and even houses as reported was anywhere near true, he was an athlete of Olympian proportions.

In a later book, the authors moved from the vagaries and mysteries of people to equally strange places, neighbourhoods, and houses with their abnormal happenings and atmospheres. Some of the places selected for us were well known: Glastonbury, Stonehenge, and Easter Island. From such locations, they led us to houses, like Llancaiach Fawr and Borley Rectory, and invited us to share their strange atmospheres and ghostly presences. They even took us to certain hills, so strange and awesome that the force of gravity seems to lose its grip there and cars left in neutral with handbrake released move upwards and not down. This book of theirs leaves no readers in doubt: people can be strange — but so can places!

To complete this trilogy of sorts, Lionel and Patricia contemplated unusual and peculiar objects, including puzzling prehistoric maps, a cursed diamond, Orffyreus's perpetual motion machine, and a weird clay monster. Their analyses of these and many other mysterious items led them — and their readers — on a journey through history and the contemporary world. Things, as much as people and places, have tales to tell.

Most of us love a good murder book. We with our unexciting, unruffled lives are content to share at arm's length the lives of others more fraught than our own. In their most recent book in this series, Lionel and Patricia reminded us of some celebrated murders: a few of them long in the past, such as Tutankhamun, Thomas Becket, and Julius Caesar. Some others were bizarre and horrible in their day and are likely never to be forgotten, such as the Jack the Ripper murders. Others were from our own day and generation but with something of the uncertain and unsolved about them. The book leaves us wondering about many things. Who was Jack the Ripper? Was young Tutankhamun killed? If so, by whom and why? Was Hanratty guilty? Did the State hang an innocent Timothy Evans? The authors give us not only facts and background, but also their own conclusions, with which their readers may or may not agree.

In this book, the authors have taken on perhaps their greatest challenge yet. They have dared us to look with them at some of the great mysteries of the sea. Such mysteries are not hard to find, but they are difficult to grasp. The seas have many secrets in their great depths. In their deepest, unfathomed waters there are undoubtedly creatures never yet seen by anyone. Leviathans of the deep are certainly not merely figments of Jules Verne's imagination. The powers of the sea can be terrifying. Almost imperceptibly, over the centuries, its tides have eaten into our coastlines, engulfing fields and houses. If there is any credence to be given to Plato's description of the island of Atlantis, with its large population and highly developed civilization, the seas have engulfed it forever as they have other islands, before and since. Only the sea can tell us where Atlantis lies now.

Humans have mood swings, as do the seas, but when the seas have them we do well to be frightened. The sea can change from a sweet, calm millpond to a raging torrent in which nothing afloat can survive. Countless wrecks lie deep beneath its waters, victims of the savage mood swings of the oceans. The seas have their secrets as we have ours. They have their phantom ships, their strange creatures, their lost vessels and crews, their sunken islands, their mermen and mermaids. These things are not, it seems, solely the imaginings of fanciful writers.

Lionel and Patricia have set them all out for us. They make few judgements. They leave that to their readers. Their research has been a fascination to them and a labour of love. It has involved much work and many journeys. Where it is still possible, they have looked with their own eyes — and what they saw and what they felt they have shared with us. Perhaps some mysteries, be they on sea or land, are destined never to be solved. At least, with the help of our authors, we know where these mysteries are. This book, and their others like it, with all the hard work involved, has left us much in their debt. It deserves and will receive our respect and admiration.

Stanley Mogford, MA
Cardiff, Wales, UK, 2004

(The authors, as ever, are deeply grateful to Canon Stanley Mogford, one of the greatest and most deservedly respected scholars in Wales, for his kindness in writing this foreword. It is always an honour and a privilege for any author to have his support.)

INTRODUCTION

The sea is a mysterious place. Enigmas lurk in its depths, riddles map its coasts, and weird anomalies appear in its behaviour. Credible witnesses report over the years that they have seen ghost ships and phantom craft of every description. Is it possible that these phantoms are connected to the equally strange accounts of inexplicable marine tragedies? Ships — including some very large ones — simply vanish without trace. On other occasions it is the people who vanish inexplicably, while their ships remain seaworthy and afloat with no one on board and no clues as to what might have happened to the missing passengers and crew.

The sturdy and seaworthy Nova Scotian brig *Amazon* was renamed *Mary Celeste* before she sailed into history without her passengers and crew in 1872. The mysterious Philadelphia Experiment possibly involved Long Island, New York, and the legendary Montauk Experimental Base said to have been located there.

Mermaids and mermen — or things that *might* be mercreatures — are often seen in the distance: in some reports, they're actually captured. Tales of ancient sea gods and demigods such as Poseidon, the Tritons, Oannes, Quinotaurs, the Sirens, and Dagon may be only mythology and legend — or they could be half-submerged, distorted memories of forgotten sea empires and their powerful rulers.

If, according to the old proverb, a cat may look at a king, then it seems only fair that a king may look at a sea monster. Among many impeccable witnesses to these bizarre phenomena was the future king George V during his days in the British navy. Alexander the Great is also alleged to have seen one many centuries earlier: perhaps sea monsters enjoy embarrassing kings and emperors. Dourly unswayed by pressure from those who tried to refute or ridicule his report in 1848, fearless Captain M'Quhae stuck to his guns about the sea serpent he had observed.

Did spiteful, insane jealousy lead to the loss of the *Lady Lovibond* on the awesome Goodwin Sands on Friday, February 13, 1748? Why have so many good ships and brave sailors died on the Goodwins? There are other dangerous and inexplicable areas, like the Bermuda Triangle and the Japanese Triangle, where more planes and ships go down and more people vanish than pure random chance can rationally explain.

The seas and oceans are also the hazardous habitat of sea wasps, sharks, the dreaded Portuguese man-of-war, the blue-ringed octopus, and huge, hungry, saltwater crocodiles.

There are persistent mysteries surrounding reports of lost islands and even lost continents. Did Atlantis really exist ten thousand years before Solon, the great Athenian statesman, first heard about it from an old Egyptian priest at Sais? Is there historical and geological truth in the Oera Linda Book, which tells of the lost island of Atland, known to Frisian sailors as Aldland, meaning "the old land." Supposedly, in ancient times, it occupied a place in the North Sea. Are the Azores the tips of mountains that once loomed above a lost land in the Atlantic? Is the beautiful Hawaiian archipelago in the Pacific the last vestige of the great continent of Lemuria? Were Atlantis and Lemuria both cradles of ancient and mysterious civilizations? The Lost Land of Lyonesse is said to lie off the coast of Cornwall in the U.K., and there are reports of church bells being sounded from long-drowned steeples beneath the North Sea where the old port of Dunwich in Suffolk, England, once stood.

Those who made pioneering circumnavigations of the globe came back trailing clouds of mystery as well as their deserved glory. Admiral Anson, whose family resided at Shugborough Hall in Staffordshire in Britain, became fabulously wealthy — and, in the eyes of some researchers, his vast treasures have never been satisfactorily explained. There are tenuous connections between the mysteries of intriguing Shugborough Hall and those surrounding Rennes-le-Château in southwestern France, where Bérenger Saunière, the enigmatic nineteenth-century priest, also became suddenly and unaccountably rich.

An archetypal hero, boldly adventurous Francis Drake also circumnavigated the world, and one of the greatest mysteries associated with his adventures was his so-called "missing time." There was a period in Drake's full and audacious career when historians find it difficult to work out where he was or what he might have been doing. It's even possible that he and a handful of loyal men were involved in creating the mysterious Money Pit on Oak Island, Nova Scotia. Could it have concealed mysterious treasure from far across the sea, which Drake stashed away in the labyrinth below Oak Island?

The other equally intriguing sea mystery associated with Sir Francis Drake is the legend of his drum — sounded when England is in great danger to summon the invincible sea hero back from the world beyond the grave. There are those with rare psychic gifts who claim to have heard it.

Statue of Sir Francis Drake at Plymouth Ho.

The oceans have their villains, pirates like Edward Teach (known as Blackbeard) and the highly successful Bartholomew Roberts, as well as their heroes, like Anson and Drake. Wreckers, smugglers, buccaneers, and slavers have all contributed to the grimmer unsolved mysteries of the sea.

There are also tragic unsolved human mysteries of the sea, like the unknown fate of Sir John Franklin and the brave explorers who accompanied him in his fatal search for the Northwest Passage in 1845 — and the three graves they left behind on Beechey Island. Were there other explorers who set out thousands of years before Franklin? Hapgood's theory of the ancient sea kings is well worth careful study, as are the contentious Piri Reis and Buache maps. In the realm of legendary voyages, the adventures of the Argonauts in search of the Golden Fleece and the colourful travels of Sinbad the Sailor have much more to them than legend alone. Didn't Thor Heyerdahl's courageous expeditions prove conclusively that even with very simple and unsophisticated ships and rafts, human courage and ingenuity could take fearless men across vast oceans?

These many unsolved mysteries of the sea have certainly fascinated and intrigued us. We hope our readers will share our enthusiasm.

Lionel & Patricia Fanthorpe
Cardiff, Wales, UK, 2004

Galley.

CHAPTER ONE

The Flying Dutchman *and Other Phantom Ships*

Many of us will already know the broad outline of the legend of the *Flying Dutchman* through Wagner's superb opera *Der fliegende Holländer*, 1843, and Coleridge's *The Rime of the Ancient Mariner*, 1798. One version of the story has a hero (or anti-hero) named Captain Falkenberg doomed to sail the North Sea forever playing an interminable dice game with Satan. In Coleridge's version, Death and Life-in-Death arrive on a weird ghost ship and play dice for the Ancient Mariner:

Was this the ship of Coleridge's strange vision?

And those her ribs through which the Sun
Did peer, as through a grate?
And is that Woman all her crew?

Is that a Death? and are there two?
Is Death that Woman's mate?

Her lips were red, her looks were free,
Her locks were yellow as gold:
Her skin was as white as leprosy,
The Nightmare Life-in-Death was she,
Who thicks man's blood with cold.

The naked hulk alongside came,
And the twain were casting dice;
"The game is done! I've won! I've won!'
Quoth she, and whistles thrice.

The Sun's rim dips; the stars rush out:
At one stride comes the dark;
With far-heard whisper, o'er the sea,
Off shot the spectre-bark.

Pandora and the Flying Dutchman, a 1950s film version of the legend, starred James Mason and Ava Gardner. Like all enduring myths and legends, there are numerous versions of the *Flying Dutchman* narrative, all of which repay careful study and research. One of the oldest may even have Norse roots. There is an account in the saga of Stote, a fearless Viking who dared to steal a precious ring from the gods themselves. When the outraged Norse gods caught up with him, he finished up as a skeleton enrobed in flames and sitting on the mast of a huge black Viking longship.

Viking runes.

The title actually refers to the Dutch skipper, rather than to the vessel herself. His name is usually rendered as Falkenberg, but he also becomes Hendrik van der Decken, Vanderdecken, Vandecker, van

Demen, van Demien, van Strachan, van Straaten, and several other similar allied spellings. When stirring adventure writers like Captain Philip Marryat create an exciting fictional version of the story, names may change. Washington Irving (1855) called his fictional Flying Dutchman Ramhout van Dam. The linguistic root of *decken* — the significant part of the legendary skipper's name — may contain some cryptic clues to the story. *Decken* can mean to cover something, to put a roof over it, to set a table, or to spread a cloth over it ready for presenting a meal, but it can also mean to disguise, to camouflage, or to conceal or hide something. In the sense that animal breeders use the word *cover* when referring to horses at stud, *decken* can also have sexual connotations meaning mating or copulating — and another version of van der Decken's story involves alleged adultery and brutal sexual jealousy as tragic and as violent as Othello's. *Die decke* used as a noun can refer to a bed covering, such as a quilt or blanket — raising the adultery perspective again. It can also mean a box or casing, or even a ceiling. It may also refer to a geological layer or stratum, a bed of clay or rock. Yet another meaning is tegument — the skin or hide of some living creature.

Whatever the skipper's name implies, most versions of the tale are centred on the challenging, storm-bedevilled water off the Cape of Good Hope. The period is late seventeenth, or early eighteenth, century, and the skipper was a man to be reckoned with — if not a man to be admired or emulated. Determination and an unbreakable will can be great virtues: they can also be doom-laden harbingers of disaster. In van der Decken's case, they were definitely the latter. One popular version of the tragedy says that he was obsessive and fanatical — and roaring drunk on top of his potentially lethal, psychological defects. Van der Decken was trying to round the Cape of Good Hope in the teeth of a force ten storm wind that put the ship, her passengers, and her crew in mortal danger. The passengers pleaded; the crew eventually mutinied. Van der Decken refused to alter course. Formidable man that he was — no Captain Bligh of the *Bounty* to be overpowered by Fletcher Christian's determined mutineers — van der Decken shot the leader of the mutineers in cold blood and tossed his body casually overboard like so much insubstantial garbage. Throughout his battle with the elements, the mighty Dutchman sang bawdy songs and cursed both God and Satan with reckless impartiality.

A shadowy figure — like Nemesis of ancient Greek tradition — appeared on the deck and reprimanded van der Decken for his fanaticism and his murderous response to the mutineers. The wild Dutchman laughed, cursed, and threatened to shoot the mysterious newcomer. In some versions, his pistol failed to work; in others, the heavy shot passed harmlessly through the insubstantial, paranormal visitor; in yet others the pistol exploded in his hand. Following his unsuccessful attempt to shoot the mysterious entity, the visitor spoke again. Van der Decken was roundly cursed: his food would be hot iron, his drink would be as bitter as gall, and he was condemned to sail the seven seas forever — with hideous animated corpses for his crew. In a slightly different version of this account, van der Decken was allowed to retain the unfortunate cabin boy for company. The lad was to be transformed into a hideous creature with the jaws of a tiger, the horns of a stag, and the skin of a dogfish.

"Damn you!" roared van der Decken. "Let it be so then. I don't care. I'm not afraid of you! Do your worst, and then to hell with you!"

Part of the Dutchman's curse was that he would bring death and disaster to all other ships his ghostly vessel encountered: food on board some of the ships that met his would instantly become corrupted and start to decay; other ships he met would be wrecked by rocks or storms; some would spring inexplicable, unstaunchable leaks and go down to Davy Jones's Locker with all hands.

There was another mysterious sea captain, a genuine historical figure this time, named Bernard Fokke, who was such a superb seaman that nautical rivals attributed his ship's great speed and his exceptional navigational skills to a deal he'd done with the devil. Captain Fokke actually disappeared at sea, and his jealous rivals nodded sagely with a knowing wink and a look that said "I told you so" — convinced that Satan had come to claim his part of the bargain.

Over the centuries, witnesses who have claimed to have seen the *Flying Dutchman* — and survived in spite of its skipper and his notorious curse — have described him as looking gaunt and wild-eyed, but strangely reformed and penitent, crouched bareheaded over the ship's bucking wheel and praying for forgiveness. Others claim to have laid eyes on his living-dead skeletal zombie crew swarming around in the rigging as they battle with torn sails and the awesome power of a supernatural wind that constantly plagues their ship.

In the Othello-type version of the legend, van der Decken was insanely, groundlessly jealous of his beautiful young wife, and after a protracted and dangerous voyage he came home obsessed by the delusion that she had been unfaithful to him. He murdered her and was sentenced to death accordingly. As he lay in the condemned cell, awaiting execution, some strange supernatural power intervened, put the guards into a trance-like sleep, and magically opened all the prison doors and gates. Van der Decken reached the harbour, where his loyal crew were waiting for him, and the *Dutchman* sailed away into legend. The insanely jealous skipper's punishment for murdering his innocent young wife was to sail the oceans until he met a woman who would love him enough to give her life for him voluntarily.

In a third version, van der Decken plays dice with the devil — betting his soul, his ship, and his crew against eternal life, eternal youth, and infinite wealth. Needless to say, throwing two ivory cubes against an opponent who has the power to control them isn't a good idea: predictably, van der Decken lost!

Sightings of the *Flying Dutchman* have been made by many reliable witnesses over the centuries. A report from a British ship in the Cape of Good Hope area in the 1830s described the *Flying Dutchman* sailing towards them on a collision course. The seamen did not realize that it was a phantom until it suddenly vanished, only seconds before what would have been a fatal collision.

The Flying Dutchman.

The most famous and probably the best-authenticated sighting of the *Flying Dutchman* took place on July 11, 1881. The future king George V of the U.K. was then a sixteen-year-old midshipman in the Royal Navy, serving aboard HMS *Inconstant*. The young prince wrote:

> At 4 a.m. the Flying Dutchman crossed our bows. She emitted a strange phosphorescent light as of a phantom ship all aglow, in the midst of which light the mast, spars and sails of a brig 200 yards distant stood out in strong relief as she came up on the port bow, where also

the Officer of the Watch from the bridge saw her, as did
the quarter-deck midshipman, who was sent forward at
once to the forecastle, but on arriving there no vestige
nor any sign whatever of any material ship was to be
seen even near or right away to the horizon, the night
being clear and the sea calm.

The information comes from a book by John H. Dalton entitled *The
Cruise of Her Majesties Ship Baccante.* The future George V and his
brother, the ill-starred Eddie, Duke of Clarence, who was a suspect in
the Jack the Ripper murders, were both aboard the *Inconstant* because
the *Baccante* had had problems with her rudder. Two other vessels were
with HMS *Inconstant* at the time: the *Tourmaline* and the *Cleopatra.*
Numerous witnesses from both ships also saw the phantom and verified
the prince's report.

As the legend emphasizes, to see the *Flying Dutchman* was considered to be the worst kind of bad luck because the doomed vessel was
allegedly carrying a fatal curse. In considering curses in general —both
on land and at sea — it is important to remember that once an event,
or a phenomenon, is *alleged* to be cursed, any tragedy that happens in
association with it will be attributed to the curse, regardless of whether
there is any statistically significant correlation.

When co-author Lionel was serving as deputy head in a very large
comprehensive high school, an unfortunate young student with hitherto unsuspected psychiatric problems was suffering from the delusion
that he was accompanied by a malevolent Egyptian mummy — invisible to all but him. He terrified several older students by telling them that
under instructions from the ghostly mummy he had cursed them. His
technique was to wait for an accident to happen, and then claim that his
curse was responsible.

Lionel gathered the frightened students together with the sadly
deluded mummy keeper, asked the boy where the mummy was standing, struck the empty air in that vicinity and said: "Come on! Do something! I think you're ugly and stupid! Now, if you have any mysterious
powers, why not bring a bolt of lightning down on me? These people are
innocent: I'm the hard man who just hit you and insulted you! Show us
what you can do, bandage-boy!" Needless to say, nothing happened. The
lad with the psychiatric problems was taken for treatment, and the for-
merly frightened students started to laugh. Lionel later reported the
incident to the head, whose revealingly anxious comment was:
"Whatever you do, don't have an accident on the way home!" That atti-

tude goes some way towards illustrating the vulnerability of the human mind when confronted with supposed curses!

After the future king George V and a dozen or so of his shipmates had witnessed the *Flying Dutchman*, the sailor who had first seen the strange apparition was killed by a fall from the mast, and the admiral died shortly afterwards. Ripper suspect Eddie, Duke of Clarence, died young in the tragic "flu" epidemic of 1892.

Of course, there is absolutely no way of proving causality, or of establishing any link with the *Dutchman's* appearance; neither is there any way of disproving causality. Some curses may, indeed, be self-fulfilling prophecies: rendered nervous and uncertain by thinking about the supposed curse, victims may have become victims by failing to concentrate and to pay proper attention to dangerous machinery or hazardous road conditions. There is nothing more likely than mental distraction to render a person vulnerable to potential accidents. An appropriate degree of concentration and sharp mental focus, combined with a confident, relaxed attitude, is a very effective shield against accidents. The mental powers of *expectation* (which we can all generate to a greater or lesser extent) also seem able to affect our environment positively or negatively. The happy and well-balanced individual who enjoys first-class health, dynamic energy, and the super-human stamina of a trans-Canada steam locomotive goes into every situation expecting to win, to succeed, to conquer, and to triumph. That powerful, positive expectation effectively reinforces the likelihood of success. The sad, tense, depressed, unhappy, negative person, low in strength, energy, and stamina and suffering from indeterminate, chronic psychosomatic illnesses, dreads the future and expects misery and failure. Again, those expectations are likely to be fulfilled.

Another world-famous witness was Grand Admiral Karl Dönitz of Germany. Born on September 16, 1891, at Grünai-bei-Berlin, Dönitz was the creator of Germany's World War II submarine fleet — in direct contravention of the Versailles Treaty, which absolutely forbade Germany to have a submarine fleet after World War I. In 1936, Dönitz became its commander. In 1943 he replaced Admiral Erich Raeder as commander-in-chief of the German navy. By 1945, with the Nazi war machine in tatters, Dönitz was made head of the North German Civil and Military Command. Hitler's last political order appointed Dönitz as his successor. Dönitz was sentenced to ten years imprisonment by the International Military Tribunal at Nüremberg in 1946, was released in 1956, and died in Aumühle on December 22, 1980 — just a few months short of his ninetieth birthday.

The report concerning the Dönitz sighting of the *Flying Dutchman* related to a German naval tour of duty "somewhere east of Suez" — a very long way from the Dutchman's traditional haunts near the Cape of Good Hope. Believers in van der Decken's prowess might have argued that the indomitable Dutchman had finally rounded the Cape, beaten the devil, and sailed in triumph up Africa's eastern seaboard past Madagascar, Mozambique, Tanzania, Kenya, and Somalia before entering the Gulf of Aden and proceeding up into the Red Sea. Was Dönitz's vessel anywhere near the Mediterranean end of the Suez Canal at the time of the reported sighting?

The *Dutchman* legend goes back to the seventeenth century, or even earlier, and, interestingly, ways of creating a water link between the Mediterranean and the Red Sea go back to ancient times. The earliest canals linked the Red Sea to the Nile and used the river to reach the Mediterranean. Pharaohs Necho and Thutmosis III have both been credited with creating the very first link, but it was the Persian Darius I who gave orders for the canal to be completed. In his day, the canals were in two parts: one connected the Great Bitter Lake to the Gulf of Suez, and the other completed the link by going to the Nile Delta and thus out into the Mediterranean. The canal worked regularly and effectively during the time of the Ptolemies, but decayed and fell into disrepair and disuse after their era. In Roman times it was refurbished while Trajan was emperor, and centuries later the great Arabian ruler Ibn-al-Aas restored it again.

It was the emperor Napoleon who first looked at the problem of connecting the Mediterranean to the Red Sea at a relatively recent date. About 1800, his engineers reported (incorrectly!) that the sea levels were different by at least ten metres, and too much land would be flooded if a direct canal was constructed. Despite the engineers' pessimism and miscalculation, Ferdinand de Lesseps, former French consul in Cairo, had the canal finished by 1867, and it was officially opened — very lavishly — on November 17, 1869, by the Egyptian Khediv Ismail.

It seems a trifle anachronistic for a seventeenth-century ghost ship to use a canal that wasn't destined to be completed for another two centuries!

On the other hand, there are reports of ghost ships to which land presents no obstacles. The phantom vessel *Goblin* has been reported many times off the coast of Porthcurno Cove, not far from St. Leven in Cornwall. Witnesses usually describe her as a black, square-rigged vessel that steers towards the coast as they watch her. However, the *Goblin* does not stop when she reaches the land but glides on over it for a fair distance and then simply vanishes. Ghost ships that fly over land, or glide just above it, are linked to the old sailors' legends of the *Ship of the Dead*. This is a strange vessel that calls to collect the souls of old, retired seamen who die ashore. It's a legend that may be as old as the Norse belief in the Valkyries, goddesses who chose the best Viking warriors and then flew with them to Valhalla after they had died fighting boldly on the battlefield.

Legends like that of the *Palatine* and the infamous *Palatine* light illustrate the complications and difficulties encountered when tracing the various versions of phantom ship stories back to their origins. Poet John Greenleaf Whittier (1807–1892) wrote a poem called "The Palatine" in which the ship of that name was wrecked on the rocks by Block Island, Rhode Island, U.S.A. This extract from the poem details the blazing ghost ship *Palatine*, which so many witnesses were certain they had seen:

> For still, on many a moonless night,
> From Kingston Head and from Montauk light
> The spectre kindles and burns in sight.
> Now low and dim, now clear and higher,
> Leaps up the terrible Ghost of Fire,
> Then, slowly, sinking, the flames expire.
> And the wise Sound skippers though skies be fine,
> Reef their sails when they see the sign
> Of the blazing wreck of the *Palatine.*

The actual tragic history behind the story of the wreck as Whittier described it seems to have referred to another vessel, the *Princess Augusta*. The passengers aboard her were Germans from the area known in those days as the Palatinates — hence the confusion over the name *Palatine*. Another contribution to the historical doubt and uncertainty is the existence on Block Island of a simple granite monument bearing the inscription "Palatine Graves — 1738." This stands on private property near the house of Simon Ray on the west side of the island. It seems likely that the name "Palatine" referred to the people who died in the tragedy rather than to their ship. The wreck of the *Princess Augusta* seems to have occurred in 1738 and not in 1752, which is frequently given as the year in which the *Palatine* met her tragic end. The immigrants aboard *Princess Augusta* were hoping to reach Philadelphia, with a view to joining the Pennsylvanian Deutsch (a German-speaking community already established there). The name "Deutsch" apparently misled some researchers into thinking that the immigrants were Dutch, and at least one otherwise reliable and factual account said that the doomed passengers of the *Princess Augusta* had set sail from Holland, not Germany.

Several accounts agree that there were many troubles and difficulties for the passengers. One version suggests that as the ship neared New England there was a dispute among the officers as to exactly where they were. The captain — said in some versions to be a savage bully, an inveterate alcoholic, and a greedy exploiter of the helpless passengers — was thrown overboard by the angry officers and crew. They then robbed the passengers and raped the women before escaping from the *Princess Augusta* in the only lifeboats — thus effectively condemning the passengers to death. If this version that includes the rape is true, it would account for the later detail of the woman who emerged from hiding only to die in the flames.

The helpless, abandoned ship drifted onto the rocks by Block Island. To their credit, local fishermen rescued as many of the passengers as they could see, helped themselves to anything of value that the crew had not already stolen, and then set fire to the sinking wreck as it drifted off the rocks, presumably floated off by the rising tide. As the blazing wreckage drifted out to sea again on its final voyage, a terrified woman passenger who had been hiding in the hold to escape the rapists ran up onto the blazing deck screaming desperately for help — but by then it was too late for the Block Island fishermen to reach her.

In 1882, an accurate and factual report of the sighting of the blazing Block Island ghost ship was given by a Long Island fishing boat owner. It actually appeared in the magazine *Scientific American*. At that time, menhaden were plentiful. These fish were an unusually oily species of herring, and their excessive oiliness is an important feature of the explanation offered in this 1882 account. The mate was unwilling to sail off Montauk Point because he claimed that he had seen mysterious glowing ships moving very late at night, although there was no discernible wind and conditions were dead calm. The skipper and the owner both ignored the mate's protests and they eventually anchored in Gardiner's Bay. In the middle of the night, the terrified mate shook the owner awake and pointed to a big schooner bearing down on them at a speed of at least ten knots — *although there was a dead calm.* They tried desperately to take evasive action — impossible when there was no wind for their sails — and prepared to jump overboard. At that second, the schooner simply vanished, just as the *Flying Dutchman* had done in the Cape of Good Hope area fifty years earlier when it seemed a collision with the British ship there was inevitable. By the time the skipper joined them there was nothing to see.

A week later, when they were fishing in the same area, the mysterious phantom light appeared again — like a strangely glowing sailing ship. The owner boldly ordered his skipper to set sail in pursuit of the ghost ship and to lower the seine net as they went. (A seine net, based on a French term, is used vertically with floats at the top and weights below. A fisherman, or a fishing boat, using such a net is referred to as a seiner.) They netted an amazing haul of menhaden as they pursued what seemed to be the glowing phantom ship.

The hypothesis seeking to explain the "ghost ship" in rational and scientific terms put forward in the 1882 article suggested that it was the huge shoal of menhaden that was responsible for the weird glow that gave the impression of a luminous ghostly vessel. As the shoal moved, it was suggested, the excessive oil exuded from the fish produced the same kind of glow that is described as will-o'-the-wisp on land. It also seemed possible that the glow effect mirrored the fishing boat, or reflected and distorted the image of any other boat in the vicinity. The fact that the "ghost ship" was able to move when there was no wind *could* be explained as the swift movement of a gigantic shoal of oily fish swimming through the water. As theories go, it's both interesting and ingenious — but it still leaves many unexplained phantom ships sailing the seven seas.

One of the most famous ghost ships, reportedly seen near Britain at fifty-year intervals, is the *Lady Lovibond*, which was reputedly involved in one of the hundreds of marine tragedies associated with the hazardous Goodwin Sands.

The Goodwin Sands are associated with the powerful Anglo-Saxon Earl Godwin, son of Wulfnoth, supporter of Danish King Cnut who became king of England in 1016. Cnut gave Wessex, one of the four great English earldoms, to Godwin, and in 1019, while accompanying Cnut on a visit to Denmark, Godwin married Gytha, sister of Ulf, the most powerful of the Danish earls. Their children included the future king Harold.

Traditionally, Godwin's vast estates once included a beautiful and fertile island named Lomea, off the coast of Kent, where the Goodwin Sands drift around so treacherously today. One of the several infamous "great storms" of the type recorded in the Anglo-Saxon Chronicle seems to have destroyed Lomea in the eleventh century — changing it into the Goodwins. Earl Godwin was blamed for failing to maintain Lomea's sea defences, according to the legend, but geological drilling on the Goodwins seems to indicate that only decayed marine matter exists between the layers of shifting sand above the chalk base, and most professional geologists think it unlikely that there was ever an island there in the first place.

The *Lady Lovibond* legend records that on February 13, 1748, the ship was on its way from London to Oporto in Portugal, carrying its newlywed skipper, Simon Peel, his lovely young bride, Annetta, and many of their wedding guests. This was in spite of the old sailors' superstition that it was unlucky to have a woman on board. The mate, however, had also been in love with the beautiful Mrs. Peel. In a fit of insane jealousy (shades of van der Decken) because of her marriage to Simon, the mate murdered Captain Peel and steered the *Lady Lovibond* onto the fatal Goodwin Sands, where she was totally wrecked, leaving no survivors.

Witnesses over the centuries have claimed not only to have seen the ship's ghostly outline, but to have heard the happy voices of the celebrating guests immediately before the phantom vessel ran onto the Goodwins. On February 13, 1798, the skipper of the *Edenbridge* made a log entry to the effect that he had almost collided with a schooner, a three-master, which was sailing straight for the Goodwins. In 1848, the lifeboat crew from Deal went to the rescue of a schooner that seemed to be in distress on the notorious sands. When they reached the spot where they had last seen it, however, there was no trace of any vessel at all. In 1898 she was seen again, and there were also reports of sightings in 1948 and 1998.

Another inexplicable spectre ship of the Goodwins was the SS *Violet,* an old, cross-channel paddle steamer that met its end on the treacherous sands during a heavy blizzard in the second half of the nineteenth century. In 1939 witnesses saw an old paddle steamer run onto the Goodwins and called out the first available lifeboat, which came from Ramsgate. They searched for an hour but found nothing. If it was the ghost of the *Violet* it had vanished back into the mysterious limbo from which it had so strangely emerged.

The legend of another ghost ship that re-enacts a centuries-old tragedy begins with the violent blood feud between the de Warrennes and the Pevenseys. In outline, the fourth Earl de Warrenne met Lord Pevensey in mortal combat at Lewes Castle and was about to be killed by him when Lady de Warrenne prayed to St. Nicholas (whose belt was a sacred relic in the care of the de Warrennes). Miraculously, her husband reversed the fortunes of the combat and killed Lord Pevensey. The triumphant de Warrennes then vowed that St. Nicholas's belt would be taken to Byzantium and placed on Saint Mary the Virgin's shrine there — *before their infant son was old enough to marry.* Years passed. The vow remained unfulfilled. Beautiful young Lady Edona was betrothed to the de Warrennes's son, Manfred, now in his twentieth year. The de Warrennes recalled their vow and sent Manfred off to Byzantium with the precious belt. A year later, so the legend of the Lewes ghost ship runs, the family were watching and waiting eagerly as young Lord Manfred's ship approached. Suddenly, she struck a rock, tilted on her side, and sank with all hands. Lady Edona collapsed and died on the spot where she had so eagerly awaited her lover. Every year, on the anniversary of her death, and Lord Manfred's, the marine tragedy is re-enacted, and the ghostly ship collides with the rock once more, keels over, and vanishes.

A very colourful ghost ship legend, which originates from the authors' home county of Norfolk, concerns a traditional Norfolk wherry called *Mayfly*: a large, cargo sailing boat intended for use on the Norfolk Broads and rivers. The skipper's name is variously rendered as Blood Stephenson, or Blood Richardson. He seems to have shared several of van der Decken's character defects — and added a few of his own. The story begins with an apparently imbecilic banker named Dormey from Beccles entrusting the fearsome and amoral Blood with a huge amount of cash and his beautiful, young, virgin daughter, Millicent, who was to go along to enjoy the scenery. Instead of taking the girl and the banker's cash safely to their destination in Yarmouth, Blood set out into the North Sea, heading for Holland (another link with van der Decken?). Not welcoming his powerful, lecherous advances, the banker's daughter screamed and struggled like the virtuous heroine of a three-volume Victorian romance.

At this point, Bert, the plucky little cabin boy, emerged from below decks and did his best to rescue her. Quite how a tiny teenaged lad and the banker's young daughter managed to fight off the gigantic, rock-hard Blood has never been realistically explained, but there was supposedly a terrific struggle in which the girl was killed and Blood himself was fatally injured. Bert managed to escape the scene of all this carnage on the blood-drenched wherry by launching the *Mayfly's* dinghy. He floated about helplessly in the North Sea for hours, and then saw a vessel approaching. Thinking he was about to be rescued, he cheered loudly and waved — *only to discover that it was the* Mayfly *with the ghosts of the screaming girl and the maniacal skipper running around the blood-soaked decks.* Not surprisingly, Bert stayed cowering in his little dinghy until the *Mayfly* vanished. Every June 24, it is said, the ghostly *Mayfly* reappears, trying, like the *Flying Dutchman,* to find her way to port.

The story in that highly colourful and not very historical form seems to have originated with an East Anglian raconteur named Bill

Soloman, who has an irrepressible sense of humour and a vivid imagination. There is, however, much more to it than merely entertaining fiction, or vividly creative exaggeration. Bill himself is the first to acknowledge that he did not create the story from scratch: there was a much older, more sinister version of the *Mayfly* tragedy before Bill embellished it for the benefit of a broadcaster who was interviewing him in the 1950s.

In sad, realistic contrast to the melodramatic tale of Blood and his wherry is the grimly factual account of the loss of the *Pamir*, a beautiful four-masted sailing ship capable of carrying over four thousand square metres of sail. In September 1957, a few hundred miles from the Azores, she was hit by Hurricane Carrie and sank. A fearless radio man, doing his vital duty to the last, gave out her position on the last distress call he was able to transmit. Ignoring the danger to their own ship, the gallant officers and men of the U.S. freighter *Saxon* raced to the *Pamir*'s last reported position and picked up six survivors: eighty of the *Pamir*'s ship's company were lost. In 1961, the spectral *Pamir* was sighted by the *Esmereld*. She was reportedly seen again near the Virgin Islands. She was also seen on later occasions by Norwegian and German witnesses and by shrewd observers aboard the *Eagle*, a ship manned by the U.S. Coast Guard — highly trained professionals who are not easy men to deceive!

When rational, reliable, objective witnesses provide convincing evidence for the existence of *something* — however unlikely that *something* seems to be — their reports deserve careful and thoughtful attention. Phenomena described as "ghost ships" — of which the *Flying Dutchman* is a prime example — come into this category. The heart of Fortean philosophy is the principle that nothing is so obvious and so apparently well-fortified by "common sense" that it should be exempt from interrogation; neither is anything so bizarre or improbable that it can be dismissed as ridiculous and never given serious examination.

The phenomenon broadly categorized as phantom vessels or ghost ships can be examined from several perspectives. First is the scientific angle on mirages.

A mirage can be defined as a refraction phenomenon. Refraction means that rays of light have been bent: turned through an angle from their original direction. When a ray of light enters a denser medium it turns towards the normal ray — the normal ray in optical science being defined as a ray that enters the surface at an angle of ninety degrees. When the ray of light leaves a dense medium for a less dense medium, it refracts away from the normal ray. For example, when light leaves air and enters water, it bends towards the normal ninety-degree ray. When it leaves water and enters air, it bends away from the normal ninety-degree ray. A long-handled spoon standing in a glass of water illustrates the basic principle of refraction due to light moving through transparent media with different densities.

Mirages are seen when the image of some distant object (for example, a ship at sea, or a pool of water on land) appears a long way away from its real, spatial position. This apparent displacement happens because of atmospheric density variations close to the surface. Mirages frequently look as if they're distorted, upside down, wavering, and shimmering. This has given them their association over many centuries with magic, faerie lore, divine intervention, and the malicious work of demons and evil spirits. Psychology plays a part here: observation is carried out with the mind as much as with the eyes, but mirages are not illusions — they can be photographed.

There are two main categories of mirage. The variety that appears in arid deserts and is popular with novelists and adventure story writers is technically referred to as an *inferior* mirage, most frequently seen today as pools of water across a highway. Inferior mirages almost invariably appear over land. The *superior* mirage is seen over expanses of water, snow, or ice. The scientific, meteorological terms *inferior* and *superior* are not qualitative in this context. An inferior mirage appears in a position that is *lower* than the real position of the material object it represents, and a superior mirage appears at a site that is *higher* than the object it mimics.

In a nutshell, mirages occur when rays of light generated by — or reflected from — some material, physical source are refracted (bent) as they pass through air layers that have different densities.

So a real oasis — a pool of water surrounded by shady fruit trees — can appear many miles away and tantalize thirsty travellers in a sun-baked desert. A real, solid East Indiaman with all sails set, battling her way through a savage gale a hundred kilometres away, could appear to be speeding towards another tall ship — barely fifty metres away, on an apparently disastrous collision course — and then vanish like a phantom at sunrise.

If mirages explain some of the famous and persistent ghost ship sightings, what of the others? Many modern physicists are far from skeptical about the possibilities of irregularities in *time*. The Norfolk Broads — especially Wroxham Broad — have curious data associated with them that might be explicable in terms of time slips. The two staid and respectable Victorian schoolteachers who had a strange experience in the gardens at Versailles over a century ago may have experienced a time slip.

There are innumerable other reports of anomalous phenomena that *might* be accounted for by some sort of time malfunction. Do ghost ships like the *Dutchman* sail across centuries as well as seas and oceans?

Another theory that experienced researchers into the paranormal would advance is that some strange sightings of ghost ships and other spectral phenomena are replays. If sound and vision can be recorded so easily and deliberately onto tapes and discs, perhaps nature has her own rather more spasmodic recording techniques. What if emotional energy is just as effective as electrical energy in creating such natural recordings? The terror of doomed passengers and crew would constitute a formidable barrage of emotional energy. Could that energy have etched its data onto the very rocks on which the ship was wrecked? Or onto other rocks far below the surface? Could that grim data of death be read — even centuries later — by observers with sufficiently intuitive and sensitive minds?

Dimensional gateways and links with those strange quasi-real *Worlds of If* — the so-called probability tracks — present the open-minded researcher with other real and serious possibilities. If event A had happened instead of event B, if decision C had been made instead of decision D in the past, the present might now be very different. If other dimensions exist — if probability tracks exist — then things from those other dimensions and probability tracks — including what look like phantom ships — might well be able to glide from their realm into ours.

It is, of course, undeniable that ghosts — even those with the theatricality of Hamlet's murdered father or Scrooge's old pal, Jacob Marley — might be surviving, intelligent entities who have travelled from the spirit world to ours with their own particular purposes to fulfil. Is van der Decken just such a psychic being — giving warnings, unloading his guilt, and trying to find peace?

There are as many possible solutions to the riddle of the ghost ship reports as there are square kilometres of salt water over which those controversial phantom vessels may wend their enigmatic way.

CHAPTER TWO

Mysterious Merpeople

Matthew Arnold (1822–1888), son of the famous Thomas Arnold, headmaster of Rugby School, graduated from Balliol College, Oxford, and spent more than thirty years as a school inspector. During those decades he also wrote a great deal of excellent and memorable poetry and was at one time professor of poetry at Oxford.

His poem "The Forsaken Merman" tells the poignant story of a merman who had married an earth girl, who subsequently — so it seems from Arnold's version — left him and their children and returned to her human kind on land. Arnold's poem begins:

> Come, dear children, let us away;
> Down and away below!
> Now my brothers call from the bay,
> Now the great winds shoreward blow,
> Now the salt tides seaward flow;
> Now the wild white horses play,
> Champ and chaff and toss in the spray.
> Children dear, let us away!
> This way, this way …

> … Call her once before you go —
> Call once yet!
> In a voice that she will know:
> "Margaret! Margaret!"

In Arnold's version of the story, however, the faithless Margaret never returns to her merman and their children. His version ends:

> … Singing: "There dwells a loved one,
> But cruel is she!
> She left lonely forever
> The kings of the sea."

In co-author Lionel's poetry anthology, *Earth, Sea and Sky,* there is a different, happier conclusion to the merman's story, entitled "The Merman's Wife Returns."

> There was an answer to the merman's call,
> A faltering step towards the beckoning sea.
> "Wait for me, children. Husband, wait for me."
> The voice they knew and loved, but faint with pain;
> Her children skim the waves to reach the shore.
> Her merman husband bounds across the sands,
> Sweeps her into his arms — his bride once more —
> Strong fingers close around her bleeding hands.
> "What have they done to you, my love, my life?"
> "They could not understand our unity.
> They hated me. They said I was unclean,
> A thing apart, because I lived with you.
> They would not let me go back to the sea,
> Our home of pearl and shell beneath the waves,
> Our lovers' wonderland of coral caves …
> But I broke free … Somehow I found the strength
> To pull my hands clear of their iron bands …
> Their prejudice, their bias and their hate …"
> The merman gently kissed her bleeding hands
> And held her very close, their children too.
> They understood the cost of her escape.
> Rejoicing in the power of her love …
> Safe in their cool, green sea they headed home,
> Their family re-united, strong, complete …
> And in the merman's heart the ocean sang.

When myths and legends are as persistent as the many stories of mermaids told and retold over thousands of years in song and story, they cannot be dismissed without serious investigation and analysis. A few years before Matthew Arnold was born, another educationalist, William Munro, a schoolmaster from Scotland, wrote a letter to the *Times*, in which he described in great detail a sighting he himself had made of "a figure resembling an unclothed human female, sitting upon a rock extending into the sea, and apparently in the action of combing its hair, which flowed around its shoulders, and was of a light brown colour …" Munro watched the strange being for some three or four minutes before it slid off its rock and down into the sea. He continued watching carefully, but it never reappeared.

The *London Mirror* of November 16, 1822, reported that John McIsaac from Corphine in Kintyre, Scotland, had made a very similar sighting in 1811. Like the creature that Munro saw, McIsaac's mermaid had long hair that it tended to comb continually.

Other early nineteenth-century mermaid observers included a girl named Mackay, whose description of what she had seen along the Caithness coast tallied closely with William Munro's account in his letter to the *Times*.

Were dugongs like this ever mistaken for mermaids?

Eighteen hundred years before either Munro or Mackay reported their mermaid sightings in Scotland, Gaius Plinius Secundus — better known as Pliny the Elder — was born in AD 23 in what was then called Transpadane Gaul (now part of modern Italy). Before his tragic death caused by volcanic fumes from Vesuvius in AD 79, Pliny had written *Natural History*, which endured as a standard reference work for centuries — until rational, scientific biologists began to express doubts about what they considered to be dubious myths and legends that Pliny had incorporated along with his factual material. In his mermaid section, Pliny wrote: "Mermaids are not fables. They are, in fact, as the artists depict them. Their bodies, however, are scaly and rough, even where they seem most human. A mermaid was seen by many witnesses close to the shore. It was dying, and the local inhabitants heard it crying pitifully."

Henry Hudson, famous for his heroic, but tragic, seventeenth-century voyages in quest of the Northwest Passage, names two of his ship's company, Thomas Hilles and Robert Rayner, as sighting a mermaid in an area then known as Novaya Zemlya.

Sir Richard Whitbourne, who originally came from Exmouth in Devonshire — famous two centuries later for the trail of mysterious footprints crossing the estuary of the River Exe — was practically a contemporary of Hudson. Whitbourne reported sighting something *similar* to a mermaid in 1610. His report is especially significant in that it describes whatever he saw as having blue streaks around its head, *resembling* hair, but he was adamant that these streaks were definitely *not* hair.

A Danish Royal Commission set out to make a serious investigation of the merfolk phenomena in 1723. Not far from the Faroe Islands, members of the commission reported that they had actually seen a merman. It submerged as they approached and then surfaced again, staring at them with a horrible, fixed intensity. This so unnerved the commission that they ordered their skipper to withdraw. Their apparent retreat caused the creature — whatever it was — to give vent to an almighty roar and submerge again, like an animal that has triumphantly defended its territorial boundaries against intruders.

Writing about merfolk in *The Natural History of Norway* (1752–3) no less a dignitary than Bishop Erik Pontoppidan himself declared: "In the Diocese of Bergen, here, and also in the Manor called Nordland, there are many honest and reliable witnesses who most strongly and positively affirm that they have seen creatures of this type."

Various reports of the infamous Amboina mermaids are also worth reporting in outline. Now named Ambon, the Indonesian island once known as Amboina, or Amboyna, is about ten kilometres off the southwestern coast of Seram Island. Its highest point is the summit of Mount Salhatu, and although Ambon is not entirely free from earthquakes, there is no volcanic activity. It does, however, have hot gas vents, called *solfataras*, as well as hot springs. The climate is tropical and rainfall is heavy. There are many varieties of fish in Teluk Bay, and some of them are bizarre, which might have given rise to the mermaid sightings.

Dutch writer Francois Valentijn compiled *The Natural History of Amboina*, which was published in 1726 and contained accounts of mermaids as well as illustrations purporting to show them. He calls them *Zee-Menschen* and *Zee-Wyven*. Valentijn's illustration had already appeared in 1718 in a book called *Poissons, Ecrivisses et Crabes ... des Isles Moluques*. The artist responsible for the picture in both volumes was Samuel Fallours, who held the rank of official artist to the Dutch East India Company.

The description accompanying Fallours's illustration said that the creature was about five feet long and resembled a siren. After being captured, the unlucky *Zee-Wyf* was kept in a barrel of water. Not surprisingly, declining to eat anything, it died about a week later — after making a few faint mewing, squeaking noises that reminded its captors of a mouse.

Tales of the mermaid of Amboina reached the illustrious ears of Tsar Peter the Great and George III of England, and Valentijn was interrogated further. In response to the Imperial interrogation, he came up with an account of an East Indies Company officer who had seen a pair of the strange merfolk swimming together near Hennetelo, a village in the Administrative District of Amboina. After several weeks these two creatures were seen again — this time by forty or more witnesses. They were described as being greyish green and shaped like human beings from the head down to the waist, below which their bodies tapered like the tail-halves of large fish.

On co-author Lionel's Channel 4 U.K. TV series, one of the mysteries investigated was an object purported to be a wizened, mummified mermaid, but under the pathologist's knife it turned out to be carved entirely from wood. A theory advanced at the time was that these carved figures were meant as votive offerings by Polynesian and other fishing peoples and were cast into the sea at appropriate places to please the gods, so ensuring a profitable catch and a safe return for the fishermen.

Other mermaids in various sideshows and exhibitions where admission fees were charged almost always turned out to have been carefully crafted by skilled taxidermists from the upper body of a monkey and the rear end of a fish.

A rather more detailed and convincing historical account comes from Orford in East Anglia in the U.K., where medieval fishermen apparently caught a merman in 1204. In those days, the port of Orford on England's east coast was relatively prosperous, Henry II having built a castle there because he was highly suspicious of the unpredictable Hugh Bigod of Bungay. The event is related by Ralph of Coggeshall, a monastic chronicler of that epoch.

According to Ralph's version of the case, a group of sturdy East Anglian fishermen were having a struggle to get their nets on board because of a large creature that had somehow become entangled with their catch. When the net finally lay in the bottom of their boat, what looked very much like a man was glaring up at them from among the squirming fish. In Ralph's account, the merman was unclothed but covered in hair — except for the top of his head, which was bald. Another very human feature was his long beard, which was described as straggly. The Orford men tried to talk to their captive, but his best replies were little more than grunting noises. Not knowing what else to do with him, the fishermen took him to the castle and handed him over to the warden, Bartholomew de Gladville. Gladville wasn't too sure about him either and decided to keep him there as a prisoner. The merman responded positively to a raw fish diet, but still refused to speak — almost certainly because he couldn't. It was noted by his jailers that when he was offered a piece of fish, he squeezed the liquid from it first and drank it.

In desperation, Gladville resorted to torture to try to get some intelligible words from his strange, aquatic prisoner, but even when he was hung upside down the merman would not, or could not, talk. On being taken to church, he showed neither knowledge of, nor interest in, religion. The humane side of Gladville coming to the top, however briefly, he ordered his men to sling nets across the harbour mouth and allow the merman to swim for a little while — probably in the hope that if their prisoner felt happier, he might say something. For a swimmer of the merman's ability, the line of nets presented no barrier at all. He simply dived under them and vanished out to sea. After one or two triumphant appearances above the waves, he left the Orford area and was never seen again.

The nature of his real identity remains an unsolved mystery today.

What might still provide clues to the enigma of the merfolk is what is alleged to be the actual grave of a mermaid in the cemetery at Nunton in the Hebrides, off the coast of Scotland. She was found dead on the beach in 1830, and was described in the traditional way — human to the waist and fish from there downwards. The human part apparently seemed so human that the sympathetic islanders felt that a decent burial was called for. With the scientific advantages of modern DNA analysis, that grave could well be worth very careful investigation.

John Smith — associated with Pocahontas in the rather controversial story of his rescue by the beautiful young Native American princess — also features as a reporter of romantic mermaid sightings. In the West Indies in 1614, Smith claimed that he had seen a mermaid so attractive that he had at first mistaken her for a human girl bathing. Closer inspection, however, revealed that she had luxuriant green hair, and in Smith's own phrasing "from below the waist the woman gave way to fish."

Christopher Columbus is also credited with sighting mermaids. He reported seeing no fewer than three of them "leaping out of the water," but it seems much more likely that what Columbus actually observed were dugongs, since he added rather disappointedly that they were "not so fair as they were said to be."

Ovid, the Roman poet also known as Naso, who was born in 43 BC, suggested imaginatively that mermaids were born from the burning galleys of the defeated Trojans. Where did they really come from?

Could the manatee and the dugong be all there is behind the innumerable mermaid legends? Or is there much more to all those reported sightings? The myths and legends of the merfolk may well be connected to the strange and ancient accounts of various marine deities such as Oannes, or demigods like the Tritons, which persist in various shapes and sizes in religious writings all over the world. These mysterious aquatic entities form the subject of our next chapter.

CHAPTER THREE

Who Were the Water Gods?

Ancient Babylonian aquatic deity: Ea or Oannes.

Academic folklorists and scholars specializing in the evolution and development of myths and legends frequently suggest links between the more recent mermaid stories and the ancient theology of various water divinities. Berosus of Chaldea, writing three hundred years before the Christian Era, described something he believed had risen from the Erythrean Sea. Berosus was intelligent, highly educated, and worked as an astronomer and a priest. His description of Ea or Oannes suggests that this extraordinary being had two heads, one underneath the other. Does this suggest diving gear to the twenty-first-century mind? Oannes also possessed human feet as well as a fish's tail — which also suggests a special aquatic suit or costume of some kind. Later carvings of Oannes, or Ea, show him with a humanoid upper body and a fish tail — rather like traditional depictions of Neptune or Poseidon.

Oannes was an exceptionally pleasant and helpful god when compared to many of his contemporaries in the Assyrio-Babylonian pantheon. Oannes taught people arts and sciences, helped with healing and fertility, and was a thoroughly benign mentor to humanity. He rose from the sea every morning and vanished back into it at night — suggesting that in the minds of some of his worshippers, at least, he was associated with the sun's rising and setting.

His feminine counterpart, Atergatis, was also known as Derceto. Early representations of her — like those of Oannes — showed a clearly humanoid body with a fish cap on the head and a fish-skin cloak, again reminiscent of modern sub-aqua gear. Later representations were closer to the modern mermaid style: human upper body and fish tail. Her priests had a keen eye for business and issued fishing licences in her name in return for an appropriate fee. Just as Oannes was tenuously associated with the sun, so Atergatis was a lunar goddess. The ebb and flow of the tides was known to be associated with the moon, so a lunar goddess like Atergatis would logically be associated with the sea.

Some later, variant myths describe her association with a human lover by whom she had a daughter, Semiramis. She seems, despite much historical controversy, to have been a genuine historical figure, and to have grown up to become a very great and politically effective queen of Assyria. According to mythology, Derceto — or Atergatis — had displeased Aphrodite, alias the Assyrian Ashtaroth, the goddess of love, who had in revenge caused Derceto to fall madly and unwisely in love with a young Syrian named Caystrus. After the birth of Semiramis, Derceto, feeling ashamed, humiliated, and betrayed, killed Caystrus and left their baby girl among the acacia bushes. Derceto then went back under the water and stayed there for a long time.

Miraculously, the baby was discovered by doves who fed her with scraps of food — much as Elijah was fed by ravens in the biblical account. Finally discovered and rescued by kind-hearted shepherds, the little girl was given the name Semiramis, meaning "she who came from among the doves." Raised by the caring shepherds, she grew into a very beautiful young woman.

King Ninus (interestingly, his name is derived from the Assyrian word *nunu*, meaning fish) sent one of his trusted senior officers, Menon, to inspect the royal flocks. He fell in love with the exquisite Semiramis and took her home with him to Nineveh, where he married her.

It was Menon's misfortune a few years later that the aging Ninus saw and fell in love with Semiramis — a parallel perhaps with the great Hebrew king David and his infatuation with Bathsheba. Ninus offered Menon one of his own beautiful daughters in exchange for Semiramis. Menon declined. Ninus then threatened to blind, torture, and kill him.

Faced with an offer he couldn't refuse, Menon reluctantly sent Semiramis to Ninus — and then committed suicide.

Fragments of historical evidence suggest that when Ninus died (perhaps Semiramis assisted in the process?) she became an extremely powerful and effective ruler. Historians are not in agreement, but there is enough evidence of the reign of Semiramis to make it more than merely myth or legend. One touching detail recorded by some historians is that she had truly loved only Menon, and even in old age she still wore and treasured a necklace that he had given her long ago when he first found her among the shepherds who had brought her up.

Was Derceto (Atergatis) perhaps also a historical person? If so, what was the real significance of her strong association with the moon and the sea, and did she have any extraordinary paranormal powers? Was it her genetic inheritance that made Semiramis so intelligent and effective?

In addition to major marine deities, the ancient theologies peopled their pantheons with sirens and water nymphs, beautiful to look at and accomplished singers and musicians. Sirens were depicted as part woman, part bird, rather than as part woman, part fish.

In mythology they were the daughters of the river god Achelous, and their numbers are given as anywhere from two to eight. Their names indicated the charm of their alluring voices: Aglaophone, for example, meant "the brilliant voice," and her sister Molpe's name meant "song." In their notorious encounter with the wily Odysseus, of Trojan Horse fame, they sang a lyric that would have turned the head of any hero: "Draw near, wonderful Odysseus, greatest and most admired of the Achaeans. Pause in your journey and come to visit our beautiful island. We know everything that happens in the world, and we know of your great deeds at Troy."

Odysseus had thoughtfully blocked the ears of his crew with wax and ordered them to tie him to the mast so that he could hear the wonderful siren sounds without succumbing to their fatal temptations.

The Sirens finally met their match when the Argonauts sailed past their island of treachery and death. Orpheus, the master musician and singer, whose powers vastly excelled theirs, defeated them, and, overwhelmed by his superior skills, the Sirens were turned into rocks — all except for Parthenope. She leapt into the sea and was drowned. Her body, according to legend, was washed ashore at the site of the future city of Naples.

In several mythologies and religious legends — including Cambodian ones — the Asparas were beautiful and seductive female water deities who played exquisite flute music and seduced scholars and academic researchers in order to distract them from studies that might have led them too close to secret truths that the gods preferred to conceal.

A colourful piece of ancient Chinese creation mythology concerns a quarrel between two gods: Gong Gong, the god of water, and Zhurong, the god of fire. A violent, catastrophic battle took place between them, and finally Gong Gong was hurled down from the heavens, which began to buckle under the strain. Shamed by defeat, he attempted to destroy himself by charging at the mountain that supported the sky — causing further major structural problems for the ancient cosmos!

Japanese and Chinese mythology also included sea dragons as well as dragon-wives and mermaids. The Japanese *Ningyo*, for example, were quasi-human, but had only a human head — rather than a full upper torso — mounted on a fish body. In Polynesian legends, the hybridized form of merperson was a combination of human form and porpoise. These aquatic semi-divinities were worshipped under the title of *Vatea*.

Greek and Roman mythology, to which so much contemporary culture is still heavily in debt, includes Neptune-Poseidon as the massively powerful sea god — often depicted with a human upper torso and a magical trident in one hand. As he rears up commandingly out of the waters he controls, many pictures show his lower body ending with a huge fish's tail. Being one of the most powerful of the ancient deities, Neptune-Poseidon could transform himself at will, and his traditional part-fish structure didn't seem to inhibit his procreational activities with human females — or with goddesses and demigoddesses of the Greco-Roman pantheon. His son Triton, who was half fish like his father, and his daughter Rhode, the patron goddess and protectress of the island of Rhodes, were born from his relationship with Amphitrite.

Triton is associated with the conch shell symbol, from which he produces a sound so terrifying that even giants run away when they hear it. Triton uses this magical conch shell to raise storms and huge waves, or to calm the sea afterwards.

As time passed, the mythology developed and expanded and the Tritons became a whole class of beings — not just one individual. Even stranger than the half-fish, half-human Tritons were the Centauro-Tritons (also known to academic mythologists and folklorists as Ichthyocentaurs). These complex beings were a mixture of horse, fish, and human being.

Real specimens of Tritons were said to have been on display in Rome and in Tangara during Roman times, according to evidence provided by the old Greek travel writer Pausanias. Born in Lydia, he toured Asia Minor, Syria, Egypt, Palestine, Epirus, and further afield. Writing between AD 143 and 180, Pausanias typically began his descriptions of the cities he visited with a short history, followed by an account of the monuments and buildings he saw, as well as references to local folklore, legends, and religious ceremonies. His careful and accurate descriptions of the places he visited so many centuries ago coincide very closely with what we know today of those landmarks that have stood the test of time and are still around. Pausanias is, therefore, regarded as a reliable chronicler. What did he really see when he described Tritons?

There are also interesting references in mythology and legends from this period, and earlier periods, to the *Nereids*. These beautiful and benign sea maidens were the daughters of Nereus, a kind of "Old Man of the Sea," but totally different from the malevolent creature who almost murdered Sinbad the Sailor. Nereus is associated with the Mediterranean in general and the Aegean in particular. His mother is Gaia, the great Earth goddess, and his father is Pontus — really just a personification of the sea itself. Kind and wise old Nereus married Doris, an Oceanid sea nymph. She herself was the daughter of Oceanus and Tethys, who were Titans. Doris became the mother of Nereus's fifty daughters — the Nereids — but apart from that did not get overly involved in the activities of the Greek pantheon. The Nereids and their father have often been credited with saving ships from wreck and their passengers and crews from death in the Aegean Sea — which is their particular responsibility. The Nereids are sometimes depicted as totally human — although sea dwellers. At other times they appear in the human-and-fish shape of classical mermaids and traditional water deities.

The U.K. also has its fair share of sea deities and aquatic demigods. What the Greeks and Romans thought of as Nereids and Oceanids were called *Merrymaids* in Cornwall and *Merrows* in Ireland. Like the Greek sea maidens of the Mediterranean and Aegean, these Irish and Cornish water nymphs were extremely beautiful. In the legends they wore "magical caps" that enabled them to pass through the water — and there are some researchers who see in the "magical cap" an advanced form of diving helmet. Were these amazing sea nymphs using a highly advanced scuba technology rather than magic? If they were, where had they come from: Atlantis, Lemuria, or some mysterious, extraterrestrial location?

The Isle of Man had its own special water god named Mannan, who was very similar to the Irish sea god Manannan mac Lir. Fishermen often prayed to them for a safe trip and a good catch:

> Manannan, Son of the Sea,
> You bless our island home,

Bless us and this boat.
May we go out well and come in better.

Although primarily a sea god, Manannan was also semi-historical. He was believed to have lived in a castle on a hill and to have been buried on the island.

The legendary sea deities from the waters around the Shetlands have ancient traditions that hint even more strongly at technological rather than magical explanations: they are said to be able to remove their marine-animal "skins" (close-fitting diving suits?) and to walk around on the land in a normal human way.

The Scandinavian water deities were known as the *Neck*, and were highly unpredictable. The males were called *Havfrue*; the females were *Havmand* and *Havfine*. In Germany, the mermaids or water nymphs and sea goddesses were called *Meerfrau* and *Melusine*. These latter had double tails.

In Russia and other maritime Eastern European cultures, the two best known water deities, or merpeople, were the *Rusalka* — malevolent female water nymphs who lured men to their deaths by drowning — and the vast and frog-like male *Vodyanoi*, who devoured their prey in the water.

France is not without its strange allusions to sea deities and curious paranormal marine beings. King Merovée, founder of the remarkable Merovingian Dynasty, reigned from 448 to 457, and was *officially* the son of King Clodion the Long-Haired. There are persistent rumours, however, to the effect that Merovée's mother was raped, or seduced, by a very unusual and mysterious sea being referred to as a Quinotaur. Was he named Merovée because the first syllable of his name, *mer*, indicates the sea? The question of who, or what, a Quinotaur might *really* have been is a controversial and complicated one: it resurrects the whole range of speculation about intelligent, amphibian aliens, or technologically advanced Atlanteans. Does the *taur* syllable of Quinotaur indicate a bull-god, like the one in the Minoan culture, or even the golden calf that Aaron permitted the Israelites to make and that caused so much trouble when Moses came back down the mountain?

Water gods like Merovée's Quinotaur and dangerous water goddesses like the Sirens are ubiquitous in myth and legend, and worldwide reports of them go back for millennia. Some researchers would suggest that the tales are based on remnants of an ancient technology, perhaps Atlantean, perhaps extraterrestrial. Others look for cryptozoological explanations, while open-minded supernaturalists give serious consideration to the possibility that these mysterious water beings really do possess assorted anomalous, magical, superhuman powers.

CHAPTER FOUR

Monsters of the Deep

Ancient Greek artwork showing Herakles fighting Ketos, a sea monster.

Two of the most famous ancient Greek accounts of sea monsters are remarkably similar: in the first, a fearless hero rescues Princess Hesione from the monster that Poseidon had sent to terrorize Troy; in the second, another hero, Perseus, rescues Andromeda from a parallel fate. So reports of marine monsters go back a very long way. Early Greek poetry, for example, referred to the battle between the mighty Herakles (Hercules) and one of the terrifying Ketea — the awesome sea monsters under Poseidon's control and sent out by him much as gangland bosses send out their hitmen today. According to these classical accounts, the creatures were insatiably hungry and resorted to cannibalism when there was no other prey readily available. The poet Oppian referred to them frequently and in detail in his work *Halieutica* — a treatise on fishing. His book warns that they appear most frequently in the Iberian Sea off the coast of Spain. These ancient Ketea are frequently described as more elongated and serpentine than normal fish.

There is a powerful and persistent nexus between Greek history and mythology and monsters of the deep. One of the most intriguing stories told about Alexander the Great is that he was an intrepid pioneer of the deep and that inside a specially constructed glass diving bell he watched a sea monster so vast that it took three full days to pass his submarine observation post.

Reports of sea monsters are also right up to date. The authors were called in by BBC TV to investigate some very interesting and accurate reports of sightings in 2003 in Pembroke Dock, Wales, U.K. We interviewed four of the eyewitnesses there and then set out for a couple of hours in the *Cleddau King* — a superb boat for the job, fully equipped with high-tech electronic search gear.

Co-author Patricia with Skipper Alun Lewis aboard his high-tech search boat
Cleddau King.

The superb Cleddau King *with ultra-high-tech electronic search gear aboard her.*

Co-author Lionel with eyewitnesses Lesley John and David Crew at the Shipwright Inn at Pembroke Dock.

Our first witness was David Crew, landlord of the Shipwright Inn, number one Front Street, Pembroke Dock, Wales, U.K. This is what David told us:

> On Wednesday, March 5, 2003, at lunchtime, I was in the kitchen. My barmaid, Lesley, was behind the bar, and a few of her customers, Peter, Tori, and Philip were in the pub. Lesley looked out of the window overlooking the Milford Haven Estuary and saw something resembling a large fin smashing through the water. She drew our attention to it and when we came out we saw something that we can only describe as a sea serpent. I would say that it was a long, dark, serpent-shaped object about five to six cars' length. Peter, one of the witnesses, quoted it as having a diamond-shaped head. He saw that diamond-shaped head rear briefly out of the water, and it disappeared again just as quickly. I would say it was five or six feet in diameter.

Lesley herself said: "It was still when I first saw it. It was just motionless in the water at that point. It was a nice bright, clear day. The thing was strange and definitely alive. I felt very shocked when I saw it. It seemed to be a big sea monster."

The next witness was Peter Thomas, a customer who had been in the Shipwright Inn at the time whatever-it-was was sighted. This is Peter's statement:

> Lesley drew my attention to something she saw in the river and I went to the window and looked out. It was something I estimated to be about ten metres in length. You could see a sort of diamond-shaped head, or what appeared to be a diamond-shaped head, out of the water and you could see the rest of it going back about thirty feet: a body moving through the water probably about the size of a beer barrel in diameter.

At this point, I asked Peter to sketch what he'd seen.

> When Lesley brought it to my attention, I went to the door and looked between the wall of the port and the Martello tower. You've got the wall down there and the tower this end. All I could see was a diamond-shaped sort of head just above the water — not erect or any-thing — and then all this turbulence back behind it. It was moving in the river at a fair amount of speed. It was obviously something moving, not anything drift-ing. ... In a matter of less than a minute it was gone ...

Co-author Lionel pointing to the area where Peter Thomas and the other witnesses saw the monster.

clean out of sight behind the port wall. It was travelling at about seven or eight knots.

Co-author Lionel with eyewitnesses Tori Crawford and Peter Thomas in the Shipwright Inn at Pembroke Dock.

Eyewitness Tori Crawford then said:

> When Lesley told us about the fin, we all proceeded to go outside. We were all together, but I was one of the last ones to get outside. There it was, just as Dave said. It was between three and five car lengths long, and there was definitely a big shadow in the water. I only saw a little bit of the diamond head, not a lot of it — what we think was the head anyway. But it was something that I'd never seen before. Never! It certainly wasn't seaweed put together, or anything like that.

Asked to draw a picture of what she'd seen, Tori provided more information as she sketched it:

> I was one of the last ones to come out, so I hardly saw anything of the head myself. But you have the wall there and the Martello tower here. And it was as if the creature had bumps like this: the large one in the middle and then a small one just coming off here. It looked like a mountain moving along, but it definitely had a smaller bit

towards the tail part, and a smaller bit towards the head. The turbulence coming from the back was unbelievable; it made you think it had flippers.

Eyewitnesses Tori Crawford and Peter Thomas in the Shipwright Inn.

Many years' experience as an investigator provides a professional researcher with the ability to weigh the reliability of witnesses to this kind of reported phenomena. Having spent several hours in their company, we are convinced that the witnesses we interviewed were very sensible, rational people making clear and accurate reports about what they had seen in the Estuary by Pembroke Dock. Precisely what the creature was remains a mystery. Possibilities range from some large, unknown species of marine animal to a miniature submarine manoeuvring in a difficult, shallow, and restricted waterway. There are Ministry of Defence activities in this area from time to time, and unconventional new designs of underwater craft *may* be tested here occasionally.

Reports of sea monsters from the past — centuries before human technology reached a point where the first relatively modern submarines appeared — would seem to require other possible explanations, unless some of the most ancient sea monster myths and legends owe their origin to underwater craft from Atlantis, Lemuria, or the advanced technology of visiting extraterrestrial amphibians.

We live in an incredibly strange universe, and the more we learn of its wonders and mysteries, the stranger and more inexplicable it becomes. What we like to refer to as "good, old-fashioned common sense" can sometimes be a million miles wide of the mark, but it is always worth looking for simple, commonsense answers before venturing into the misty and uncertain vistas of Von Daniken Land. William of Occam's famous medieval philosophical Razor taught much the same set of truths! His basic principle was that we should never make more assumptions than the minimum necessary to explain any phenomenon being studied. It's also referred to as the Principle of Parsimony. Despite its medieval origins it underlies much of our contemporary thought. Occam's Razor recommends that we metaphorically shave off anything that isn't absolutely essential to explain the phenomenon we're investigating — or the model of it that we're building.

Although the widely and persistently reported Loch Ness phenomena do not strictly relate to *sea* monsters, the Loch Ness sightings are too important to be omitted from any serious study of marine cryptozoology. If sea monsters really exist, a detailed survey of Loch Ness will provide the researcher with valuable clues.

A report from as long ago as the year 565 records how Saint Columba, while travelling up to Inverness on a missionary journey to the Picts, rescued a man in danger on Loch Ness. The original account reports that "a strange beast rose from the water." The geological history of Loch Ness suggests that it was at one time connected to the North Sea, a fact that would support the argument that members of the plesiosaur group are reasonably strong claimants for being the Loch Ness monster — if there is one at all. To add detail to the 565 account, it was said that Columba and his followers knew that a local swimmer had been fatally mauled by *something* big and dangerous in the Loch. Despite this, one of Columba's followers had valiantly started swimming to retrieve a boat. Suddenly, a huge creature reared up out of the water and made towards the terrified swimmer. Some early accounts, which give the monster its Gaelic name, Niseag, describe it as resembling an enormous frog. This would link it with the vodyanoi of Finland.

Columba himself ran fearlessly into the water to save his companion, shouting sternly to the monster, "Go no farther! Touch not thou that man." Columba was a powerful man in mind and body, as well as a good and courageous one. Whether it was the saint's forceful voice or some paranormal power of holiness surrounding him, the monster decided that on this occasion it had more than met its match and that discretion was definitely the better part of valour: it retreated ignominiously. Could the creature even have been a thought-form like the Tibetan *tulpa*, which retreated when attacked by a powerful mind like Columba's?

The Loch is about 35 kilometres long and 250 metres deep: a spacious enough home for the largest sea monster. Duncan McDonald, a diver, was working there in 1880 (albeit with the rather primitive equipment then available). As he carried out his salvage operations on a wrecked ship in the Loch, he claimed that he saw the monster swimming past him. In his report he paid particular note to the monster's eyes, saying that they were small, grey, and baleful. They gave him the impression that annoying or interfering with Nessie would not be prudent.

Fifty-odd years after Duncan McDonald's encounter, George Spicer and his wife were driving along the south bank of Loch Ness when they saw a strange creature on land, actually emerging from the bracken beside the road. The Spicers said that it appeared to have a long, undulating neck resembling an elephant's trunk. The head was disproportionately small, but big enough for the monster to hold an animal in its mouth. As the Spicers watched, whatever the thing was lumbered down the bank and into the Loch, where it vanished below the water with a loud splash. In a later interview with a journalist, George said that it had made him think of an enormous snail with a long neck and small head.

During the 1930s, excitement over reports of Nessie reached fever pitch. Among hundreds of reported sightings at that time was one from an AA motorcycle patrolman. His description coincided closely with what George Spicer had reported. Hugh Gray, an engineer, actually managed to get a photograph of it — but although it was agreed by the scientific experts that the picture had not been tampered with, it was not sufficiently clear and distinct for the creature to be zoologically identified.

Alexander Campbell, a journalist, described his sighting in the summer of 1934. His cottage was situated beside the Loch, and, as he left home one morning, he saw the creature rear up out of the water, looking remarkably like a prehistoric monster. He confirmed the descriptions of the long, serpentine neck given by other witnesses, and added that he had seen a flat tail as well. Alexander said that where the neck and body joined there was a hump. He watched it sunbathing for some moments until the sound of a boat on the Caledonian Canal apparently unnerved it. Its sudden dive into deeper water produced a miniature tidal wave.

Saint Columba was by no means the only holy man to see the monster. Some fourteen centuries after Columba rescued the intrepid swimmer, Brother Richard Horan, a monk from St. Benedict's Abbey at Fort Augustus, also saw the creature. He said that it was in clear view for almost half an hour, and added that the head and neck were thrust out of the water at an angle of about forty-five degrees and were silvery grey. Just as a boat had disturbed the monster when Alexander Campbell saw it, so Brother Horan's view of it ended when a motorboat went past. At the sound of the engine, the monster sank back into the impenetrable darkness of the Loch.

There have been so many reliable and sensibly reported sightings over so many years that it is not easy to dismiss Nessie as a figment of the imagination, an optical illusion, or a shrewd publicity stunt. Space prevents more than a few of the hundreds of such reports appearing here, but among the most notable ones are:

- 1895: Several fishermen, timber workers, and a hotelier reported what they described as something "very big and horrible" surfacing not far from them in Loch Ness.

- 1903: Three witnesses in a rowboat tried very bravely to get closer to it but failed to narrow the distance between the creature and their boat. They reported the humped contour of what they saw.

- 1908: John Macleod reported seeing something more than twelve metres long with a body that he described as "eel-like and tapering." According to John's account it seemed to be floating on, or very close to, the surface. After a few moments, it moved away.

- 1923: Miller and MacGillivray had a good clear view of something in the Loch and described its distinct hump.

- 1929: Mrs. Cummings and another witness saw a humped creature on the surface for a few moments. As they watched, it submerged.

- 1930: Ian Milne saw something inexplicable in the Loch very early in the morning. He reported that it was moving fast — close to twenty knots — and he was sure he saw two or three of the characteristic humps along its back.

- 1943: Something at least ten metres long was observed submerged but clearly discernible just below the surface of the Loch. It was very early in the morning and the witness was sure that he saw at least one large hump.

- 1947: The MacIver family and two or three other witnesses reported something very big and very strange moving fast across the Loch.
- 1953: A group of timber cutters working beside the Loch reported seeing the creature for two or three minutes.
- 1954: A fishing boat's echo-sounder detected something about 20 metres long at a depth of 170 metres.
- 1960: Torquil MacLeod and his wife reported seeing it while they were in the Invermorriston area. They had it in view for almost ten minutes as it sat on the opposite shore, and they described it as grey with skin like an elephant or hippopotamus. They also noted its paddle-shaped flippers.
- Tim Dinsdale took a very significant ciné-film of it in the same year. He gave up his profession as an aircraft engineer in order to devote all his time to investigating the creature.
- 1961: A large group of guests — nearly twenty of them — at a hotel overlooking the Loch reported observing something over ten metres long. It rose from the water and they had a clear view of it for five or six minutes. Those witnesses were convinced that they could clearly see the monster's humps, which were frequently reported during previous sightings.
- 1962: Sir Peter Scott (1909–1990), son of the famous polar explorer, was renowned for his high intelligence, his skills as an artist, his services to natural science — and his dry sense of humour. He helped to found the Loch Ness Phenomena Investigation Bureau and named the creature being sought: *Nessiteras Rhombopteryx*. That sounds like an excellent piece of scientific nomenclature, but it can be broken down into an anagram of the type that delights advanced crossword enthusiasts. The seemingly dignified, scientific Latin name that Sir Peter awarded to

Nessie can be made to spell *Monster hoax by Sir Peter S.* Was that a deliberate anagram or just a curious coincidence? Cryptographers and code-breaking professionals know just how easy it is for what seems like a clever anagram to be mere chance. No great mathematician from the depths of mathematical history ever decided to call a decimal point a decimal point simply because the anagram *A decimal point = I'm a dot in place* existed. Sir Peter's naming of the monster might have been as accidental and innocent as the decimal point example. There are also a great many bluffs and counter-bluffs in the archives of investigations into anomalous phenomena: things that seemed inexplicable at first turn out to have simple, mundane explanations, but the next set of investigations shows that the so-called simple and rational explanations were themselves wrong — and there *is* an anomaly to be investigated after all! It might well have appealed to Sir Peter's mischievous sense of humour to *pretend* that there was only a hoax in Loch Ness, not a mystery. As a dedicated conservationist, it might also have occurred to him that the best way to keep prospective monster hunters away from the Loch was to pretend that it was all a hoax.

- 1969: Four members of the Craven family watched a creature ten metres long surface, disturb the water significantly, and then sink down into the depths again.
- 1970: Dr. Robert Rines of the Academy of Applied Sciences in Belmont, Massachusetts, spent time investigating the Loch and was convinced that the creature — or creatures — existed.
- 1971: Dinsdale's team reported something very mysterious and very much alive rearing up out of the Loch.
- 1972: Former paratrooper Frank Searle investigated carefully and reported several significant sightings. He believes that there's a colony of at least a dozen of the strange creatures living in the Loch.

- 1974: Henry Wilson and Andy Call described a creature twenty metres long with an equine head. They saw it surface and thresh the water for ten or fifteen minutes while they watched.
- 1975: On June 20, Dr. Rines's team took some very interesting and convincing pictures deep in the Loch.
- 1996: Witness Bill Kinder described something odd rising up from the Loch with two humps clearly visible.
- 2003: Witnesses on the Royal Scot train during the early afternoon saw something big and inexplicable moving at an estimated twenty-five knots along the Loch. They also reported that the weather was calm at the time, so there was no wind to account for the movement of some casually floating, inanimate object.

Leaving Occam's Razor oiled, sharpened, and ready in its waterproof case for the sake of wider, more complex and imaginative arguments, what speculative explanations might be available? The first possibility is the survival of something like a prehistoric plesiosaur: the general description of the plesiosaur included flippers, humps, a long neck, and a tail. The second theory comes within the sphere of phenomenalism, a philosophical theory that suggests there are hard, scientific, material facts at one end of the spectrum of phenomena — things such as bricks, mortar, and Newton's Laws of Motion. At the other end are pure imaginings and fantasies, such as dreams of riding up cider waterfalls in canoes made of chocolate pulled by gigantic sugary dragonflies. Phenomenalists hypothesize that between these two extremes there are some intermediate observations that are neither hard, provable fact nor pure, subjective fantasy. Without necessarily including it in their theories, phenomenalists would entertain the ancillary possibility that things like the Loch Ness monster, ghosts, apparitions, and phantoms might have a quasi-existence — perhaps gliding between timeframes or probability tracks to impinge upon what we fondly call "reality." This realm of speculation also includes tulpa-like thought-forms.

There are other theorists who regard the Loch Ness monster as something paranormal, sinister, negative, and threatening: perhaps a primitive, elemental spirit being — taking on quasi-physical appearances as and when it chooses.

There are also the mechanical theories — that the supposed monster is really an artifact of some kind. According to these speculations, the more modern appearances may be due to tests of secret inventions of the Ministry of Defence, such as small submarines. The ancient appearances, if mechanical, would have to tiptoe into Von Daniken Land and incorporate theories about highly intelligent aliens from the stars, Atlantis, or Lemuria, equipped with a technology that included submarines.

Interest in the Loch is as fresh today as it ever was — and some is truly heart-warming. Lloyd Scott suffered from chronic myeloid leukaemia until a life-saving bone marrow transplant put things right for him in 1989. Determined to help others in similar circumstances, Lloyd became a record-holding charity marathon runner, completing the London Marathon in an ancient diving suit with a copper helmet. His latest charity venture on behalf of children suffering from leukaemia is to walk all around the edges of Loch Ness, on the narrow ledges a few feet underwater, in his famous antique copper-helmeted diving suit.

The authors warmly congratulate him and wish him every success. Co-author Lionel wore a similar outfit while filming an episode of *Fortean TV* on the U.K.'s Channel 4. The director wanted him to get into a tank full of fish in the Yarmouth, Norfolk, U.K., aquarium, submerge, then surface to introduce an item about a mysterious diver. The genuine antique diving suit supplied by a theatrical costume company had long since lost its original lead-soled boots, so when Lionel submerged, his feet shot upwards. The big copper helmet filled with water and held him upside down. Fortunately, Alf, his stalwart guitarist, was also in the tank and fished him out none the worse for wear!

Almost as famous as the Loch Ness phenomenon is the account of the sea serpent observed by Captain Peter M'Quhae and his crew on board the frigate *Daedalus* on August 6, 1848. They were between the island of St. Helena (where Napoleon *reputedly* died — but that's another strange mystery) and the Cape of Good Hope (notorious for its connection with the *Flying Dutchman*). It was five o'clock in the afternoon, and visibility was not ideal: the weather was described as dull and showery. A young midshipman reported that he had seen what he described as a "strange creature" moving towards the *Daedalus*'s starboard bow. Various shipmates — including the officer of the watch, the navigator, and the captain himself — responded to the midshipman's call. A total of seven experienced naval men were now watching the creature. Their reports clearly indicated *something* serpentine estimated at well over thirty metres long and travelling at about twelve knots. With the aid of telescopes, they kept it in sight for nearly half an hour. Despite the poor visibility caused by the dull, damp weather, M'Quhae reckoned that he and his crew were able to see the monster reasonably well. He said that if the thing had been a person whom he knew, he would have been able to recognize him — the creature was as close and as clear as that! M'Quhae referred to the face and head as "distinctly snake-like." According to his account, the neck supporting this serpentine head was about forty centimetres in diameter, and the body went back a long way. The head was just above the water, and the underside of the neck was a whitish yellow. The rest of the creature, as M'Quhae and his team described it, was very dark brown, almost black.

The men of the *Daedalus* were somewhat puzzled by the creature's ability to maintain its speed and course without any apparent means of propulsion. They said that as far as they were able to ascertain it neither paddled with submerged flippers nor undulated its lengthy body from side to side, as many marine serpents do when swimming. The thing M'Quhae and his men reported bore a striking resemblance to the sea serpent described by Bishop Pontoppidan a century earlier in his book *A Natural History of Norway*. Pontoppidan had also described merfolk, as noted in our earlier chapter. Media reports in 1848 were not necessarily accurate, and although the *Times* of October 10 reported that M'Quhae and his men had seen a beast with a huge mouth full of dangerous teeth, they themselves did not seem to have said anything about its dentition.

Although their accounts differed in certain details — as honest, independent accounts normally do — the witnesses agreed that the thing they had seen had not struck them as threatening or hostile to the *Daedalus* in any way. Neither had it seemed to be afraid of the ship. The general impression it gave them was that it was totally preoccupied with some purpose of its own — perhaps something as demanding as searching for a mate, or as simple as a quest for nourishment. M'Quhae made sketches of it, which were eventually reproduced in the *Illustrated London News* on October 28 — after the *Times* had told the story on October 13.

Various theories were put forward as to what M'Quhae's monster might have been. Suggestions included the gigantic variety of seal, *phoca proboscidea*, referred to as a "sea-elephant" — but M'Quhae, who had seen one, was adamant that the creature observed from the *Daedalus* was very definitely not an elephant seal.

Brilliant professional underwater cinematographer Jonathan Bird encountered an oarfish (*Regalecus glesne*) in the Bahamas recently. Although this was by no means as long as the monster that M'Quhae and his team described, it was certainly similar to it, and the specimen Jonathan saw was about fifteen metres long. The oarfish is very elongated and has yellow lures on the ends of its strange antennae. It swims in an upright position using its dorsal fin only — not its entire body:

that also sounds like the movement of the weird creature that the men of the *Daedalus* reported.

A report from 1953 — about a century after the adventure of the *Daedalus* — came from a diver working in the South Pacific and attempting to establish a new depth record. He said that he was keeping a wary eye on a shark that was taking an unhealthy interest in him and wondering just how far it would attempt to follow him down. His explorations took him to the edge of a vast submarine chasm vanishing down into awesome, unknown depths. He said that the water became markedly colder. The temperature drop was very significant, and it continued to get more pronounced. Clinging tightly to his ledge — to have dropped into the chasm would have been fatal — the diver saw a huge black shadowy *something* rising very slowly towards him. About the size of a soccer field and dark brown in colour, the *thing* pulsated as it floated gradually higher and higher — convincing the diver that it was definitely a living creature of some type.

As it drew level with his ledge, he reported that the coldness became even more bitter. The weird mass drifted ever closer to the shark, which the diver felt was immobilized either by the cold or by pure terror. The outer edges of the sheet-like thing from the depths touched the motionless shark. It convulsed but made no attempt to resist or escape. Its weird attacker drew the doomed shark down into itself like an amoeba surrounding and digesting its prey and then sank slowly back into the abyss. The diver who reported this episode added that he remained motionless on his perilous submarine ledge until the horrific thing from the abyss had vanished again into the depths.

Could whatever that thing was have been responsible for the tragic disappearance of several divers in that area in the late 1930s? The *Melbourne Leader* at that time reported that the Japanese captain of the *Yamta Maru* had gone down to salvage pearls from a wreck and had given an urgent signal to his crew to haul him up fast. All that reached the surface was his helmet and lifeline; of the fearless captain himself there was no trace. It happened again in 1938. This time it was Masao Matsumo, another Japanese diver, who went down from the *Felton* and was never seen again. Like the skipper of the *Yamta Maru*, Masao gave the signal to be hauled up. His shipmates recovered only his empty helmet and a basket of shells. Fearlessly, his diving colleagues then went down over seventy metres looking for him — but Masao had vanished as completely as the ill-fated captain of the *Yamta Maru*.

There is a remote possibility that the weird, sheet-like, shark-killing *thing* seen in 1953 might have had some connection with another oddity reported in the *Daily Mail* on April 2, 2002. In this press account, it was stated that a huge dark blob — even bigger than the thing that allegedly came up from the chasm and disposed of the shark — was seen drifting towards Florida. Scientists put forward the theory that this particular "monster" was actually a huge cloud of algae. Scientific expeditions sent out to investigate the thing noticed that other marine life seemed to be avoiding it assiduously. Observed from space satellites, it looked very dark, almost black, but when examined from the scientists' boat it was dark green. Marine chemist Dr. Richard Pierce explained that the algae cloud would remove oxygen from the water around it after dark, and marine life avoiding the strange, discoloured patch might be doing so because they sensed that the water in its vicinity was low in vital oxygen.

Of all the great sea monsters of myth, legend, and prehistory, the dreaded Kraken holds the most prominent place. Tennyson's famous poem captures the atmosphere perfectly:

> Below the thunders of the upper deep;
> Far far beneath in the abysmal sea,
> His ancient, dreamless, uninvaded sleep
> The Kraken sleepeth: faintest sunlights flee
> About his shadowy sides: above him swell
> Huge sponges of millennial growth and height;
> And far away into the sickly light,
> From many a wondrous grot and secret cell
> Unnumber'd and enormous polypi
> Winnow with giant fins the slumbering green.
> There hath he lain for ages and will lie
> Battening upon huge seaworms in his sleep
> Until the latter fire shall heat the deep;
> Then once by men and angels to be seen,
> In roaring he shall rise and on the surface die.

Something that was described as a Kraken-type monster at the time was encountered by the crew of a French gunboat, the *Alecton*, on November 30, 1861. They fired cannon shot into it and discharged various small arms, but nothing seemed to affect it very much. Finally, they harpooned it and attempted to get a line around it. The rope slipped until it jammed against the creature's dorsal fin, but as the sailors tried to haul it aboard, the body of their monster disintegrated, leaving them with only a relatively small portion of its tail section.

Arriving with the trophy at Tenerife, the captain contacted the French Consul, displayed the evidence, and made a full report. By December 30, this evidence reached the French Academy of Sciences, where Arthur Mangin, among other highly traditional and formal orthodox scientists, proceeded to ridicule the evidence provided by the *Alecton's* curious catch: "No wise person, especially the man of science, would permit stories of these extraordinary creatures into the catalogue."

With a few honourable exceptions, it was automatically assumed by the ultra-cautious, traditional, scientific elite of the mid-nineteenth century that reports of things that did not fit their schemata were deliberate lies, hoaxes, wild exaggerations, or hallucinations.

Erik Pontoppidan, Bishop of Bergen, who was an indefatigable chronicler of weird and wonderful aquatic lifeforms, described something Krakenesque in his *Natural History of Norway* (1752–3). The bishop believed his beast was two and a half kilometres around, with arms (or tentacles) long enough and strong enough to drag the biggest warship of his day straight to the bottom of the ocean. He appears to have had something like a very large representative of the giant squid tribe in mind, and that certainly fits in well with an account from Dingle Bay in Ireland dating from 1673 — almost a century before Pontoppidan's book appeared. The Irish broadsheet describing the Dingle Bay monster said that it had been killed by James Steward "when it came up at him out of the sea." The picturesque language of the broadsheet was surprisingly accurate in its description of the creature as having eight long "horns" covered with hundreds of "buttons": very squid-like to the modern marine biologist.

Shortly after the Irish adventure in Dingle Bay, another Kraken of vast size ventured onto some rocks off the Norwegian coast, failed to free itself, and died there in 1680. Contemporary accounts said that the stench from its decaying carcass cleared the area for miles around more effectively than any fear of it while alive might have done.

Another Kraken spotter was the famous Hans Egede. He was born on January 31, 1686, at Harrestad in Norway. He took a bachelor of theology degree at the University of Copenhagen in 1705 and was greatly influenced by the then-popular religious movement known as Pietism. (It is necessary to understand Egede's character and faith in order to evaluate his evidence. He seems to have been a man of great intelligence and integrity, which makes him a highly reliable reporter.) The Pietists advocated intensive Bible study and believed that priesthood was universal among Christian believers, which meant that the laity should have an equal share in Church government. Pietists also believed that Christian practice of goodness and kindness in everyday life was essential, and that instead of criticizing those with different beliefs, or with no beliefs at all, the Church should do all it could to help them and make them welcome. Pietists also wanted to reorganize the universities and give religion in them a higher priority. In addition, they wanted to revolutionize preaching so that it concentrated on building people up and increasing their faith.

At the age of thirty-five, in 1721, Egede went to work in Greenland as a missionary and stayed there for fifteen years. In 1734 he reported a "Kraken" seen in the Greenland area. Egede said that it was so vast that when it came up out of the water it reared up as high as the top of the mainmast and that it was of about the same girth as the ship — and several times longer. He described its broad "paws" and long, pointed snout. He said that the ragged, uneven skin of the huge body seemed to be covered in shells. Assuming Egede was making an accurate report, could these have been barnacles?

Johan Streenstrup, a Danish researcher, found evidence of a beached Kraken going back to Iceland in 1639. He lectured on his findings to the Society of Scandinavian Naturalists in 1847 and later backed up his archival evidence with parts of specimens washed up in Jutland. He gave his discovered "Kraken" the scientific name *Architeuthis*, which has stayed with it ever since. Recent scientific studies of *Architeuthis* describe it as having a probable maximum length of twenty metres and a body mass of approximately one tonne. It lives at an average depth of about six hundred metres, and its diet seems to be fish and smaller squids. The eyes are among the largest found in any living creature — up to thirty centimetres across. Study of the brain has been limited because of the rarity of specimens available for examination, but what scientists have learned is rather disconcerting: the brain appears to be very large and complex. The *Architeuthis*'s funnel is an amazing, all-purpose organ capable of producing a powerful jet, expelling eggs, squirting defensive ink, breathing, and waste disposal!

Nondescript monsters — Krakens or otherwise — made several appearances along the eastern seaboard of Canada and the U.S. in the early years of the nineteenth century. In June 1815, to cite just one widely publicized example, something over thirty metres long and proudly displaying a series of the traditional undulating humps was seen ploughing its way southwards through Gloucester Bay. Its head was described as equine.

Bostonian Sam Cabot saw a member of the same species — or the same one that had caused the disturbance in Gloucester Bay — when he was in Nahant in 1816. The one he saw also had a horse-like head and undulating humps. Sam thought it was about thirty metres long. The following year another very confident expert witness had a high-quality telescope with him and said that the horse-headed marine creature he saw through it was definitely not a whale or an enormous member of the dolphin family. He was adamant that nothing he had ever seen among the giant cetaceans had an undulating back like the marine beast of Nahant.

Nova Scotia also made many contributions to the history of eastern seaboard monster sightings during this period. One typical case involved two men from Peggy's Cove who were out fishing: John Bockner and his teacher friend, James Wilson. They later reported their encounter with a sea serpent in St. Margaret's Bay to the Reverend John Ambrose, who subsequently saw one himself and contributed a scientific paper to the Nova Scotia Institute of Natural Sciences. Among Rev. Ambrose's accounts was an episode that took place in 1849 involving Joseph Holland, Jacob Keddy, and two of their colleagues. On South West Island on the west side of the entrance to St. Margaret's Bay, they observed something like a gigantic sea snake propelling itself through the water not far from the shore. They launched a boat to get a better view of it and managed to get close to it, apparently without being seen by it. The men said that it was eel-like. They were close enough to see that its huge body was covered in scales, each about fifteen centimetres long by seven or eight centimetres wide. The longer part of the scales pointed along the length of the sea serpent's body, which was black in colour. When the monster became aware of the observers' boat, it turned towards them and opened its huge jaws. The witnesses were close enough to see its great teeth all too distinctly, and decided to row as fast as they could towards the shore.

After this narrow escape in 1849, there were many other sightings in St. Margaret's Bay. Some of the men who had observed at least one of the sea serpents closely wondered whether there were two at least, and perhaps they were a breeding pair.

Ten years later, in 1855, something in the sea off Green Harbour was described as "a hideous length of undulating terror," and more detailed accounts of it published in *Ballou's* magazine reported that it made a noise like escaping steam and moved through the water with a series of vertical curves. It was also said to have malevolent eyes protected by bony ridges, and jaws full of dangerous-looking teeth.

Another important Nova Scotia sighting was not recorded in the *Zoologist* magazine until 1847, although the events had taken place in 1833. Henry Ince was the ordnance storekeeper at Halifax, Nova Scotia, at the time. He recorded that on May 31 that year he had been one of a party of five on a fishing trip in Mahone Bay, where intriguing Oak

Island and its famous unsolved Money Pit mystery is also situated. The morning was cloudy, the wind in the south-southeast and rising. The other four on board were Captain Sullivan, lieutenants Malcolm and MacLachlan from the Rifle Brigade, and Artillery Lieutenant Lyster. They saw what Henry Ince described as "a true and veritable sea-serpent" about thirty metres in length and undulating through the water.

Another episode occurred on October 26, 1873, when a "Kraken" in the guise of a giant squid attacked two sturdy Canadian fishermen in a small boat in Conception Bay — not noted for the depth of its water. They were just on the north side of the Avalon Peninsula in Newfoundland when the weird marine beast went for them. Lesser men would have succumbed, but the powerful Canadians fought back courageously. They came away victorious and still very much alive — with a severed tentacle as a souvenir. They estimated that, including its tentacles, the beast had been a good fifteen metres long overall, with a three-metre body and a metre-long head.

Canadian lakes, like Loch Ness in Scotland, are often deep and mysterious, and have been the source of as many monster sightings as the seas and oceans. Geologists frequently make the point that what are now technically lakes may once well have been connected to the sea, later isolated from greater bodies of water by geological upheavals caused by movements of the tectonic plates. Many of these very deep lakes lie between the Rockies and the Pacific, and Lake Okanagan — home of the Ogopogo, also known as Naitaka — is typical of them.

When filming the episode of *Fortean TV* that included research into the Ogopogo, co-author Patricia provided a little light relief in her Ogopogo costume, while co-author Lionel was dressed as an RCMP officer for that same episode.

Co-author Patricia in her Ogopogo costume while filming
Fortean TV *for U.K. TV's Channel 4.*

*Co-author Lionel in RCMP officer's uniform while filming the
Ogopogo episode for U.K. Channel 4's* Fortean TV.

Modern interest in Ogopogo or Naitaka sightings dates from 1854, when a traveller was taking horses across Lake Okanagan. In his account of the attack by the aquatic monster, he said it was like being seized by a gigantic hand that was trying to pull him and his horses down under the water. He was powerful and agile enough to fight his way out of the deadly grip of whatever lived in Lake Okanagan, but his horses fell victim to it. Some years later, another traveller, John McDougal, was also crossing the lake with horses when he was attacked in a very similar manner. Once again the man survived, although his horses were lost.

Another account of a sighting from the later years of the nineteenth century was reported by a timber transporter named Postill in 1880. While the lumber was being worked on and a raft constructed, the Ogopogo was sighted. Postill was certain that whatever lived in the mysterious lake came up out of the depths and watched him working on the raft. In that same year, a woman, Mrs. Allison from Sunnyside, also saw something resembling a huge log floating in the lake — *but it was going in the opposite direction from the prevailing wind and current.*

One of the saddest and most sinister episodes recorded in the annals of Lake Okanagan is the unsolved disappearance of powerful swimmer Henry Murdoch, who was practising for a forthcoming marathon. As far as is known, he had planned to swim from the old Eldorado Hotel to the Maud Roxby Bird Sanctuary. His good and trusted friend John Ackland was rowing a pilot boat for him. John took a few moments' rest and bent forward out of the wind to light a cigarette. In those few seconds, Henry vanished without trace — and despite an intensive police search and two days of dragging the lake for his body *he was never seen again.* The water in that location was barely three metres deep and beautifully clear — yet of Henry Murdoch there was no sign. It needs to be emphasized that he was a very strong swimmer and a professional lifeguard, so an accident was almost impossible. Unless something very big and powerful had taken him, there was no way to account for his sudden disappearance — but how does that square with the water being clear and barely three metres deep at that point?

More recently, Ogopogo was described as resembling a telegraph pole with a sheep's head at one end. He was also said to have had a forked tail, only one-half of which came out of the water as he moved. The *Vernon Advertiser* dated July 20, 1959, carried an interesting and well-authenticated account of an Ogopogo sighting by R.H. Millar. He had been cruising on the lake at about eight knots when he saw Ogopogo through his binoculars about eighty metres away. He was surprised by its speed, as it was going twice as fast as the ship, making about fifteen or sixteen knots. The snakelike head was only a few centimetres above the water, and Millar noted several undulating humps. He guessed — although he couldn't see them — that the monster had fins or paddles of some kind underneath.

Some of the most recently reported sightings from the Gellatly Road area, near the Gellatly Cemetery, suggest that Ogopogo is undoubtedly real, and undoubtedly somewhere in the Okanagan Lake area.

Very wisely, the Canadian authorities have declared Ogopogo to be a protected species under the Federal Law and Fisheries Act and the Wildlife Act.

In the early 1930s, when Nessie was hitting the world headlines following various reported sightings in Scotland, British Columbia newspaper editor Archie Willis christened a formidable Canadian sea monster *Cadborosaurus* — soon to be known as Caddy. Earliest reports of Caddy go back many centuries and cover the sea areas between Alaska and Oregon. Marine biologists and oceanographers have drawn up scientific criteria that point in the direction of something totally real and classifiable inhabiting those waters. Caddies seem to vary in length, with an average of about ten metres, and their bodies are serpentine, like gigantic eels. The head is variously described as resembling a horse or camel — definitely not snake-like or fish-like. The neck is long, and the body adjoining it is either humped or undulating — or perhaps both. There are powerful flippers that must be highly effective, as Caddies have been clocked at well over thirty knots when swimming on the surface.

The northwest Pacific coast where Caddies are regularly sighted is close to a *very, very deep* submarine trench where almost anything of any size could live undetected for millions of years. Is Caddy a survivor from the distant past, like the coelacanth? It seems highly likely. He also appears to have close relatives in Wales and Cornwall in the U.K.

Another monster, Morgawr, was reported off the Cornish coast in 1975 and was closely associated with the work of the famous Doc Shiels and his daughters, who were at that time widely recognized and acknowledged as expert and knowledgeable practitioners of the "Old Religion."

The basic *physical* descriptions of Morgawr, the Cornish sea monster, are very similar to the descriptions of Nessie, Caddy, and other large aquatic beasts reported as broadly resembling plesiosaurs. There are, however, some strange and intriguing *metaphysical* questions raised by the apparent nexus between Old Religion practitioners and their monster-summoning spells on the one hand, and the reported sightings of monsters *subsequent* to those "magical works" on the other. In this connection, however, it is wise to remember the importance of the *post hoc ergo propter hoc* fallacy (*after this, therefore because of this*).

Lyall Watson, whose scientific theorizing is rigorous, adventurous, and of the highest quality, has also wondered seriously about this possible connection. In his brilliant book *The Romeo Error,* he argues that certain very gifted people can produce physical effects at a distance — purely by mental power. Watson also wonders whether magnetic flaws in specific locations may assist this process. He conjectures that dragons, elves, fairies, and UFOs may all exist, but that those who say these things are all in the mind might be right, too, because these strange tulpa-type phenomena *could* be produced at what Watson calls the second, or etheric, level. The aberrant behaviour of these phenomena gives Watson cause to wonder whether they are subject to laws that differ from the laws and principles of the natural sciences as we understand them in the twenty-first century. When psychic or other anomalous phenomena behave in ways that support the theories of those who examine and explore them, Watson suggests that this indicates a degree of influence from the mind of the participant observer over the external phenomena themselves. He feels that if these two ideas could be studied seriously together, they would go some way towards explaining many phenomena that are currently regarded as anomalous.

There is a considerable body of evidence to suggest that Alexandra David-Neel's reported episode with a tulpa in Tibet was a perfectly genuine and objective experience. According to mystical Tibetan wisdom, a tulpa is an entity created by an act of imagination. A parallel may be drawn with the author or scriptwriter who creates a fictional character with words. Tulpas do not have to be written down; they are creatures of the mind. The technique of tulpa creation is a protracted one that requires very powerful concentration and visualization, but Alexandra was almost *too* successful. Her tulpa began as an entirely benign and innocuous monk-like figure, plump and smiling. After a while other members of the party reported seeing him, too, but as time passed he became leaner and lost his benign smile. He had apparently managed to escape from Alexandra's conscious control and was only disposed of with great effort and difficulty.

There are researchers into the various sea monster phenomena who subscribe to the idea that Nessie, Caddy, and some of their weird companions may be akin to tulpas — quasi-solid thought-forms with an objectivity that can be influenced by group contemplation of the type involved in the experiments conducted by Doc Shiels, his daughters, and their colleagues. If the tulpa-creation theory can be applied to *some* sea and lake monsters, it would be one possible explanation for the success St. Columba had in rescuing the man being threatened by Nessie. The very powerful, sharply focused mind of the benign but formidable saint would have shattered a quasi-real thought-form like a sledgehammer going through an egg shell.

CHAPTER FIVE

Mysterious Disappearances and Appearances

One of the strangest unsolved sea mysteries of all time occurred in 1900 and involved the disappearance of three lighthouse keepers from Eilean Mor, the largest of the seven Flannan Isles. They were probably named after St. Flannan, one-time bishop of Killaloe and Kilfenora, whose own sea miracles are worthy of inclusion. It was said, for example, that when he set out for Rome to meet Pope John he sailed there on a floating stone. Another legend credits him with attracting vast shoals of fish to the shores to feed his people.

The Flannan lighthouse is situated 58°17' north and 07°35' west, which puts it roughly thirty-two hundred kilometres east of Canada and twenty-seven kilometres west of the Outer Hebrides. The vast expanse of the northern Atlantic provides an awesome opportunity for waves to reach a prodigious size when wind, ocean currents, and tidal conditions are appropriate.

The sturdy lighthouse on Eilean Mor was designed in 1899 by an engineer named Alan Stevenson. George Lawson carried out the actual work, which cost almost £7,000 — a huge sum in those days. The construction work included constructing landing stages and steps leading up to them. Lawson was also commissioned to build homes for the lighthouse keepers and their families at Breasclete on the Isle of Lewis, and this cost a further £3,500. Breasclete was chosen because of its proximity to Loch Roag, where there was safe anchorage for the lighthouse boat that carried the keepers to and from Eilean Mor. What is referred to technically in lighthouse language as the "character" of the signal is that it flashes two white beams every thirty seconds. The lighthouse building itself is well over twenty metres tall and stands more than one hundred metres above sea level. Its lamp has a candlepower of one hundred thousand, and the nominal range of the light it provides is over thirty kilometres.

The Flannans are also known as the Seven Hunters, and there is one popular old tradition (similar to the tale of the Man in the Moon being sent there for gathering sticks on a Sunday!) that these seven impious men had dared to hunt on the Sabbath, and were accordingly turned into seven remote, storm-lashed islands. Eilean Mor shows a few traces of ancient habitation centuries before the erection of the lighthouse. Historians and other academic record-keepers are generally agreed that two ruins, described as the "Bothies of the Clan McPhail," are actually an ancient dwelling and an equally ancient chapel.

Many strange, sinister legends are associated with the Flannans. Some say that evil forces lurk there still, and that those who trespass on the lonely rocks will be changed into seabirds. Fairies were said to inhabit them; they were also thought to be the abode of kelpies. In Scottish mythology, kelpies were cannibalistic water demons who ate their own kind, human beings, and even deer that had fallen into the water. Descriptions of the sinister kelpies varied. In some accounts they were webbed; in other versions they had the manes and tails of horses. They were also alleged to be shape-shifters, able to assume human form when it suited their grim purposes. There were those even in 1900 who attributed the tragedy of the missing keepers to kelpy activity.

When the light was established on Eilean Mor in those early days, there was no radio communication available, so Roderick MacKenzie, a gamekeeper, was paid eight pounds a year to keep a watchful eye on the Eilean Mor installation in case the keepers signalled for help or the light went out. Roderick's observation post was Gallan Head on the Isle of Lewis, about thirty kilometers southeast of Eilean Mor.

There were four keepers who manned the Eilean Mor lighthouse: Joseph Moore (who was on leave on shore near Loch Roag when tragedy struck his companions), James Ducat, Donald McArthur, and Thomas Marshall. James Ducat was the principal keeper, and Don McArthur was the occasional keeper, replacing William Ross, the first assistant keeper, who was absent on sick leave at the time of the tragedy.

When Captain Holman of the steamer *Archtor* passed the Flannans on the night of December 15, he was certain that he was close enough to the islands to have seen the light had it been on. He saw nothing and duly logged that the light was not visible. This fact was incorporated into the official report of Superintendent Robert Muirhead, which was completed and filed on January 8, 1901.

Captain Harvie was in charge of the lighthouse supply tender *Hesperus*, which sailed out to Eilean Mor on December 26, 1900, arriving at noon. To the surprise of Harvie and his second mate, McCormack, no preparations had been made to receive the supplies the *Hesperus* was carrying. They sounded the siren and steam whistle of the *Hesperus* — but there was still no response from the keepers. Finally, a signal rocket was fired from *Hesperus* — but still there was no response. The *Hesperus* then sent a boat to the east landing stage of Eilean Mor, but nothing could be seen or heard of the three keepers. Joseph Moore, now very anxious indeed about the safety of his three colleagues — who were very much his friends as well — scrambled ashore with some difficulty and went to explore. He found the entrance gate and the outside door were closed. When he got inside he observed that the clock had stopped and the fire was out. He quickly examined the bedrooms to see if his companions had been taken ill: the beds were empty. Moore then ran back to the boat for help. Second Mate McCormack and one of the sailors jumped ashore, having the same trouble in landing that Moore had experienced. All three men then made a thorough search of the lighthouse: there was no sign at all of the missing men, and no clues as to what might have happened to them. Captain Harvie asked Moore to stay on Eilean Mor to tend the vitally important light. Seamen Campbell and Lamont volunteered to stay to help him, and Buoymaster MacDonald, who was also on board the *Hesperus* at the time, volunteered to stay with them until proper, permanent arrangements could be made. These four got the light going again, while Captain Harvie took the *Hesperus* back to Breasclete and sent a report through to Lighthouse Headquarters.

Part of Harvie's message ran: "A dreadful accident has occurred at the Flannans. The three Keepers, Ducat, Marshall and the Occasional have disappeared…"

The emergency team on Eilean Mor made another thorough exploration of the lighthouse and found the log slate that Ducat had made up for the morning of Saturday, December, 15, 1900. The emergency crew also found that the oil fountains and oil storage vessels were all properly filled. The lenses were clear and the necessary lantern mechanisms were also properly cleaned and lubricated. Everything was as it should be — *except for the three missing keepers*. Whichever of the three had been acting as cook on the fateful day had carefully cleaned away the pots, pans, and crockery after lunch, so everything had apparently been as normal at the start of the afternoon.

The two landing places — one at the east and one at the west — had been built so that one would always have a lee shore for men and supplies to land, no matter which way a storm might be blowing. When the search party went around to the west landing place, however, things were very far from normal. A toolbox containing ropes and other essential equipment was usually stored on a ledge thirty-five metres up the cliff. That toolbox had been smashed by the wind and waves, and some of its rope contents (still properly coiled) were found draped around a crane on its platform a dozen metres lower down. This crane platform had strong iron railings around it, for the keepers' safety in foul weather: *these sturdy iron railings were now twisted.* Furthermore, a block of stone weighing at least a ton had been dislodged by *something*, and had fallen to the pathway below. What kind of diabolical weather must have hit the western side of Eilean Mor on that fateful day?

When the protective clothing was examined, it was found that Ducat had been wearing his waterproof gear and sea boots when he vanished, and Marshall's sea boots and oilskin were also missing. Presumably they had put their protective clothing on to go down to do some work on the jetties, probably to make certain that everything was safely stowed down there before the worst of the storm hit Eilean Mor.

It may be deduced from the missing oilskins that Donald McArthur, a loyal and fearless companion, risked his life — and lost it — in a valiant but vain attempt to save the other two men. If he had been the duty cook and tableman that day, he would have stayed in the light-house clearing up, washing the crockery and cutlery, and cleaning and putting away the pots and pans while the other two donned their protective gear and went outside to secure the tools and equipment on the western jetty. His observation point is now far higher than theirs. He sits at the table to relax for a few minutes and sees an enormous wave — enormous even by Flannan standards — bearing down on the island. He leaps up and races out after his fellow keepers. We can almost imagine him yelling at the top of his voice: "Come up! Come up! There's a huge wave heading for us!" Over the wind and the storm and the fatal roaring of the sea, Ducat and Marshall fail to hear their friend's warning. Determined to do everything he can, McArthur runs down the dangerously wet, storm-swept steps, shouting his warning again and again as he descends. His gallant self-sacrifice is all in vain. The wave hits the western edge of Eilean Mor, shatters the toolbox, hurls its contents down the steps, twists the strong iron railings as if they were putty, and then sweeps the three keepers to their deaths.

Superintendent Robert Muirhead went to see what extra information he could glean from Roderick Mackenzie, the official observer on Lewis. Mackenzie was away, but he had left the observations in the hands of his two responsible and intelligent teenaged sons. They showed Muirhead the records their father kept and added their own extra information. At a distance of thirty kilometres, Eilean Mor was not always visible — neither was the light visible when weather conditions were adverse. Mackenzie's records showed that, even with the aid of a powerful telescope, the lighthouse tower had not been visible from December 7 to 29. Neither was the light seen from December 8 to 11 inclusive. It had been observed on the 12, but was not seen again until Moore and his volunteer crew renewed it on the 26.

So what really happened to the three brave keepers on Eilean Mor on December 15, 1900? Was it a huge storm, creating waves nearly sixty metres high that tore them off the granite cliffs and sent them to their deaths? Or were there sinister supernatural forces on the Flannans? Is it even possible that kelpies exist and attack human beings? Although much of the rational evidence points towards a natural marine disaster, the hint of some paranormal evil never quite vanishes — after all, the Flannans have been notoriously mysterious for many centuries.

The disappearance of Glen Miller, the famous bandleader, officially happened on December 15, 1944. He was said to have gone down in a small plane called a Norseman while flying from England to Paris. According to what may well have been only an elaborate (and badly perforated!) cover story, Miller and Flight Officer John R.S. Morgan took off at 1:40 p.m. that day in their small, propeller-driven plane, and were never seen again. It was recorded that the weather was atrocious when they left. Later investigations seemed to show that the plane had developed engine trouble while heading for Dieppe and ditched in the sea. A report from 1973 stated that a plane — possibly Morgan and Miller's — had been located by a diver, who found that the propeller was missing. Aviation history experts are aware of a technical problem with propeller-driven aircraft of the forties — if there's a leak, or other failure, in the hydraulics, the propeller can malfunction in a way that's technically referred to as *overspeed,* which in the worst-case scenario can make it fall off. Apparently that's what may have happened to the little Norseman allegedly carrying Miller and Flight Officer John Morgan.

There is strong evidence of some kind of cover-up over the whole account of Glen Miller's disappearance. Using Occam's Razor once again to strip away the most imaginative of the conspiracy theories, the question of what *might* have happened to the Norseman remains at the centre of the mystery. One theory suggests that allied aircraft, returning in fog or thick cloud on December 15, jettisoned their bombs over the channel, and one of those bombs took Miller's little plane out of the sky. Other aviation disaster theories suggest that the Norseman iced up and came down in the water — it was, after all, a cold December day. So theory number one is simply that there was a perfectly normal, explicable crash into the sea, and that was the end of the brilliantly talented and gallant musician. Co-author Lionel was living in France, first in Boulogne-sur-mer and then in Paris, in 1949, and spectacular rumours of what had happened — or what *might* have happened — to the great Glen Miller were still buzzing, especially in Paris, five years after the tragedy. In particular, those rumours were still very much alive in Pigalle — the erogenous zone of Paris nightlife. It was said there that Miller had never been on the Norseman on December 15, but instead had flown into Paris two days earlier and had been fatally injured in a fight in a Pigalle brothel. In order to safeguard his reputation, he had been flown more dead than alive back to a hospital in the U.S. where, soon after his arrival, he succumbed to the major skull fracture acquired in the brothel brawl.

Another rumour suggested that chain-smoking Miller had died of lung cancer, and that it had been his dying wish to go out as a hero on active service rather than as a sick man in bed. Accordingly, he had been falsely entered as a passenger on the missing plane.

The wildest rumours of all maintained that one of his lady friends in Paris had been a Pigalle brothel madame, and that Miller had been so enamoured of her that he decided to stage his own death, change his identity, and set up a new business with her in Nice. The verdict on that one is "highly unlikely," but nothing was totally impossible in the traumatized and disorganized world of post-war Europe in the late forties.

Ex-RAF officer John Edwards did everything possible to get to the bottom of the mystery of whether or not Miller was on the ill-fated Norseman. There was an official form called a 201 that should have cleared up the matter once and for all. Edwards tried to get it, was told it had probably been lost in a records office fire, and met a stone wall of stolid denial of its existence. Squadron Leader Jack Taylor also investigated — but the form he located was almost unreadable and had an illegible signature. If it had been just a tragic, straightforward crash that killed Miller, why all the difficulty with the records?

It is also rather curious that there did not seem to have been any proper *search* for the missing bandleader. Miller was rightly world famous; surely with the war in Europe almost over the Allies would have had time and spare capacity to instigate a proper search? *Unless it was already known in high places that — wherever else he was — Miller was not dead in the wreckage under the Channel.*

Wilbur Wright (not the pioneer aviator, but a contemporary author and expert on Glen Miller) wrote two excellent books about the famous bandleader's disappearance. He carried out painstaking investigations as recently as 1986 and met with another blank wall of evasion and subterfuge from the authorities. He became justifiably convinced that some sort of major cover-up was shrouding the truth behind Miller's death. He wrote to President Reagan for help, but even that didn't crack the cover-up. He finally obtained — and recorded — an admission from the appropriate records office in the U.S. that the Miller files existed but were strictly off-limits. So there almost certainly *was* a massive cover-up over Miller's disappearance — but the great mystery is *why.* Was it a mystery of the sea, as the official records suggested — or a mysterious brawl leading to a fatal head injury in a Pigalle brothel?

Second only to the mystery of the *Mary Celeste,* which deserves a complete chapter to itself, is the mystery of the *Waratah.* Built on the Clyde by Barclay Curle and Company in 1908, she became the flagship of Lund's Blue Anchor Line. Coal-fired and twin-screwed, the *Waratah* had a gross displacement of 9,339 tons. Her purpose was to serve as a combined cargo-passenger liner on what was then the very popular emigration route to New Zealand and Australia. She was named after the flower that is the emblem of New South Wales in Australia. Known botanically as *telopea speciossima,* the waratah's flowers are bright red, and its wedge-shaped or oblong leaves are a very deep green and heavily veined. They are leathery and can achieve a length of twenty centimetres. The strong, upright stems are woody. The waratah bush or shrub can grow to a height of three metres, with a corresponding spread of two metres.

There are some researchers of anomalous phenomena who are particularly interested in the mysteries associated with omens, portents, and premonitions. They wonder whether the blood red waratah flowers brought the ominous threat of blood and death to the ill-fated *Waratah* liner. Omens or not, she was sometimes described as "the ship without a soul," and her history was never a happy one. Blue Anchor had done well commercially with the *Waratah's* sister ship, *Geelong,* which was why the *Waratah* had been built to almost identical specifications. Like the *Titanic,* the *Waratah* was well equipped with allegedly watertight compartments — eight of them — and was believed to be unsinkable. Omen enthusiasts might be interested in that proud claim. The ancient Greek sin against their pantheon was *hubris* — the foolish pride of trying to equal, or surpass, the gods. It was almost as if some jealous and sinister oceanic deity resented the claim and set out to disprove it!

The *Waratah* was capable of thirteen knots (yet another omen?).

Her captain, an able and experienced veteran named Joshua E. Ilbery, with thirty years of maritime skill behind him, was not happy with the *Waratah's* performance on her maiden voyage. Ilbery was said to have been unhappy with her stability when she sailed from England to Australia on November 5, 1908. There were 689 emigrants tightly packed into the third-class dormitories down in her various holds, plus 67 first-class passengers in far more spacious and comfortable conditions on the upper decks. The ship made calls at Adelaide, Melbourne, and Sydney without any trouble, and most of her passengers were set down in Australia. Because of his misgivings about the *Waratah's* overall balance and stability, Captain Ilbery was said to have personally supervised the loading and stowing of the cargo — nearly seven thousand tons of it including corn, frozen meat, and hides. It is also recorded that the *Waratah* was checked in dry dock and pronounced perfectly seaworthy and fit to sail.

She set out on April 27, 1909, Durban being her first port of call. It's at this juncture that the most intriguing part of the *Waratah's* tragedy took place. One passenger was an engineer named Claude Sawyer, a veteran of many lengthy sea voyages. He felt distinctly uneasy about the *Waratah's* stability. Reports tend to vary slightly, but Sawyer clearly had some sort of premonition in the form of a dream, or dreams. In a few accounts, he is supposed to have said that he had seen a weird, semi-human figure at the porthole of his cabin, waving a bloodstained rag at him. In other versions, the sinister figure who came to warn him was dressed like Hendrik van der Decken, the Flying Dutchman — who had, in legend, come to grief in that same area of ocean near the Cape of Good Hope. So disturbed was Sawyer by these weird dreams, or hallucinations, that he disembarked at Durban and booked a passage home on a different vessel. He actually told the booking manager of the Union Castle Line that he had had a horrendous dream the previous night in which he saw the *Waratah* struggling through huge waves. In Sawyer's dream, one vast wave went over her bow and pressed her down into the sea. Then he saw the vessel roll over towards starboard. After that, she went straight down, disappearing completely. So much for the eight vaunted watertight compartments and the myth of the *Waratah's* unsinkability.

Documentary evidence of Sawyer's grave doubts about the *Waratah's* sea-worthiness existed in the form of a telegram he sent to his wife in London: "Thought 'Waratah' top heavy, landed Durban."

On the evening of July 26, 1909, the *Waratah* left Durban en route to London. The next morning she overtook the *Clan MacIntyre,* a much slower, smaller vessel. They exchanged signals:

Clan MacIntyre:	What ship?
Waratah:	*Waratah* for London.
Clan MacIntyre:	*Clan MacIntyre* for London. What weather did you have from Australia?
Waratah:	Strong south-westerly to southerly winds across.
Clan MacIntyre:	Thanks. Goodbye. Pleasant passage.
Waratah:	Thanks. Same to you. Goodbye.

The *Waratah* steamed on her way, leaving the little *Clan MacIntyre* far behind. The crew of the smaller vessel watched the *Waratah* fade over the horizon. That was the last certain sighting of her. At approximately nine-thirty on the evening of July 27, 1909, the Union Castle liner *Guelph* was heading for Durban in the opposite direction from the *Waratah* when she exchanged light signals with a large, unidentified vessel. Because of poor visibility, the *Guelph* was able to read only the last three letters of the bigger vessel's name: those highly significant letters were *T A H.* The mystery deepened. If it was the *Waratah* the *Guelph* had encountered, she would have covered only seventy or eighty sea miles since exchanging greetings with the *Clan MacIntyre* about fifteen hours previously. For a ship capable of thirteen knots, even if bad weather had brought her down to ten knots, the *Waratah* should have covered at least twice that distance. Had she developed engine trouble, making her vulnerable to storms and heavy seas, if she could not make normal headway against them?

Another major peril of the area was the Agulhas Current and the hazardous oceanic phenomenon associated with it: the Agulhas Retroflection. Large low-pressure systems come from Antarctica accompanied by driving rain and fierce winds — and they come very fast. Moist, warm air from the African coast collides with chilled Antarctic air and results in heavy cloud cover, making conditions at sea even more perilous. A combination of the Agulhas Current and the Agulhas Retroflection are capable of producing gigantic rogue waves — some well over thirty metres high — that can threaten to engulf ships the size of super-tankers.

The fast, warm Agulhas Current runs south and west from the Indian Ocean and then collides with the icy-cold Benguela Current near the Cape of Good Hope. Second only to the Gulf Stream in speed, the Agulhas splits up and surges in one direction through the narrow channel between Mozambique and Madagascar. Winds with speeds of nearly two hundred kilometres per hour are not unknown in the area. When they blow from the west or southwest — *opposing* the Agulhas Current — they produce gargantuan waves (as described above) beyond the survival capacity of almost all ships.

As well as the definite sighting by the *Clan MacIntyre* and the probable sighting by the *Guelph*, the *Waratah* may also have been spotted by the *Harlow*. Her captain reported seeing smoke on the horizon where the *Waratah* might have been. He also reported what he thought were her masthead lights, then flashes like distress flares — or an explosion.

Ominously, some time after the *Waratah* went missing, there were reports from the *Insizwa* and the *Tottenham* that they had seen bodies in the water over five hundred kilometres southwest of Durban.

There were prolonged searches for the *Waratah*, as some expert mariners believed that she had not sunk but was disabled and drifting.

Two British Royal Navy ships — HMS *Pandora* and HMS *Forte* — based at Port Natal, Durban, joined in the search, but without any success. HMS *Hermes* also took part, but with no better luck than the two earlier search vessels. The very determined Australians persisted with the theory that the *Waratah* might still be afloat. There were enough provisions on board to keep the passengers and crew alive for eighteen months or more, and there had been a strange case in 1899 when the *Waikato* had been disabled and drifted for nearly four months until she reached the remote Island of St. Paul's in the Indian Ocean. Accordingly, the Australian government sent out the *Sabine* to search for the *Waratah*. The *Sabine* hunted hopefully for three months and covered over twenty thousand kilometres. She failed to find any trace of the *Waratah*. Still not prepared to abandon their loved ones and friends, the relatives of the *Waratah*'s passengers and crew chartered the *Wakefield* in 1910 and conducted another painstaking three-month search. Once again, no trace of the missing *Waratah* was found.

As recently as 1989, Emlyn Brown chartered the *Meiring Naude* and used what was then the latest and most sophisticated submersible camera equipment to search wreckage that might have been the *Waratah*. Powerful currents swept the cameras away from his objective. Fearless and determined, Brown and his team have not yet given up their underwater search, but the wreck of the *Waratah* has still not been discovered.

One of the strangest rumours and legends associated with the mystery is that a group of white-skinned children had turned up in a badly damaged lifeboat at a remote area of the South African Transkei coast in 1909. According to this rumour, they were nursed and cared for by the friendly and hospitable local people, and eventually assimilated into their community.

Perhaps one of the saddest and most poignant mysteries of vanished ships is the loss of the *Erna,* a fine Canadian vessel from St. John's, Newfoundland. Her loss was so heavily overshadowed by the tragedy of the *Titanic,* which happened at the same time in 1912, that only the bereaved families and friends in St. John's really knew about it. Unlike the mighty *Titanic,* the *Erna* went down without a trace and left no survivors to tell the traumatic tale of her dying moments. But was there something singularly sinister and significant about the early months of 1912? Were there abnormal ocean conditions? Not only the *Erna* and *Titanic* went down that year: at least six other sturdy and seaworthy Canadian ships from Conception Bay and St. John's also vanished into the Atlantic. These included *Arkansas, Aureola, Beatrice, Dorothy Louise, Grace,* and *Reliance.*

The three-thousand-ton *Erna* was predominantly a sealing ship, the property of her skipper, Captain Thomas Linklater. Born in Scotland, Linklater had worked with Gulf Line steamers, and had been happily settled in St. John's, Newfoundland, for more than ten years.

Erna left Scotland, heading for St. John's, on February 26, 1912. The captain's wife and nine-year-old son were aboard, along with three other passengers — including one who had been a survivor of the *Aureola.* Also aboard were Captain Jacob Winsor of Wesleyville and thirty crewmen. Linklater was planning to disembark at St. John's with his family, and Captain Winsor and the crew would continue on from there to the sealing grounds to undertake work there. In all, thirty-seven souls were lost with the *Erna* when she vanished somewhere in the North Atlantic on her way from Scotland to St. John's. Freak weather? Collision with an iceberg — just like the *Titanic?* Or was some stranger, more terrible force at work in the hazardous North Atlantic in 1912?

There were said to be strange psychic happenings aboard the SS *Borodino* back in the 1950s when she was on a regular run between Denmark and Hull. A seaman named Percy MacDonald had suffered a grim accident in the engine room and had lost both legs there. A young steward was so traumatized by what he reported as *an apparition with no legs* that floated outside his cabin door that he left the ship at Hull.

The four-masted *Pamir,* built in 1905 at the Blom and Voss shipyards in Hamburg, was one of the loveliest and most impressive tall ships ever launched: with four masts and over four thousand square metres of canvas, she was nearly three hundred feet long. In the 1950s she served as a training ship. She encountered Hurricane Carrie on September 20, 1957, just a few hundred miles from the Azores. Her final radio distress call reported a forty-five-degree list and all sails lost. The U.S. freighter *Saxon* responded by steaming at top speed towards the *Pamir's* last reported position. They found five survivors in a lifeboat and saved one more the following day. Eighty of her complement had gone down with her, many of them teenaged sea cadets. Many strange reports were made over the years of sighting the *Pamir* again as a ghost ship. The crew of the *Esmereld*, battling a gale herself in the English Channel, claimed that they saw the spectral *Pamir* with her dead crew lining the rail. Famous yachtsman Reed Byers reported sighting the phantom *Pamir* near the Virgin Islands, and other reports of the ghost-ly vessel were made by observers on the *Gorch Foch* and the *Christian Radich*. Yet another report of the spectral *Pamir* came from U.S. Coast Guards on board the *Eagle*.

One of the weirdest marine encounters of all time took place in 1774. A whaler named the *Herald* saw an ice-encrusted hulk drifting not far from the coast of Greenland. Just as was to be the case with the *Mary Celeste* almost a century later, the captain of the *Herald* did his duty and sent a search party out to the derelict. She turned out to be the *Octavius*, which had once been bound for China. She had left England in 1761 — thirteen years before the *Herald* found her. The *Octavius's* log showed that she had been trapped in the ice near Alaska. How had she made her way through the infamous Northwest Passage and somehow emerged near Greenland — *on the eastern side of Canada?* There were forty-eight dead seamen, fully dressed as though for duty, frozen solid in the fo'c'sle. The captain sat in his cabin, hands on the desk in front of him. Like his men, the dead skipper was frozen solid.

The tragic tableau in the adjoining cabin brought the search party close to tears. The frozen body of an attractive young mother rested almost casually with her head propped up on one elbow. Her husband was a little way from her, beside a pile of wood shavings that he had been vainly trying to light. Wrapped carefully in the warm clothing his devoted parents had placed around him was the frozen body of their young son.

There was something in those sad victims reminiscent of the corpses found after the volcano destroyed Pompeii.

There is also a tragic mystery surrounding the final disappearance of Henry Hudson, the pioneering navigator who gave his name to Hudson Bay. The Muscovy Company, which he had helped to found, sent him to look for the Northwest Passage in 1607 and again in 1608. Both trips were unsuccessful: Hudson was stopped by the ice floes. In 1609, the Dutch East India Company hired him to try again. He set off in the eighty-ton *Half Moon* with a crew of twenty Dutch and English mariners. After yet another unsuccessful trip, the *Half Moon* reached England again in November. With a different group of wealthy London sponsors anxious to find a shorter, cheaper route to what they called the Spice Islands, Hudson was sent off again in a new vessel named the *Discovery*. Trapped for long months in the ice in James Bay, the crew quarrelled and then mutinied. Hudson with his son and a handful of men who were still loyal to him were set adrift in a small, open boat. *They were never seen again.*

The account of another mysterious missing vessel, the *Marlborough,* is sometimes questioned and may need further verification. As far as can be ascertained, however, she was built by Robert Duncan of Glasgow and launched in 1876. Her main function was to carry passengers from the U.K. to New Zealand and cargoes of frozen lamb on the way back. She was a fine vessel of over eleven hundred tons. Having made many successful voyages under Captain Anderson, she was in the hands of another expert skipper, Captain Herd, when she vanished without trace on a voyage from Lyttleton, New Zealand, to the U.K. early in 1890.

There were reports that a ship passing one of the islands near Cape Horn in 1891 recorded seeing what looked like a group of marooned mariners on the island signalling for help. The report went on to say that the weather was appalling and there was no possibility of reaching the stranded survivors. Had they come from the missing *Marlborough*? Another possible clue to the mystery was reported in 1913, when a Seattle pilot named Burley alleged that he had seen the wreck of the *Marlborough* — or possibly another vessel with the same name — in a lonely cove. He vividly described her dereliction and said that he had observed twenty or so skeletons near her, surrounded by heaps of empty seashells, as though the starving mariners had survived on shellfish for as long as they could.

Another report states that the remains of the *Marlborough* were found by the British steamer *Johnson* off the coast of Chile. Her paint was peeling, her sails had rotted, and a boarding party from the *Johnson* discovered the skeletons of nineteen men and one woman. Could the *Marlborough* really have drifted for twenty-three years after leaving Lyttleton?

A very similar mystery surrounds the tragic loss of the *Dunedin*. Having made nearly twenty successful and uneventful trips between New Zealand and the U.K., the *Dunedin* vanished without a trace in the vicinity of Cape Horn only a matter of days after the ill-fated *Marlborough* disappeared. The *Dunedin* had a crew of over thirty and she was loaded with wool and frozen meat when she sailed on her last journey from Oamaru in New Zealand. (Incidentally, the town is famous today as the home of a magnificent blue penguin colony.)

Another strange marine spectre, one that haunted the *Port Pirie,* was unusually benign. In 1948 one of her crew was killed when a boiler ran dry and exploded. A while later, one of her engineers was checking things and was concerned because of a sinister knocking sound in the feed pump supplying the boiler. The gauge showed that the boiler was full — yet the sinister knocking continued. As a last resort, the engineer checked the gauge and found that it was wildly faulty — the boiler was almost empty and about to explode. The regular crew were convinced that it was the spirit of the dead man looking after them. Those who had been there with him when the fatal accident took place said that he had sworn that if it was within his powers in the Next World, no shipmate would ever die on board the *Port Pirie* as he had suffered when the boiler exploded.

The alleged ghost that troubled and jinxed the *Great Eastern,* however, was far from benign. Brunel designed the ship, and some idea of her size relative to other vessels in 1857 can be gleaned from the difficulty that was experienced when an attempt to launch her (sideways!) was made on November 7 that year. The nineteen-thousand-ton vessel travelled about a metre and stuck fast. It wasn't until January 30, 1858, that they finally got her floated. The trouble that dogged her had begun! For over a year, she simply floated there, without any move being made to her complete her: this cost a fortune. One reason for building her so big was the problem of refuelling normal-sized steamers on the Australia run. The *Great Eastern* could carry enough fuel to get her to Calcutta in one stage. Her enormous size was also an attempt to beat the problem of rolling and the seasickness that accompanied it. It was argued (not unreasonably) that if a vessel was longer than the length of the largest wave known to seafarers, she would not roll. It was all right as a theory — it just didn't work in practice. The *Great Eastern* was a more powerful emetic than anything used by the Roman Emperors at their orgies!

When she was on her sea trials in 1859, there was a devastating explosion, and several men were scalded. In agonizing pain, one of these victims hurled himself over the side and was crushed to death by the great paddle wheels. One thing after another went wrong for the *Great Eastern* until she was finally sold for scrap in 1888. While the demolition men were taking her to pieces, they found the skeleton of a workman who had mysteriously vanished when the ship was being built in the 1850s. He had somehow become trapped between the thick plates of her double hulls. The grisly find caused speculations that it was this dead man's vengeful spirit that had jinxed the *Great Eastern*.

Another disappearing ship mystery centred around the *President*, which sailed from New York heading for Liverpool on March 11, 1841. Her Fawcett-Preston engines, made in Liverpool, were among the biggest and most advanced of their day. Their great eighty-one-inch cylinders accommodated a stroke of nearly eight feet. Tyrone Power, Sr., ancestor of the famous Hollywood star of the same name, was also a great actor. He had just completed a successful trans-Atlantic theatrical tour and was heading home. Among his close friends in the profession was theatre manager Ben Webster, who lived in a luxurious mansion in Blackheath, London. Two days after the *President* had left New York, Ben's butler was roused by a loud and insistent knocking during the early hours of the morning. He asked who was knocking at such an unusual time and what the trouble was. A voice he knew well and recognized as that of Tyrone Power said, "Mr. Webster, I am drowned in the rain." Not wanting to open the door in case a dangerous criminal was trying to get in and rob them, the butler roused his master. He told Ben that he thought it was their friend Mr. Power. The two of them returned to the front door together and Ben opened it expecting to see his actor friend, *but there was no one there.* They looked around carefully, but no one was in the garden, either. Webster asked his butler to go over the facts again. Both men were very puzzled and disturbed by the event, especially when they realized that having left New York only on March 11 there was no way that Tyrone Power could have reached London by March 13.

Several other vessels that had left New York after the *President* docked safely in the U.K., but of Power's ship there was no sign. The air was filled with rumours and false reports — but the ship was never seen again.

More controversial and hotly disputed than the questions raised in connection with the *Marlborough* are the varying accounts of what might, or might not, have happened to the German U-boat UB-65. According to the popular versions of the mystery, while the UB-65 was being constructed in 1916, a steel girder swung out of control, killing one shipbuilder and fatally injuring another. Others died when poisoned by engine room fumes. Ballast tanks and re-inflation equipment failed, nearly suffocating all on board. Another explosion killed the second officer — whose ghost was later seen — and so the grim story of one misadventure after another went on. Finally, the sub was alleged to have exploded spontaneously, killing all on board. One fact does emerge clearly from the strange rumours of accidents and paranormal phenomena surrounding the UB-65. On July 10, 1918, a U.S. submarine, the AL-2, was on patrol near Fastnet in U.K. waters. Lieutenant Forster observed the UB-65 and prepared to torpedo it. Before he could fire, however, observers on the AL-2 saw the U-boat explode on its own — without any input from the American submariners.

If the paranormal reports surrounding her were suspect, where did they come from? One theory held by some reliable researchers is that a British Intelligence officer created the whole myth of a doomed, cursed, haunted submarine to discourage the German navy in World War I and so reduce their morale. This ingenious Allied propagandist was Hector C. Bywater — but trying to trace him and his very significant contribution to the war is as difficult as trying to establish all the real facts connected with the UB-65.

CHAPTER SIX

The Philadelphia Experiment

There are certain curious psychological quirks of the human mind that in Darwinian terms are probably useful survival mechanisms. When strange new phenomena appear to challenge the deductions we have made about practical, commonsense, everyday life — deductions based on our observations and experiences of it — we tend to respond in one of three distinct ways. First, we ignore the phenomena, pretending that they don't exist or suggesting that they're merely the product of someone's fevered imagination. Our second response is to regard them as false alarms in good faith. The mysterious alien in the UFO that stopped our car engine, using a technology beyond our present understanding of the laws of natural science, was really nothing more than a coincidental odd alignment of unusually bright planets — plus a weather balloon or two — combined with the car's faulty high-tension lead falling off the distributor at the critical moment. Third, we put these phenomena into a kind of limbo. We store them in a flexible compartment of the mind labelled: *Things I can neither prove nor disprove. They're really interesting, but they're also awesomely strange and potentially life-changing, and I don't think I really want to deal with them.*

There are cases in which we do our best to be honest, open-minded, and objective. We don't use dismissal methods one and two in these instances because we recognize the genuine possibility that these phenomena might be real. Instead, we put the investigation off indefinitely — by mowing the lawn, washing the car, or changing the guest room curtains. For many researchers and investigators, the Philadelphia Experiment goes into that mental box. If it actually happened, the world will never be the same again, and its potential scientific significance is at least equal to that of splitting the atom, genetic engineering, and cloning. Some of us are not entirely sure that we want to contemplate that — so we leave the USS *Eldridge* on the back burner, something to study in greater depth and in sharper focus *at some indeterminate future time.* But that time is *now.* The *Eldridge* and all who sailed in her are demanding a fair hearing. Like Schrödinger's unfortunate cat in the hypothetical metaphysical experiment, they want to get out of the box: *dead or alive.*

What are the basic points that can be collected, analyzed, and evaluated from the various accounts of the Philadelphia Experiment?

Morris Jessup, an astronomer who had already produced academic work on astrophysics, wrote *The Case for the UFO* in 1955. His book attracted a strange series of letters, curiously written with different coloured pencils and ink. The letters, signed *Carl M. Allen,* claimed that in 1943 the USS *Eldridge,* a destroyer, had become invisible as a result of applying Einstein's Unified Field Theory. Tesla, the strange genius with exceptional knowledge of all things electrical, was also said to have been involved — with Einstein himself — in the invisibility work, officially named Project Rainbow.

The amount of subsequent covering up, denials, counter-denials, and the dissemination of misleading statements from many quarters makes it almost impossible to sift the facts from the fiction and to get any clear picture of what — if anything — ever happened to the USS *Eldridge.* The problem is complicated still further by the strong possibility that several witness were perfectly honest and sincere — but powerfully deluded.

The USS *Eldridge* seems to have pulled into Delaware Bay in July 1943. The invisibility experiment involved wrapping wire — like an electric coil — all around her. The apparent theory behind this technique was that it would degauss the ship, cancel her magnetic field, and thus make her invisible to magnetic mines, which, broadly speaking, depended on a victim's magnetic field to detonate them. One of the main reasons it is so difficult to get to the truth about what really happened there more than half a century ago is the apparently deliberate and opaque veil of secrecy that was draped over the whole Project Rainbow story almost immediately after the alleged events occurred.

Another interesting idea — and a more or less sensible and matter-of-fact one — was that something rather more ambitious than "magnetic invisibility" (via the degaussing process) was being tried out on the USS *Eldridge.* According to this hypothesis, an attempt was being made to make her truly invisible as far as normal optical surveillance was concerned. There was no reference to space-time warps, electronic journeys into unknown dimensions, or any of the other paraphernalia enjoyed by the readers and writers of good, imaginative science fiction. Nothing more elaborate than high-frequency generators were required. When they went into action, the air and water in the vicinity of the *Eldridge* would heat up enough to cause a mirage. Quite how viable that idea was may raise a few technological question marks, but in theory it was supposed to generate a greenish grey fog and make the *Eldridge* invisible.

High-frequency generators have a reputation — deserved or otherwise — for causing headaches and nausea, and if half the crew of the *Eldridge* felt bilious and generally unwell, that would provide fertile soil in which the seeds of rumour could grow.

These fairly simplistic theories of degaussing and of using high-frequency generators to create the right conditions for mirages are vulnerable to two serious counter-arguments: why was it reported that the *Eldridge* was seen in Norfolk, Virginia, at the same moment that she vanished in Philadelphia? And what about the sinister reports of some unfortunate crew members being inseparable from the fabric of the *Eldridge* while others allegedly vanished permanently after the experiment?

There has been considerable evidence for such mysterious vanishings over many centuries. Were any of these due to time warps, or trips through hyperspace? What is usually ascribed to aliens in UFOs today was ascribed to fairies or similar supernatural beings in earlier times, when they were part of the contemporary culture and belief systems — while UFOs were not.

A case reported from 1678 is typical. Dr. Moore and three of his friends were touring Ireland and were staying at an inn in Dromgreagh in Wicklow. Moore was a firm believer in fairy abductions, claiming that he had been taken as a child on more than one occasion and had been rescued by the superior magic of a local wise man or woman. He was in the middle of these accounts when — almost as if speaking of them had made them happen again — his three friends saw him being pulled up out of his chair by some invisible, irresistible force. They made a grab at him, but whatever the force was, it was much more powerful than they were. Despite their best efforts, Moore disappeared into the wild darkness of that Irish night. On the landlord's advice, Moore's friends sent for the local wise woman, who duly arrived and explained that her powers had revealed that the good doctor was being held prisoner by fairies in a neighbouring wood. She further explained that she could save him only if he ate and drank nothing while in their hands.

This is reminiscent of the abduction of Persephone, daughter of Demeter, in Greek mythology. Persephone was carried away by Hades, god of the underworld, and, following negotiations between Demeter and Zeus, was allowed to return for only six months each year, as she had eaten six pomegranate seeds while in captivity. The theme of being entrapped by eating while a prisoner seems to go all the way back to this Greek legend.

The Irish wise woman duly carried out her magical rituals and at dawn Dr. Moore staggered back to the inn. He was very hungry and thirsty and told his friends that during his captivity an invisible force had knocked all food and drink from his hands. This suggested that the wise woman's spell had been powerful enough to protect him, and that, defeated by it, his abductors had released him. As dawn broke he had suddenly found himself outside the inn. If the fairy elements are removed from the account, it might almost be argued that Dr. Moore seems to have been transported through hyperspace — as some of the *Eldridge*'s crew were said to have been.

No reference to scientific mysteries such as time warps and hyperspace could be complete without involving the enigma of Nikola Tesla. Perhaps the least acknowledged super-genius of the nineteenth and twentieth centuries, Tesla was always linked by rumour with the mysterious Philadelphia Experiment. He was *supposed* to have died of a heart attack. It allegedly happened sometime between the night of Tuesday, January 5, and the morning of Friday, January 8, 1943, when what was *said* to be Tesla's body was discovered by the maid who went into his hotel room. One octogenarian corpse looks remarkably similar to another. Was a suitable unclaimed cadaver from the city morgue smuggled in?

There was a great deal of palaver centred on opening Tesla's safe and extracting various books and papers. Was this because Tesla was still very much alive and well and needed those papers because he was working secretly with Einstein on Project Rainbow in Philadelphia? Tesla's nephew, Sava Kosanovich, a refugee from Yugoslavia then living in the U.S., was his only known relative. He turned up with a locksmith and took *something* from the safe. The FBI, understandably because World War II was raging, were said to be watching Kosanovich in case he was a German spy. But was he really their secret contact with Tesla? Was he the go-between for Tesla, Einstein, and the FBI on the amazing invisibility experiment? Whatever their real role in the matter, the FBI very soon knew what was happening concerning the vitally important safe and its contents, and they supposedly contacted Alien Property Control to retrieve whatever Kosanovich had taken.

The mystery then deepened: officially, no one was absolutely certain what had gone from the safe, or where the vital parts of it went afterwards.

The relevance of Tesla's supposed death in January 1943 to the Philadelphia Experiment is central to the mystery surrounding Project Rainbow. Tesla and Einstein together were a formidable combination. Einstein, born on March 14, 1879, lived until April 18, 1955 — more than ten years after Tesla's supposed death. Einstein was very much around and still closely involved in avant-garde science when the *Eldridge* allegedly vanished — but if the body in the hotel was *not* Tesla's, it's more than possible that the two super-geniuses were still working on Project Rainbow together in July 1943.

Another intriguing scientific ingredient of the supposed Philadelphia Experiment came in the person of David Hilbert, who developed a very complex system of mathematics known later as Hilbert Space. Hilbert's work with the brilliant Dr. John von Neumann in 1926 led to further amazing developments in very advanced maths and physics. Einstein described Neumann as the most brilliant mathematician of all time. His great special abilities led him to apply abstract mathematical concepts to the so-called *real* physical environment.

What Hilbert and Neumann initiated was also worked over by Dr. Levinson, creator of the Levinson Time Equations, including the Levinson Recursion. This is basically a method for solving equations and is practically an equivalent to a recurrence relation in orthogonal polynomial theory. Although Levinson developed it for use with a single time series, it can easily be adapted to work with multiple time series. The combination of Hilbert Space, Neumann's brilliant calculations, and the advanced Levinson Recursion for multiple time series revives the question of whether the leading physicists and mathematicians of their day were the secret driving force behind something far more serious than a simple degaussing process to protect a ship like the *Eldridge* from magnetic mines. The united mental powers of Einstein, Hilbert, Tesla, Neumann, and Levinson *might* have been sufficient to send the *Eldridge* hurtling invisibly through hyperspace from Philadelphia to Norfolk, Virginia. If anyone could do it, they could.

In Jack London's fascinating early science fiction story *The Shadow and the Flash*, two intense rivals, Lloyd Inwood and Paul Tichlorne, approach the problem of invisibility from different directions. One works on the theory that absolute transparency — like the transparency of the gases forming Earth's atmosphere — is the best route; the other works on the theory that perfect blackness — reflecting no light at all — will solve the problem. Both finally succeed and meet in battle.

The observers can see only an occasional flash from the transparent fighter and an intermittent shadow from the other one. The invisibility theory that seems to have been associated with the *Eldridge* was very different from the ideas put forward in Jack London's story.

The Project Rainbow hypothesis was alleged to have been that light rays had to be bent around the ship in order to render her invisible. It was theorized that if enough coils of wire were wrapped around the vessel, and a powerful electric current was sent through those coils, an enormous magnetic field would form around the *Eldridge*. If all went according to plan, this would bend the light so that objects behind the ship would be visible because the light was detouring around the vessel.

The corollary to this theory, however, was that a force powerful enough to bend light rays would also be powerful enough to bend space and time simultaneously. To paraphrase, abbreviate, and simplify Einstein's profound ideas: Matter tells space how to curve, and space tells matter how to move. If the magnetic field around the *Eldridge* (always assuming that something *did* happen in Philadelphia that day) was powerful enough, then it would have affected time and space as well as the simple light rays on which visibility depended.

According to the basic accounts put forward by various Philadelphia Experiment researchers, the first experiment was only a partial success. The *Eldridge* did not vanish entirely. Witnesses allegedly saw a vague and hazy outline of her in the water. A second experiment with more current (and perhaps more coils?) was said to have been traumatically successful: not only did the ship disappear in a mysterious green haze in Philadelphia — she reappeared in Norfolk, Virginia.

Some of her crew were missing entirely. Some were said to have combusted spontaneously. Some were reported to have become seriously mentally ill. Others were occupying the same space as parts of the ship's structure — with dire consequences for the flesh, blood, and bone that were competing with steel. Those who escaped sane and intact seemed to be carrying strange residual powers with them, as though what had happened to the *Eldridge*'s normal space-time behaviour had infected them, too. This is reminiscent of the reports of some investigators who have apparently brought poltergeists, or other ghostly phenomena, home with them after visiting reputedly haunted sites. One *Eldridge* survivor was said to have been involved in a barroom brawl, and when sufficient emotional and physical energy were being released there during the roughhouse *everything froze as though time itself had suddenly stopped.*

In the course of their comprehensive studies of the Philadelphia Experiment, William Moore and Charles Berlitz were sent a curious document purporting to be an article from a 1943 Philadelphia newspaper. It expanded and modified the story of the brawling fighters being frozen in time and said that two sailors (presumably ex-crewmen of the *Eldridge*) had not merely been frozen in time *but had totally vanished*. The supposed press article, however, has been difficult, if not impossible, to trace back to any 1943 Philadelphia newspaper or magazine with any degree of certainty. It wasn't dated, and it had no publication's name on it.

Returning to the strange letters Morris Jessup received from the writer calling himself Carl M. Allen, claims were made that these residual effects were not limited to the ability to freeze time. Allen maintained that some of the survivors had acquired the ability to walk through walls. Differences of space-time and dimensional irregularities might conceivably make this possible, and it is particularly interesting to note that in the vast majority of reports of paranormal, psychic phenomena, the psychic entities described do glide through walls, locked doors, and other apparently solid matter. The mysterious Carl M. Allen — also known as Carlos Miguel Allende — claimed to have been on board a nearby ship and to have seen what happened to the *Eldridge* from there.

Three senior naval officers became interested in the mystery when they examined a copy of Jessup's book *The Case for the UFO*, which had been heavily annotated with cryptic references to space, time, other dimensions, and invisibility. Jessup himself was dead by 1969, when the mysterious Carlos Miguel Allende was interviewed by the three keenly interested naval researchers. Allende made a number of odd statements to them, allegedly confessing that the whole thing was a hoax, that nothing had happened to the *Eldridge* or any of her crew. He said that he himself had become very frightened when he read Jessup's ideas about invisibility and force fields and had made up the myth of the *Eldridge* ostensibly to scare Jessup and to prevent him from writing any more material about UFOs. As an argument, Allende's reasoning seems about as sequential as an Escher staircase.

Opponents of the theory that something very curious happened to the *Eldridge* in 1943 allege that there was a reunion of former *Eldridge* personnel as recently as 1999 — most of them would then have been in their late seventies or early eighties — and that none of them recalled anything odd happening at any time. It was further postulated by opponents of the Philadelphia Experiment mystery that the *Eldridge* had not even been in Philadelphia in 1943. If there was, in fact, a massive cover-up at the highest level, it would have been the easiest thing in the world to alter the records of the ship's whereabouts. If a conspiracy of silence and a cover-up really *did* take place, then the desired degree of secrecy could have been enhanced by denying that the ship was ever in the location where the so-called Philadelphia Experiment was said to have been conducted. The mystery of whether there *was* a conspiracy of silence is almost as great as the mystery of the invisibility and space-time distortion theory.

When the previously unimaginable is written in a clear, concise, matter-of-fact manner, backed up by a formidable array of logic and sequential, rational thought, it becomes imaginable. When that logic is backed by substantial scientific and historical knowledge, the imaginable starts edging its way towards the possible. *The Montauk Project: Experiments in Time* by Preston B. Nichols and Peter Moon was as epoch-making in its theories of time in 1992 as Dunne's time theory books were seventy years earlier. Nichols and Moon's hypotheses are both fascinating and challenging. When we were investigating on Long Island, New York, where the Montauk Project was based, we interviewed one of the team who worked with Nichols and Moon. His ideas on time, like theirs, were extremely interesting and innovative — but so far in advance of conventional thinking on the subject that they confronted orthodox science and metaphysics.

According to the evidence available to Nichols and Moon and their research associates, UFOs were sighted over the *Eldridge* shortly before the switch was thrown to energize the amazing invisibility experiment. According to this evidence, one of the UFOs was affected as well as the *Eldridge* herself and was hurled through hyperspace, ending up in Montauk, in a top secret research area well below the surface of Long Island.

The two engineers credited with actually throwing the fateful switch were named by these researchers as Edward and Duncan Cameron. The most amazing part of the account is that the brothers were dragged through a time tunnel and found themselves inside the Montauk Project on Long Island. They were then involved in a scenario that would do justice to a science fiction film. Several time journeys to and from 1943 to 1983 were undertaken, and delicate and complex equipment was retrieved for aliens they met on their travels through time and space. The mysteries become even more fantastic when a process of mind-body transfer is included.

What seems at first sight like a brilliantly imaginative episode from *Sinbad, The Golden Fleece,* or *The Adventures of Baron Munchausen*

becomes challengingly real and factual when studied in more depth —
threatening to overturn the comfortable, secure, commonsense world
inside which we feel *reasonably* safe most of the time. In *Fortean* terms,
we need to tread delicately on the thin crust called reality.

We, the jury, are left with three possible choices of verdict rather
than the two traditional ones the law offers: first, nothing happened at
all — the Philadelphia Experiment was just a wild rumour with no basis
in fact whatsoever; second, there were some simple and clearly understood degaussing procedures that were subsequently mystified,
coloured, and exaggerated out of all proportion; or third, it really happened, extraterrestrials were involved, time and hyperspace were used
like the freeway between Montauk and Philadelphia — and the universe
turns out to be unimaginably stranger than we thought.

CHAPTER SEVEN

The Disappearance of the Crew of the Mary Celeste

Nova Scotian shipwrights still deservedly enjoy the highest professional reputation for their skill and expertise. The sturdy brigantines that were launched from Joshua Davis's yard on Spencer's Island, Nova Scotia, in the 1850s and 1860s were among the best in the world. The *Mary Celeste* was originally named *Amazon* when she was launched there in 1861 — the first of twenty-seven identical vessels Joshua built. The best Nova Scotian beech, birch, spruce, and maple had gone into her, and her cabins were pine-finished. Just under one hundred feet long, and approximately a quarter of that in width, her depth was approximately twelve feet and her displacement about two hundred tons.

A brigantine resembling Amazon, *renamed* Mary Celeste, *1861–1884.*

A vessel can be either clinker-built, where the planks of her hull overlap one another, or corvel-built, where they fit tightly edge to edge. *Amazon* was corvel-built. She was a two-masted brigantine, although officially listed as a half-brig in the records of the Atlantic Mutual Insurance Company. Her official registration took place at Parrsboro — a very interesting and important Nova Scotia town, always well worth a visit. It stands at latitude 45°22' and longitude 65°20' on the coast of the Bay of Fundy with its astonishing, record-breaking tides that can vary by as much as 16.8 metres (54.6 feet).

In addition to its significant role in the story of the *Mary Celeste,* Parrsboro deserves to be cross-referenced with investigations into sea monsters: in 1985 the biggest fossil find in Canada was discovered on the North Shore of Minas Basin, close to Parrsboro — this find included a unique track of dinosaur footprints.

Parrsboro was known as Partridge Island in 1776 and was already an important settlement then. In 1784, it was given its present name in honour of Lieutenant Colonel John Parr, governor of Nova Scotia at that time.

When the authors were in Nova Scotia researching *The Oak Island Mystery,* they were fascinated by the accounts of the great Micmac hero Glooscap, who *might* have been one of the noble Sinclair family from the ancient Orkney Kingdom near Scotland. The Sinclairs were of Norse descent and were believed to have crossed the Atlantic long before Columbus. They were also believed to have befriended the fearless Templars when that great and noble Order was treacherously attacked by Philip IV in 1307. If the Lost Fleet of the Templars reached Oak Island, it is *possible* that either one of their leaders — or Earl Sinclair of Orkney — became Glooscap, friend and guide of the Micmacs. Parrsboro is an ideal centre for tracing the Glooscap Trail. As well as the one off the coast of Chester on the Mahone Bay side of Nova Scotia, there was also *another* Oak Island on the Bay of Fundy not far from Parrsboro — a full account of that theory can be found in the authors' *The Oak Island Mystery.*

So famous and successful was Parrsboro in the days of sail that stout ships like the *Amazon,* sturdily built of stout Nova Scotian timber and carrying the Parrsboro registration, were to be found in almost every port in the world.

Some experienced sailors — practical men with plenty of sound common sense — often wonder whether certain vessels carry a jinx, or curse. There were plenty of them in the late nineteenth century who had their doubts about the *Amazon.* Her first skipper was a Scotsman

named Robert McLellan who died within two days of taking command
of her — not exactly a promising start! On her maiden voyage she was
badly gashed down one side when she collided with a fishing boat off
the coast of Maine. While this was being repaired, fire broke out on
board and inflicted further severe damage. John Nutting Parker, her
skipper, was sacked.

The *Amazon* did manage to cross the Atlantic uneventfully, but collided with a similar brig near Dover, England, and sank it. This led to yet
another change of skipper. In 1867, under her new captain's command,
she ran aground just off Cow Bay, part of Cape Breton Island, Nova
Scotia, and was originally regarded as a total wreck. Haines and McBean
tried unsuccessfully to salvage her, and went bankrupt in the process.
The jinx seemed to extend to financial ventures as well as nautical ones.
John Beatty of New York bought her next and passed her on to James H.
Winchester and his associates, Sylvester Goodwin and Daniel Sampson.

By this time major structural changes had been made in her. Her
length had been increased to 103 feet, and her width by only a few inch-
es. Her displacement had been raised to 282 tons. She was now
American owned and registered, and she flew the Stars and Stripes.
Most significantly of all, her name had been changed: the old *Amazon*
had been re-christened the *Mary Celeste*. Lloyds of London had once
logged her as the *Marie Celeste* instead, and there were strange rumours
that her new name had been intended to be *Mary Sellers*. Careful searching of genealogical records shows that there *was* a real Mary Sellers,
daughter of John and Sarah Sellers. Mary was born in 1843 in
Covington County, Mississippi, U.S. She was killed in a tragic accident
involving a horse when she was only twenty-seven. Was the ill-fated
Mary Celeste intended to have been re-christened *Mary Sellers* to honour her memory by a ship-owner who knew and loved her?

Winchester and his associates discovered that the ship had dry rot
in her hull. The bottom was rebuilt and reinforced with a strong copper
lining. In their capable hands, the *Mary Celeste* became as stout and seaworthy as any vessel of her size in the 1870s. Her first skipper after the
rebuilding was Rufus Fowler, who was a co-owner of the vessel. On
October 29, 1872, he was replaced by Captain Benjamin Spooner Briggs,
who, like Fowler, was also a part-owner of the ship. Benjamin had been
born at Wareham, a coastal town on Buzzards Bay, Massachusetts, on
April 24, 1835, making him just eight years older than the tragic Mary
Sellers of Mississippi. Was it possible that this well-travelled seaman had
met her on one of his voyages? *Was that the connection between her and
the changed name of the ship?*

Ben was the product of a puritanical New England seafaring family. He was the second of the five sons of Captain Nathan Briggs and his wife, Sophia. His brothers also followed their father's proud seagoing tradition. By the time Ben took over the *Mary Celeste* he had already successfully commanded three other ships: *Forest King, Arthur,* and *Sea Foam.*

Just before she sailed into history, the *Mary Celeste* had been anchored at Pier 44 in New York's East River. On Saturday, November 2, 1872, she was loaded with over seventeen hundred red oak casks filled with commercial alcohol, and everything was made safe and secure in the hold. These casks were destined for H. Mascerenhas and Co. of Genoa in Italy. The shippers were a firm of New York merchants, Meissner Arckerman and Co.

The Sandy Hook pilot ship took the *Mary Celeste* from Pier 44 to Staten Island's Lower Bay on November 5, but the Atlantic weather was so unwelcoming that Briggs wisely decided to wait a couple of days before taking his ship out into open waters on November 7.

In addition to his crew, Briggs was accompanied by his lovely thirty-year-old wife, Sarah Elizabeth, daughter of the Reverend Cobb, the Congregationalist minister in Marion, Massachusetts, and their toddler daughter, Sophia Matilda. Their son, seven-year-old Arthur Stanley, was being cared for by Nathan and Sophia Briggs, his paternal grandparents. Poignantly, in her last letter, posted from Staten Island, Sarah Briggs said how much she was looking forward to getting a letter from her young son.

Briggs' first mate was Albert G. Richardson. He was twenty-eight years old and had served as a soldier in the American Civil War. His wife was the niece of James H. Winchester, principle shareholder in the *Mary Celeste*. He and Briggs had sailed together before, and Richardson was known to be a brave, honest, and reliable seaman — although there were rumours of a clandestine romance between him and the attractive Sarah Briggs.

Andrew Gilling, who was three years younger than Richardson, served as second mate and was also known as a loyal and reliable sailor. He was a New Yorker with Danish ancestors. Twenty-three-year-old Edward William Head served as the ship's cook and steward. He was a Brooklyn man who enjoyed the same high reputation as the three officers. The remaining crew members were German. Volkert Lorensen and his brother, Boy, were in their twenties. Gottlieb Goodschall was in the same age range as the Lorensens. Arien Martens was the mystery man. At thirty-five years old — not much younger than Captain Briggs himself — Arien was a good sailor with a good reputation; furthermore, he was fully qualified as a mate — but he had signed on the *Mary Celeste* as an ordinary seaman. *Why?*

Before setting sail on what was to be their fateful last journey, Ben and Sarah had dinner with Captain and Mrs. Morehouse at Astor House. Morehouse was an old friend of the Briggs family and was in command of the *Dei Gratia*. They were bound for Gibraltar with a cargo of petroleum. His wife and Sarah Briggs were also good friends. By a strange, ironic twist of fate, it was the *Dei Gratia* that later discovered the empty *Mary Celeste*.

On November 7, 1872, the *Mary Celeste* duly set out from New York, heading for Genoa. Eight days later the *Dei Gratia* weighed anchor and set out for Gibraltar. Her log revealed that for ten days or so her voyage was uneventful and routine. Then, at one o'clock on the afternoon of December 5, helmsman John Johnson saw a ship approximately five miles off the *Dei Gratia*'s port bow. Their position at the time was 38°20' north by 17°15' west, approximately six hundred miles off the coast of Portugal. Johnson, an intelligent, experienced seaman, suspected almost immediately that there was something strangely wrong with the distant ship. She was yawing appreciably, and there was something odd about her sails.

Johnson called to Second Mate John Wright, who peered intently at the mysterious ship and then decided to report it to the skipper. Captain Morehouse trained his telescope on the distant ship and then decided that it definitely needed help. Accordingly, by three o'clock, the *Dei Gratia* was within four hundred metres of the enigmatic vessel. Morehouse hailed her several times but received no answer, so he sent a boat over to investigate. Oliver Deveau, the first mate of the *Dei Gratia*, went across with John Johnson and John Wright. As they drew closer, they saw that the ship they were trying to help was the *Mary Celeste*, which had left New York some eight days ahead of them. That alone was conclusive evidence that something was seriously wrong on board her. Johnson remained in charge of the dinghy, while Deveau and Wright clambered aboard the *Mary Celeste*. Deveau, who played a leading and heroic role in the mystery, was a big, muscular man who feared nothing.

They searched the *Mary Celeste* from end to end but found no trace of anyone aboard — *alive or dead*. They sounded the pumps to see how much water she'd taken into her hold: one pump had already been withdrawn to let down a sounding rod, so the *Dei Gratia*'s officers used the other one. Not surprisingly, recent storms had left a significant amount of water between the *Mary Celeste*'s decks, but not enough to threaten the ship's buoyancy and stability. Deveau and Wright took careful note of the sails. They found the main staysail lying across the forward housing, but the upper foresail and the foresail itself had apparently been torn away by the recent storms. They concluded that these sails must have been washed overboard since the *Mary Celeste* had been abandoned. The jib was set, and so were the fore-topmast staysails and the lower topsail; all the other sails were furled. The running rigging was in a chaotic mess: much of it was fouled, some was dangling forlornly over the side, and the rest had apparently been blown away and lost like the foresails.

The vitally important main peak halyard, which was almost one hundred metres long, had snapped off short — and the greater part of it simply wasn't there. Its normal use was to hoist the outer end of the gaff sail. Did that missing halyard provide a major clue to the tragedy?

The binnacle had been blown over — or knocked over by storm-lashed debris — and the compass was smashed. The helm was spinning wildly as wind and tide moved the rudder at random.

The main hatch cover was securely in place — if it hadn't been properly fastened, the water below decks would have been a much more serious problem. Several auxiliary hatches were open, however, and their covers were lying on the deck. Wright and Deveau inspected the galley carefully. It held less than a foot of water. There was an ample supply of fresh drinking water, and most of the *Mary Celeste*'s provisions were still intact and edible.

When their search took them to the cabin that Ben and Sarah had shared, they found the temporary, or slate, log. It recorded that on Monday, November 25, the *Mary Celeste* had been near St. Mary's Island in the Azores, sailing on a bearing of east-southeast. By eight o'clock that same day they had been within six miles of Eastern Point and moving on a bearing of south-southwest.

It was of great significance in trying to piece together the clues to the tragedy that Sarah's sewing machine had not been put away, and there was a partly completed child's garment in it. A sewing machine was a very expensive and important piece of household equipment in 1872. Its owner would take great care of it — except in some dire emergency. *What had made Sarah abandon it?*

The evidence in the mate's cabin also provided clues to the suddenness of whatever had disturbed the passengers and crew so dramatically. A navigational calculation remained partially finished. In the days before electronic calculators became ubiquitous, it was very important for a navigator to complete the mathematical work he was doing. Courses were checked and rechecked by hand — the hard way. You didn't leave a half-finished calculation unless something really important had called you away from it. This cabin also contained a tracing of the

Mary Celeste's track up until November 24, when she had been about one hundred miles southwest of San Miguel Island in the Azores.

Other telltale signs of sudden departure in the crew's quarters included razors left out unwiped. These expensive items could last a lifetime with care. No one on sailor's pay in 1872 would carelessly leave his razor out to rust. Other treasured possessions, including pipes, tobacco pouches, and protective oilskins, had also been abandoned. There was even a bottle of medicine without its cork. Someone had felt that the disturbance — whatever it was — was so urgent that there wasn't time to replace a cork! Sea chests had also been abandoned — a thing no nineteenth-century sailor would do except in dire emergency. Newly washed underwear was hanging out to dry on a line slung across the crew's quarters.

One of the popular misconceptions about the mystery of the *Mary Celeste* can be traced back to a sentence from Conan Doyle's short story "J. Habakuk Jephson's Statement," which was published in *Cornhill Magazine* in 1883. This fictional version of the abandoned vessel contained the sentence: "The boats were intact and slung upon the davits; and the cargo, consisting of tallow and American clocks, was untouched."

The borders between fact and fiction are not well guarded. When the story of the *Mary Celeste* was repeatedly told and retold, Conan Doyle's reference to the intact lifeboats (plural in his yarn) being in their places was deliciously mystifying. If the captain, his family, and his crew had *not* gone in the boats, *how had they gone*?

Lifeboat suspended on its davits.

The historical facts were very different: the boat (singular) was a small yawl, normally kept above the main hatch cover. It was missing; the clear implication was that the people had left the *Mary Celeste* in it. In fact, two sections of the ship's rail had been removed, presumably to launch it. Further indications that at least some of the ship's personnel had left in the boat were that they seemed to have taken the bill of lading, the navigation book, the sextant, and the chronometer with them. Taking these items suggested that whoever was in the inadequate little yawl had been hoping to navigate her either into a main shipping lane to be rescued, or to get her to the nearest land.

After their careful inspection of the abandoned *Mary Celeste*, Deveau, Johnson, and Wright returned to the *Dei Gratia* to report their findings to Captain Morehouse. A decision had to made. Salvage money was a big incentive — but trying to run *both* brigantines with too few men on each risked total disaster. It was finally agreed that Deveau with two good men to help him could *probably* get the *Mary Celeste* as far as Gibraltar. Oliver was, after all, an exceptionally powerful man and an exceptionally good sailor. Morehouse had complete confidence in him. Accompanied by Augustus Anderson and Charles Lund, Deveau took command of the derelict *Mary Celeste*.

The risks were significant: each vessel had barely more than a skeleton crew. If there was an emergency, or if the weather turned really foul, it would mean desperate trouble. They decided to travel in convoy, keeping within clear signalling distance of each other. All went well at first, but a fierce storm separated them as they entered the Straits of Gibraltar. The *Dei Gratia* docked in Gibraltar on the evening of December 12. The magnificent Oliver Deveau and his two fearless crewmen struggled in about twelve hours later.

Between them, Morehouse and Deveau had accomplished an almost impossible and highly dangerous task. They had saved a valuable ship and her expensive cargo. They richly deserved a hero's welcome and generous salvage money as a reward. What actually happened was almost unbelievable.

A preposterous little bureaucrat named Frederick Solly Flood held the grandiloquent title of Attorney General for Gibraltar and Advocate General for the Queen in her Office of Admiralty. Unfortunately, Fred, a neurotic control freak, was obsessed with the notion that some form of trickery must have taken place. He simply could not get his microscopic mind around the simple fact that the *Mary Celeste* had been found abandoned. Her Majesty's very inadequate Advocate General formulated the theory that the crew of the *Mary Celeste* had broached the alcohol cargo in the hold, become dangerously drunk, murdered Captain Briggs and his family and then one another, before the last man standing had — presumably — fallen overboard. It was explained to him in simple language that raw industrial alcohol is extremely unpalatable, and that it causes acute abdominal pain long before it causes intoxication. Reluctantly, Fred gave up his crew-got-drunk theory and sought other criminal explanations.

Undaunted, he arranged for marine surveyors to make a thorough examination of the *Mary Celeste*. They said she was in excellent condition, with no sign of any collision damage. However, their reports included one curious detail. There was a long groove running along each side of her bows — as though it had been deliberately cut there. One marine carpentry expert, Captain Schufeldt, said he thought the grooves were simply the result of natural weathering.

Having found nothing on the *Mary Celeste*'s structure to support his paranoid suspicions, Fred's next line of enquiry was to suggest that some curious reddish-brown stains on the deck were blood. He also became intensely curious about some stains on an antique Italian sword found in Captain Briggs's cabin. He had both sets of stains analyzed — and the forensic chemistry of the 1870s was capable of achieving quite commendable results. Having had a report from the analysts, however, Fred decided to keep it to himself. This almost certainly indicates that it *wasn't* blood. Had the stains supported his theories, Fred would have trumpeted them from the housetops.

It was fortunate for Morehouse, Deveau, and their crew that the members of the Admiralty Court were sensible and experienced seamen. Despite Fred's attempts to discredit them, Morehouse and his men were awarded £1,700 in salvage money: a tidy sum for the 1870s, but only a fraction of what they should have been awarded.

The fate of Briggs, his family, and the crew of the *Mary Celeste* remains an unsolved mystery of the sea. Theories abound; proof is missing. Only statistical probabilities of different strengths exist — attached to a wide variety of hypotheses. What theories have been put forward over the years?

Ergotine poisoning could have been responsible. Ergot is a parasitic fungus: scientific name *claviceps purpurea*. It turns up on various cereal grasses, including wheat and barley, but rye seems to be its favourite host. Individual ergots in the form of purple-black sclerotia (club-shaped bodies) get to the tops of the cereal grass where its seeds are produced. These sclerotia then give rise to the fungal fruiting bodies of the *claviceps purpurea*. Typically, these fungal fruiting parts have bulbous heads mounted on long stalks. The ergot alkaloids they produce include: beta-ergocryptine, ergocryptine, ergocristine, ergocornine, beta-ergotine, ergotomine, and ergotine itself. These different varieties all have hallucinogenic properties to a greater or lesser extent. They are also vasoconstrictive, interfering with the blood supply, and can cause gangrene in the body's extremities.

Medieval hygiene being very limited, outbreaks of ergotine poisoning with its accompanying hallucinations were all too common. A very severe outbreak in France as recently as the 1950s led patients to report that they were being chased by hideous monsters. The relevance of ergotine to the unsolved mystery of the *Mary Celeste* is clear: if the food was contaminated, the passengers and crew would have hallucinated and left the ship in wild panic — some in the boat, some by leaping overboard to escape the "hideous monsters" they thought were pursuing them.

Some ergotine hallucinations are reportedly aetiological in character: they seek to "explain" the environment in unreal ways. If another human being — nurse, doctor, or caregiver — is approaching a hallucinating ergotine poisoning victim, the patient will imagine that the approaching figure is a vampire, a were-beast, a zombie, a demon, or a homicidal extraterrestrial being. The agonizing pain felt in the victim's intestines because of the toxicity of the ergotine will be imagined to be caused by the monster's claws, or a blast from the alien's laser gun — depending upon the cultural expectations of the patient.

We can imagine the Briggs family and the crew of the *Mary Celeste*, infected with hallucinogenic ergotine toxins, "explaining" their fellow sufferers in terms of wild-eyed homicidal pirates, sea monsters, mermen, Tritons, Atlanteans, or Quinotaurs. The ergotine theory is tenable but unproven.

Piracy was not totally unknown in 1872. Although the heyday of the trade was over, a few pirates and white slavers still functioned spasmodically along the notorious Barbary Coast. Was it remotely possible that beautiful young Sarah Briggs met what nineteenth-century New England puritans would have coyly described as "a fate worse than death"? Was she sold into a North African brothel, or to swell an emir's harem, while her husband and his crew grimly ended their days as slave labourers? The problem with that theory is that pirate slave traders would not have left anything of value on the *Mary Celeste*. They would certainly have taken the money that was still on board when the *Dei Gratia* found her, and they would have seriously considered taking the entire ship herself. A change of flag and nameplate and the *Mary Celeste* could have been sold quickly, quietly, and profitably in a port where difficult questions were not asked and paperwork was minimal.

The slaver theory is, however, curiously supported by the evidence of a man named Demetrius. He breathed nothing about the tragedy until 1913 — forty years after the event — because of his own alleged role in the crime. Demetrius claimed that he had actually *been* one of the slavers who had captured the *Mary Celeste*'s complement. As she approached the Azores, his ship had flown signals: "Short of provisions. Starving." Briggs had responded humanely by signalling to them to send a boat. When it approached the *Mary Celeste* there seemed to be only one man aboard it, plus some provision cases covered with a tarpaulin. Too late, Briggs and his crew realized that the other heavily armed slavers were hidden below the sheeting. Briggs and his crew were all transferred to the slaver, and the *Mary Celeste* was abandoned. Demetrius went on to recount that fever had decimated the pirates and their prisoners until scarcely anyone was left alive on board the slaving vessel. He concluded his tale by reporting that a large steamer had subsequently collided with the slaver and sunk her — without stopping — and that he, Demetrius, was the sole survivor. His strange account was just possible, perhaps, but it sounds more like a tall tale than the truth about a tall ship!

Another dramatic theory involved sea monsters. Did some dark denizen of the deep reach up with its grim tentacles and pluck Ben, his family, and the crew of the *Mary Celeste* from their ship? It seems highly improbable, and yet the theory cannot be entirely dismissed as idle fantasy.

The oceans are vast, and *things* dwell within them that would have been more than capable of destroying the personnel of the *Mary Celeste* without necessarily destroying their ship as well. It is far more probable, however, that such a Krakenesque assailant would have taken the ship itself down rather than merely picked off the crew — but the theory is not an impossible one.

Yet another theory that might have sprung from the quaintly officious little mind of Fred Flood concerned a pack of dangerously intoxicated rats. It was suggested that they had broached the industrial alcohol in the hold, rather enjoyed it, and turned as a psychotic rodent horde on Briggs, his family, and the crew, who leapt overboard to escape. Presumably, the alcoholic rats had leapt after them, lemming-like, into the Atlantic — because Oliver Deveau and his companions found no trace of them when they explored the *Mary Celeste* and then sailed her successfully to Gibraltar.

A similar theory blames a plague of flesh-eating crabs rather than rodents. This hypothesis suggests that they popped up buoyantly out of the Atlantic, swarmed aboard the *Mary Celeste,* and swiftly devoured everyone before jumping back, replete, into the ocean. That story is reminiscent of the work of the brilliant horror writer Guy N. Smith, whose *Night of the Crabs* is one of the most effectively bloodcurdling yarns in that genre.

The next theory involves vanishing islands. They have a long tradition. Classical accounts tell of enormous whales sleeping peacefully while partially submerged. In these versions, sailors land on the supposed island and light a fire to cook their food. Not surprisingly the gigantic whale wakes up and plunges down into the depths — taking them with him. It seems highly improbable that the personnel of the *Mary Celeste* decided to hold a picnic and barbecue on a sleeping whale in November — but the idea was once put forward.

Natural disasters and unusual geological and meteorological phenomena may have had a hand in the tragedy. There is evidence that on November 5, 1872, the seismological recording equipment in Zurich, Switzerland, noted a very large earthquake with its epicentre in the Atlantic Ocean *in the vicinity of where the* Mary Celeste *would have been.* Could that submarine seaquake have been responsible in any way for the ship's abandonment?

Waterspouts threatening a sailing ship.

Whirlwinds and waterspouts were also blamed by some theorists. It seems highly improbable, however, that any waterspout would have been so selective that it siphoned off all the human beings but left the ship relatively undamaged.

An exceptionally neat and consistent explanation is usually labelled "The Stowaway's Story" and takes account of the curious groove running along each side of the *Mary Celeste*'s bows. According to the unnamed stowaway, who claimed to be an eyewitness, there was a great deal of friendly rivalry between Briggs and his first mate. Each claimed that he was the stronger and faster swimmer, and, with little else to do, they decided to settle the matter by having a swimming race around the ship — starting at the bows and finishing the circuit there.

Active little Sophia, the Briggs's toddler daughter, caused her parents much anxiety by slipping away occasionally and trying to climb out along the bowsprit to watch the water racing by. The ship's carpenter built a neat little safety platform for the child immediately under the bowsprit, which accounted for the two grooves where he had let it securely into the ship's timbers.

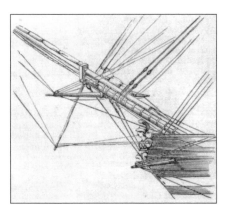

Bowsprit: below here the two grooves ran along the bows.

The swimming race began. Briggs and Richardson were neck and neck all the way. Everyone stopped whatever he, or she, was doing and ran up on deck to watch. The curvature of the bows, sloping down towards the waterline, restricted their vital view of the finish. The spectators clambered onto the little platform to get a better look: it promptly collapsed on top of Briggs and Richardson as they finished their race. Everyone was drowning while their ship went heedlessly on her way.

The stowaway storyteller cut two pieces of rail away to launch the yawl to try to save them. He risked punishment and imprisonment by revealing himself and trying to help them, but he did his best. Just as he got the yawl into the water, however, a squall hit the *Mary Celeste*. She sped away from the tragedy, while the stowaway found it almost impossible to handle the yawl on his own. He did eventually get it back to the spot where the accident had happened — but only the pathetic little play-platform floated forlornly in the water: there was no sign of a living soul.

A more salacious version of the swimming race hypothesis was that Richardson was Sarah's lover, and that he and Benjamin had decided to settle the matter honourably — with a swimming race rather than a duel. Sarah, in love with both, had agreed to go exclusively with the winner, while the loser would quietly move out of her life once they reached port. It's a million light years from the ethics of the nineteenth-century New England puritan culture to which they all belonged — but stranger things have happened.

The stowaway in the yawl finally made it to a lonely part of the Azores, gave a false name, told a vague and confused story about being shipwrecked — but said not a word about the *Mary Celeste* in case of punishment for stowing away.

It was a beautifully *neat* story — and perhaps that's where its main weakness lies. Truth is often stranger than fiction, but truth tends to have loose ends and an untidy structure. It is well-crafted fiction that fits together precisely.

The mysterious bow grooves are also explained by the hypothesis of extraterrestrials in a UFO. By a curious coincidence one of our early science fiction novels, called *Fiends*, published in the 1950s by Badger Books of Hammersmith, involved a UFO with a gigantic gripper as part of its equipment. This was used to immobilize the *Mary Celeste* while the extraterrestrials abducted her people. Needless to say, it was that alien gripper that left the marks on the bows.

Time travel features in another theory. First-class, avant-garde physicists are still undecided about the true nature of time even in our highly technological twenty-first century. It may well be that time can slip, warp, bend, distort, and behave in other odd and unexpected ways. Because we human beings are vividly aware of time, it might, perhaps, be argued that metaphysical time, subjective time-consciousness, and intelligent self-awareness are all inextricably integrated. If some sort of weird time irregularity occurred in the vicinity of the *Mary Celeste* during that fateful November of 1872, it is feasible to conjecture that it would have affected her passengers and crew rather than the vessel herself. Were the Briggs family and their companions snatched away into another time, or even another probability track — one of the intriguing *Worlds of If?*

Another whimsical theory even concerned mermaids. Going back to classical concepts of the irresistible songs of the malevolent Sirens luring mariners to their deaths, it was suggested that similar marine temptresses lured Briggs and the sailors overboard, while Sarah and Sophia — impervious to those gender-directed songs — were abandoned to their fate. Sarah, realizing that she could not hope to handle the brigantine alone, decided that she and her tiny daughter would have more chance in the yawl, which one strong woman could just about handle. Accordingly, she cut away the rails and committed herself and her precious child to the Atlantic. If slave traders found them in their tiny lifeboat, we are back to the scenario of a Barbary Coast bordello.

Yet another theory — along the lines of the unpleasant thoughts that lurked in the suspicious mind of Freddy Flood — was that there had been some sort of intrigue and collusion between Briggs and

Morehouse. According to this theory, Morehouse took the *Mary Celeste* personnel to a remote part of the Azores and left them there, then went on to collect the salvage money, which would be shared later among the conspirators. The insuperable objection to this hypothesis is that Briggs was a deeply moral, ethical, and sincerely religious man who could no more participate in a confidence trick than he could rob a blind beggar.

Even his profound and sincere religion was turned against him in the next theory. His deeply held New England Puritanism was said to have been a form of dangerous religious mania, and, deciding that his crew were all sinners deserving death, he had seen himself as the divine instrument of slaughter and butchered them all. He had also slaughtered his wife and child in a sort of ritual sacrifice before throwing himself over the side. That strikes us as far less likely than even the Sirens theory!

Turning from wild conjecture to common sense and rationality, what was the most likely explanation for this weird unsolved mystery of the sea? There were no signs of foul play. There were no signs of attack by pirates, slavers, or sea serpents. There was little or no chance that such good and honest men as Briggs and Morehouse were involved in a conspiracy to defraud the insurers. Time slips and aliens in UFOs are not totally impossible, but they don't seem very probable. So what *really* happened to those eleven people?

If we analyze the story a detail at a time, we realize several important things. Briggs was a competent and experienced captain, but he had not — according to such records as are available — carried a large cargo of industrial alcohol before. Those who had were not keen on it. The liquid was volatile, and the containers were not perfectly airtight and watertight. Mariners who had carried industrial alcohol reported that its fumes tended to escape and had on occasion blown hatch covers off.

Briggs was not sailing as a solitary captain. Two of the people he loved best were on board with him, sharing any risks to which the *Mary Celeste* was exposed. In general, we tend to take greater risks on our own than when we are taking care of those we love. (Co-author Lionel, for example, hammers his big Harley Davidson far harder around tight bends on his own than when co-author Patricia is on the pillion!) Ben Briggs would have taken risks for himself that he would never have shared with Sarah and Sophia. On this voyage, he is being hyper-cautious.

The alcohol in the hold emits dangerous vapours. A hatch cover blows. Briggs imagines (wrongly) that the whole lot is about to explode. He gives emergency orders to launch the yawl. Everyone abandons whatever he, or she, is doing and gets the tiny boat into the sea. It's dangerously overcrowded and barely seaworthy, but as far as

Briggs is concerned it offers a better survival chance than the risk of being blown to hell by exploding alcohol in the hold of the *Mary Celeste*. They secure the yawl to the stern of the empty ship with the longest line they've got: the peak halyard. All goes well for a while. The alcohol has *not* exploded. Briggs begins to wonder whether the dangerous vapours have blown clear. Is it safe to go back on board? Then a savage squall hits the ship. The *Mary Celeste* leaps forward as the wind takes her sails. The peak halyard snaps. They row the overloaded boat frantically in pursuit — but the pursuit is hopeless. The *Mary Celeste* pulls further and further ahead of them — and vanishes into the gloom. Just a few hours later the inevitable tragedy happens: the inadequate little yawl overturns and sinks. All eleven people are lost. Like El Cid, the empty *Mary Celeste* sails out of history and into legend.

After the lengthy and totally unnecessary objections raised by the unpleasant Freddy Flood in Gibraltar, the *Mary Celeste* was sent back to James Winchester, and her new skipper, Captain George W. Blatchford, safely delivered her cargo to Genoa. Glad to be clear of the problem and half-believing that there really *was* a jinx on the *Mary Celeste*, Winchester sold her at a loss. Everything seemed to go downhill from there as far as the *Mary Celeste* was concerned. During the following thirteen years, she had seventeen different owners before she was bought in 1884 by a Boston consortium who paid very little for her.

The new owners insured her cargo for a suspiciously high amount, claiming that it included bread, beef, ale, cutlery, and furniture. Near the coast of the notorious Voodoo Island of Haiti, her captain, Gilman C. Parker, ordered the helmsman to run her aground on a coral reef. This was a particularly stupid way to try to dispose of a ship with barratry in mind — jammed on a coral reef, the *Mary Celeste* was wide open to insurance inspectors, and, in the circumstances, they came with alacrity. The expensive cutlery turned out to be cheap dog collars; the beer bottles were full of water. Charges were brought against Parker and his mate — who both died rather conveniently before going to court. Was it natural causes, or was someone higher up in the murky organization afraid of what they might say to save their own skins? Several companies involved in that Haiti reef swindle went bankrupt. Another of the conspirators *allegedly* committed suicide — but like Parker and the mate, he might have received a little assistance from someone who preferred his silence to his evidence. Her tragic end so close to Voodoo Island provided plenty of material for those who believed in the jinx that had followed the *Amazon/Mary Celeste* from the day she was launched until her death on the reef.

CHAPTER EIGHT

Some Strange and Dangerous Denizens of the Deep

Oliver Goldsmith (1728–1774) was a doctor, a poet, and a playwright. His famous work *A History of Animated Nature* contains some unforgettable words about the sea and its inhabitants:

> The ocean is a great receptacle of fishes. It has been thought, by some, that all fish are naturally of the salt element; and that they have mounted up into fresh water by some accidental migration. A few still swim up rivers to deposit their spawn; but of the great body of fishes, of which the size is enormous and the shoals are endless, those all keep to the sea, and would quickly expire in fresh water. In that extensive and undiscovered abode, millions reside, whose manners are a secret to us, and whose very form is unknown. The curiosity of mankind, indeed, has drawn some from their depths, and his wants many more: with the figure of these at least he is acquainted; but for their pursuits, migrations, societies, antipathies, pleasures, times of gestation, and manner of bringing forth, these are all hidden in the turbulent element that protects them .... Most fish offer us the same external form, sharp at either end and swelling in the middle, by which they are enabled to transverse the fluid which they inhabit with greater celerity and ease. That peculiar shape, which nature has granted to most fishes, we endeavour to imitate in such vessels as are designed to sail with the

greatest swiftness: however, the progress of a machine, moved forward in the water by human contrivance, is nothing to the rapidity of an animal destined by nature to reside there. Any of the large fish overtake a ship in full sail, with great ease, play around it without effort and outstrip it at pleasure.

Goldsmith's eighteenth-century representation of a codfish.

The passing centuries have added vast stores of knowledge to the pioneering marine biology of Goldsmith's eighteenth century, but his great statement "In that extensive and undiscovered abode, millions reside, whose manners are a secret to us, and whose very form is unknown" remains awesomely true. Many of the most impressive unsolved mysteries of the sea live in it. What Goldsmith said so profoundly about the sea and its many strange inhabitants in the eighteenth century is being reinforced and expanded by outstanding Canadian marine biologists and other leading Canadian ocean scientists in our twenty-first century.

Professor Paul Hebert, for example, who holds the Chair in Molecular Biodiversity in the Department of Zoology in the highly prestigious Guelph University in Ontario, has done brilliant work on DNA bar-coding. Professor Ransom Myers, who holds the Killam Chair in Ocean Studies at the celebrated and influential University of Dalhousie in Halifax, Nova Scotia, works with Dr. Boris Worm of the German Institute of Marine Science. They have issued a very significant and serious warning concerning the loss of huge numbers of large marine life forms.

Chimera monstrosa.

There are still many species waiting to be found and classified by scientists and researchers. An example is the weird-looking *Chimera monstrosa*, which has been described in some colourful eyewitness accounts as a cross between a shark and a unicorn. It is an odd-looking bottom-feeder, hauled up occasionally from great depths by fishermen working off the French coast. How many uncles, aunts, and cousins has the *Chimera monstrosa* got down there with him?

Almost as strange in appearance, but relatively better known, is the edible and nutritious doree, also called dory, John Dory, and St. Peter's fish. Its pigments are olive and yellow, with glimpses of blue, silver, and gold. According to legend, the large dark spots on each side are where the saint took hold of it: the coin found in its mouth (hence the *gold* and *silver* markings) paid the temple tax collector (Matthew 17: 27).

Doree, or dory, St. Peter's fish (Zeus faber).

The sea wasp, also called the box jellyfish, is known scientifically as *Chironex fleckeri Southcott*. With a mass of two or three kilograms, it's one of the sea's deadliest toxic stingers, with a big, translucent, bell-shaped body that can reach sizes of up to half a metre across. Sixteen tentacles, which can each be four metres long, trail out behind this bucket-shaped body. Each tentacle carries millions of capsules filled with venomous toxin that the sea wasp discharges enthusiastically into anything that makes contact with it. In humans, the sea wasp's poison causes agonizing pain, restricts breathing, hinders the circulation, and induces a fatal heart attack. The toxin also damages the skin badly, causing marks that look like the wheals left by a whip. Victims can survive, however, if an antidote to the toxin is administered very soon after the attack.

Portuguese man-of-war.

The Portuguese man-of-war is more widely distributed than the sea wasp, which is mainly a problem in Australian waters, and — although unpleasant — the man-of-war is considerably less dangerous than the sea wasp. They have been found in Hawaii, Japan, the Mediterranean, and even in the Canadian Bay of Fundy. The Portuguese man-of-war is not a single marine entity but a complete colony of polyps attached to a blue float, which gives the man-of-war its nickname, bluebottle. This inflated blue bladder rises well above the water and acts as a sail when the colonial polyps travel. The polyps are equipped with tentacles armed with stinging cells called *nematocysts*. The poison from these cells causes respiratory problems and weakness of the muscles. It can easily knock out small fish. The sting causes sharp pain to human victims, but is not normally lethal.

The blue-ringed octopus — small but deadly — is one of the nastiest marine creatures around. Two varieties of them are found in Australian waters: *Hapalochlaena lunulata* is slightly larger than *Hapalochlaena maculosa*. Both of them lurk in tidal pools, as well as in the sea itself. Although they barely reach twenty centimetres from tentacle tip to tentacle tip, weight for weight they are about as dangerous an opponent as the unwary bather can have the misfortune to encounter.

When frightened, disturbed, or taken up out of the water, the blue-ringed octopus shows the brilliant blue rings from which it gets its name. It can deliver its potent venom either through biting, like a poisonous snake does, or by squirting it at its victim. The main result is respiratory failure and malfunction of the nervous system. There is numbness, blurred vision, loss of tactile sensation, difficulty in speaking and swallowing, paralysis, and nausea. Unless given immediate medical help, the victim can die of lack of oxygen or heart failure — or a sinister combination of the two.

Just as deadly — but vastly bigger, and brutally powerful rather than toxic — is the awesome sea crocodile. *Crocodylus porosus* is particularly dangerous because, despite his simplistic appearance, he's as cunning as the proverbial fox and has few — if any — natural enemies. If this abnormal and unexpected brainpower somehow makes him aware that human beings are dangerous to him because they can stab, harpoon, or shoot him, it may perhaps account for his tendency to attack people without provocation. A recent example (November 2003) of crocodile intelligence comes from Hong Kong, where crocodile expert John Lever of Queensland, Australia, finally admitted defeat after two weeks of hunting. He had laid special traps for the elusive crocodile terrorizing the area. At the time of writing, two Chinese experts, He Zhanzhao and Li Mingjian, have taken over the search. Before Lever came to help them, local Hong Kong conservationists, armed with tranquillizer guns, had also searched for the croc unsuccessfully; they'd even laid traps for it.

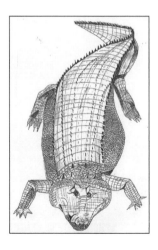

Adult saltwater crocodile, nine metres long.

Saltwater crocs can grow up to eight or nine metres long and live for more than one hundred years. They prowl the coastal areas, venturing into creeks, rivers, and lakes, lurking and lying in wait for the next victim to walk, wade, or swim past. They harbour in mangrove swamps, and their powerful jaws will take birds, fish, animals, and people indiscriminately. *Crocodylus porosus* is an omnivore and proud of it.

He looks incapable of any sort of speed on land — but that's dangerously deceptive. Over twenty- or thirty-metre sprints he's as fast as a horse, and in addition to his powerful jaws and formidable teeth he has a flexible muscular tail that can bring most prey down with one deadly sideways blow.

Crocodylus porosus has unpleasant dietary habits. Having despatched his victims, he likes to hide them in his underwater mangrove larder until they have rotted down nicely before eating them.

The sea anemone looks beautiful and flower-like — but doesn't behave that way! It's very common in the tidal pools of Hawaii and extends out to deep offshore waters as well. Some anemones enjoy symbiotic relationships with crabs. The crab carries the anemone around on its back from one profitable feeding place to another, and the anemone reimburses its carrier by acting as a weapon if the crab is attacked. Some marine biologists report that the boxer crab, *Lybia tesselata*, holds the anemone in its claws on these occasions and seems to use it as a combination of sword and shield. The stinging cells in the anemone's tentacles deter most predators. *Majidae dochlea*, commonly known as the spider crab, also carries anemones around, as does *Dorippe facchino*, the porter crab.

This type of marine relationship is one of the many unsolved biological mysteries relating to numerous strange denizens of the deep. Symbiosis can be subdivided into mutualism, where both partners get something out of the relationship; commensalism, where one creature gets considerable advantages from being on the team but the other doesn't — although the non-benefiting partner is not harmed by the arrangement; and crude, undeniable parasitism, where the parasitic partner wins and the host loses. Some marine biologists also include the idea of mimicry as a form of symbiosis at a distance. The harlequin snake eel, for example, is about as innocuous a sea creature as you can hope to meet — but it mimics the powerfully venomous banded sea snake, *Laticauda colubrine,* in order to dissuade potential attackers.

Many other mysterious examples of symbiosis abound in the sea and oceans. *Astropyga radiate* is an unpleasantly toxic sea urchin among whose spines its little goby partners lurk for protection. Other varieties of sea urchin are interesting rather than toxic.

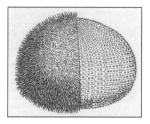

*Sea urchin (*Echinus radiate*).*

Toxicity can help a species to survive, but rarely seems effective for the toxic individual when it's essentially posthumous! The puffer fish is easy enough to catch, but is likely to take its revenge on the successful angler if he, or she, eats it. The flesh and organs of a puffer can be toxic enough to interfere with breathing, and, even at its least serious, induces very unpleasant sickness.

The actual poison inside the puffer fish is tetrodotoxin, and Canadian scientists, working with colleagues in Britain and China, have isolated one of its ingredients, which may soon become the world's most effective painkiller, thousands of times stronger than morphine. It will hopefully be able to ease the pain of terminally ill patients for whom even morphine is no longer effective.

*Puffer fish (*Lagocephalus*).*

Cone snails, which inhabit tidal pools and beach areas, as well as offshore habitats, are also venomously toxic. They have a device not unlike a built-in hypodermic needle that helps them to kill their prey. If injected into a human being, their toxin can induce severe pain, loss of sensation, heart attack, and unconsciousness.

The moray eel isn't one of the marine toxic team, but its powerful jaws and a set of teeth that combine the most dangerous features of razors and stilettos make him an unpleasant guy to encounter. He inhabits crevices, tidal pools, the undersides of rocks — almost any location where he's not generally expected. Dead fish, or a few drops of blood from an angler's hook-in-the-finger type injury, will attract him powerfully. Those formidable teeth can do more than superficial tissue damage: the moray eel's dentition will get through a victim's nerves and tendons if they come within range.

Artist's impression of dangerous eel-type creature, or ribbon fish.

Needle fish stay near the surface as a rule and turn up in bays, inlets, estuaries, and open waters. As the name suggests, they have a very long, pointed jaw — another of the sea's many biological mysteries. They are attracted by light and by any bright, gleaming, or glittering objects. When that long, abnormally pointed jaw pierces a victim, it tends to break off in the wound. Another strangely elongated jaw belongs to the tobacco-pipe fish (*Fistularia tabacaria*).

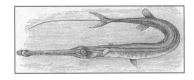

*Tobacco-pipe fish (*Fistularia tabacaria*).*

Dinosaurs are venerable, but the coelacanth is older still. It was thought to have become extinct when they did around 65 million years ago — but it didn't! The reappearance of the amazing — not to mention controversial — coelacanth with its 400-million-year pedigree took place in 1938. A highly intelligent and proactive museum curator, Marjorie Courtenay Latimer, worked in the port of East London, situated northeast of Cape Town, South Africa. Her friend Captain Hendrick Goosen commanded the trawler *Nerine.* An arrangement they had that was of great benefit to Marjorie's museum was that whenever the *Nerine* docked in East London, Hendrick invited her over to inspect the cargo in case there were any unusual or interesting specimens among his newly caught fish. On December 23, 1938, there most certainly was!

The *Nerine* had been trawling off the mouth of the River Chalumna, and as Marjorie inspected the pile of dead fish she spotted an unusual blue fin sticking out. Moving sharks and rays aside to reveal the late owner of that mysterious and intriguing blue fin, Marjorie saw the unforgettable bluish-purple body and iridescent silver markings of what could only have been a coelacanth. She took it back to her museum, sketched it, and sent the sketch to an eminent ichthyologist, Professor J.L.B. Smith of Rhodes University. He sent back the now famous cable: "Most important preserve skeleton and gills." When he reached East London and examined what was left of the coelacanth he described it as the most important zoological find of the century.

Reward notices were posted everywhere in the area in the hope of finding more specimens, but it was not until 1952 that the next coelacanth was discovered. Captain Eric Hunt of the *Nduwaro* was doing all he could to locate one as he traded among the Comoros Islands in the Mozambique Channel. As a result of Hunt's work in spreading Professor Smith's reward notices, two local men, Ahamadi Abdallah and his friend Affane Mohamed, duly brought in a coelacanth. Ahamadi had caught it on his handline. Although not common, the species was well enough known to the Comorians of Anjouan Island, who referred to them as Gombessa or mame fish.

Urgent messages to Professor Smith brought him flying over in a DC3 Dakota. He confirmed that Ahamadi had indeed caught a coelacanth. Worldwide publicity and great excitement naturally followed.

The tragic corollary to the story is the mysterious disappearance of boldly adventurous Captain Eric Hunt of the *Nduwaro.* Four years after being instrumental in bringing Professor Smith's wonderful ichthyological dream to life, Hunt's ship was wrecked on the dangerous Geyser Bank between Madagascar and the Comoros. Hunt was never found.

The stingray — another mystery of the sea — is one of a vast range of cartilaginous fish (*Elasmobranchii*) including many other rays, skate, ratfish, and sharks. The ray's pedigree covers millions of years: fossils of their earliest antecedents go back to Jurassic times — 150 million years ago. Their powerful, flexible bodies are supported by tough, fibrous cartilage instead of bone. Rays are related to sharks, from which they evolved. The stingray has spines on its tail capable of poisoning an attacker. In some species the tail is long and moves like a whip. In others, it is little more than a stump. The rays vary enormously in colour: sometimes males and females of the same species are differently pigmented.

Elasmobranchii — *a typical member of the ray family.*

The smallest known ray is referred to as the short-nosed electric ray, weighing about half a kilogram and being only ten centimetres in diameter. The biggest of its cousins is the mighty manta ray (*Manta birostris*), with a diameter of nine metres and a mass of several tonnes. Despite its vast size, the manta ray is a swift and elegant swimmer — although its style differs from that of most normal fish. Its wing-like pectoral fins propel it by rippling and flapping. These big pectoral fins make it possible for it to glide through the water, rather as gliding birds go through the air. The diet of this enormous denizen of the deep consists of minute fish and microscopic plankton, enlivened with a sprinkling of very small crustaceans. It directs food into its mouth by using the cephalic lobes situated just ahead of its eyes.

Other rays eat fish, molluscs, worms, and crustaceans. Some hunt for their prey on the ocean floor. Others stun it with an electric charge. Rays are remarkably talented — the mangrove stingray, for example, can even jump out of the water! Their feats in the water — including the speed with which they swim — are due in part to some species being coated with slippery mucous that greatly reduces water-drag. Most fish have a swim bladder, which controls the depth at which they swim. Rays — like sharks — don't have one. Their buoyancy is controlled by their large, oily livers, but when they stop swimming, rays sink down to the ocean floor.

The strangely misnamed angelfish, also called monkfish and fiddle fish, is a voracious predator equipped with five rows of very effective teeth in a mouth — unlike the mouths of its cousins — situated at the far end of its large head. It claims kinship with the plagiostomi, the fish group that includes rays and sharks and other creatures that can reach a length of three metres.

Squatina angelus — *known as angelfish, fiddle fish, and monkfish.*

As far as can be ascertained, some plagiostomi, including rays, are highly intelligent — and some are amazingly gregarious and sociable, living together in colonies thousands strong. Others, hermit-like, prefer to be loners. They usually express curiosity when divers approach them, although they can survive at astounding depths — up to three thousand metres below sea level — far beyond normal diving range! The blind electric ray (*Typhlonarke aysoni*) can also survive at phenomenal depths. Specimens are said to exist as far down as nine hundred metres. Visibility is very restricted at that level, and, consequently, its eyes appear to be almost non-functional, but it "sees" using electro-receptors and is capable of delivering powerful electric shocks.

The mangrove stingray's ability to leap out of the water is impressive, but it pales into insignificance beside the aerial antics of flying fish. Known technically as *Exocoetidae*, flying fish are gregarious, swimming in schools or shoals. In length they range from eighteen to thirty centimetres, and they possess pectoral fins that rival the wings of birds. Many species also have pelvic fins that are much larger than those of traditional fish.

Technically, flying fish do not actually *fly* like birds, but rather *glide*. They get airborne by approaching the surface of the sea at speeds of up to fifty kilometres an hour. Then they taxi along the surface like small aircraft attempting a takeoff by using their remarkable tail fins almost like rear-end propellers! Unlike its cousins, the characin flying fish found around the Amazon Basin really does fly by using its fins like wings and buzzing them like a bumblebee. It's the misfortune of the flying fish to be appetizing to dolphins, mackerel, and tuna — and their aeronautics are essential to their survival when these predators are after them.

*Flying fish (*Exocoetidae*).*

Among the strangest and most mysterious denizens of the deep are the angler fish. There are well over two hundred species of them, named because of their technique of what resembles fishing. Their "fishing rods" are actually spines of their dorsal fins, with a lure — often luminous — dangling on the end. Prey, fascinated by this "bait," comes too close — and is promptly eaten.

The sex life of the angler fish is even stranger than its food-gathering techniques. Only the female has the built-in fishing tackle. The male is much smaller than his mate and lives on her as a permanent parasite. The nuptials consist of the male giving the female a hearty bite and attaching himself. His mouth adheres to her skin and they are literally inseparable thereafter. He blends his bloodstream with hers and becomes totally dependent on her for nourishment. As time passes, he loses his

Angler fish.

eyes, followed by his internal organs — and remains solely as a source of sperm: the ultimate example, perhaps, of Darwinian survival mechanisms at their most economical!

One of the largely mythical terrors of the deep is the giant clam, *Tridacna gigas*, which is supposedly able to trap a diver's legs and drown him. Admittedly, the giant clam can reach a width of well over a metre and a weight of 250 kilograms, but it would be hard pressed to trap a diver between its bivalvular shells because it has to empty its water chamber before it can get the shells to close — and this takes several seconds! Unless the diver who has been careless enough to put his foot between the giant clam's two shells has a reaction speed that makes a sloth look like Billy the Kid drawing a Colt .45, he ought to be well clear of the closure hazard before the clam has got a quarter of its water chamber empty. Human beings are of more danger to the giant clam than it is to us. There are reports of souvenir giant clam shells being used as birdbaths and baptismal fonts in churches. Furthermore, some gourmets regard the clam's flesh as both a delicacy and an aphrodisiac— a reputation that does nothing for its life expectancy.

Best known — and most feared — of all marine predators are the members of the sinister shark family. They come in a wide range of shapes and sizes, the hammerhead being one of the more spectacular. Big hammerheads can reach a length of six metres and a weight of 250 kilograms. They are ferocious predators with voracious appetites. Their diet includes squid, octopus, crustaceans, rays, and other sharks. Hammerheads are migratory and travel to cooler waters in summer. They give birth to live young, averaging about thirty pups, with an average length of seventy-five centimetres.

*Hammerhead shark (*Zygaena malleus*). The great hammerhead is* Sphyrna mokarran.

The most dangerous of all sharks is the great white. Big specimens can reach a length of seven metres and a mass of well over three tonnes:

the females are bigger than the males! Their diet is rather more varied than the hammerhead's menu and can include otters, seals, and sea lions as well as belugas and sea turtles: nothing edible is safe! Despite possessing about three thousand teeth, which move around into place as required, great whites don't chew their food — they simply rip it into suitably sized pieces and swallow it whole. They can also go for a week or two between meals.

This shark's ability to sense even the tiniest drop of blood in the water is phenomenal — a concentration of one part blood in ten million parts of water is apparently detectable to a great white's nostrils. They can also pick up minute electrical charges from prospective prey, so being detected by one is all too easy if you're swimming anywhere in its vicinity — especially if it hasn't eaten anything substantial for a month or two! They have fewer simultaneous pups than the hammerheads: a great white manages only about ten at a time. Their life spans are not known with any certainty, but some marine biologists estimate they can probably live for about a century.

Early nineteenth-century artist's impression of a great white shark.

Big and dangerous as the great whites undeniably are, the biggest of all creatures are the whales. They are members of the cetacean family, which includes nearly eighty species of whales, porpoises, and dolphins. One of this great family, the blue whale, is the largest living creature that has ever existed on Earth — including the mightiest of the dinosaurs. Blue whales are about thirty metres long.

Many of the sea's biological mysteries centre on whales. Their behaviour includes *logging*, where they rest just below the surface with part of the huge back and head exposed above the water and the tail resting in the downwards position. The many semi-legendary, but very persistent, stories of mariners landing on what they *thought* were small islands could be based on sailors' stories of actual landings on logging whales. Other mysterious whale activities include *lob-tailing*, where they slap the water with their tails; *spy-hopping*, where they lift their heads out of the water and rotate as though looking around; and *breaching*, where they leap clear out of the water — a prodigious feat considering the vast body mass involved.

Nineteenth-century concepts of whaling.

Unlike baby sharks, which have to fend for themselves as soon as they're born, baby whales — referred to as calves — are nursed and protected by their mothers for at least a year and often significantly longer. Whales are highly intelligent and often gregarious, frequently moving around together in what are known as *pods*. It is practically certain that they have systems of social relationships, too. The famous whale song — part of that social behaviour — can last for more than half an hour and can carry over great expanses of water.

Although killer whales attack smaller members of the family, human beings are the only known predators of the giant whales, and it seems to the authors that the hunting and killing of these magnificent, intelligent, and sociable ocean giants is not only morally questionable but an inadequate commercial use of a unique natural resource. Sea film safaris and whale-spotting holiday tours would produce ten times the income available from whale hunting. Co-author Lionel makes that statement authoritatively and categorically as a practising professional management consultant and a fellow of the Chartered Institute of Management. The whale has to face enough natural hazards without the human race adding to them unnecessarily. As recently as November 2003, for example, more than one hundred pilot whales were found dead at Point Hibbs on the Tasmanian coast. Had they gone too far inshore during a feeding frenzy? Or had they been trying to escape from predators?

A beached whale.

Another great mystery of whales is the question of where they originated. Just as many sea creatures gradually emerged from the water during evolutionary millennia, so whales appear to have gone the other way — from the land to the sea. One interesting theory of whale development is that they came from land mammals with hooves. About 50 million years ago there was a land-dweller, known to science as *Mesonychid,* that *may* have returned to the sea and become the whale's ancestor.

So we conclude this chapter with a reference to Goldsmith's pioneering work in the eighteenth century, and a salute to the prominent pioneering Canadian marine scientists of our own day, Professor Myers and Professor Hebert: *In that extensive and undiscovered abode, millions reside, whose manners are a secret to us, and whose very form is unknown.*

CHAPTER NINE

Perilous Waters

Draw three lines connecting Miami, Bermuda, and Puerto Rico. Some researchers have called the area inside those lines the "Devil's Triangle." To others it was the "Hoodoo Sea." The name that seems to have adhered to it best during the past century is the "Bermuda Triangle." Like all prominent mysteries — from land, sky, sea, or space — the Bermuda Triangle initiates fierce and wide-ranging controversy. To those who are prepared to be totally objective, receptive, and open-minded, it might be a star gate, a doorway to hyperspace, an access point to unknown dimensions, a time portal, a vestigial remnant of ancient Atlantean technology, or the hiding place of extraterrestrial beings.

To cynics and skeptics — whose views are vital when genuine mysteries are being investigated seriously and scientifically — the area is naturally dangerous, and the hazards there may well include geological and meteorological features that can affect magnetic compasses. The area is always susceptible to sudden and unexpected air turbulence. A plane can be flying smoothly and normally one minute and bouncing around like a tennis ball the next. The weather within and surrounding the Bermuda Triangle is unpredictable. Meteorologists know well that a relatively minor storm can become a deadly, dangerous hurricane if the time, speed, and fetch are all that way inclined. (The fetch indicates the area over which the wind is able to blow uninterruptedly; the other two storm-to-hurricane transformation inducers are the time the storm has to develop and build up its power and the speed with which it's travelling.) Relatively modest thunderstorms can be transformed in a very short time into what meteorologists call meso-meteorological storms of great power. These small, sudden, violently escalating and very hazardous storms are exacerbated by the meteorological conditions that pertain to the Bermuda Triangle: cold airstreams there encounter hot ones, and they react to each other like rival tomcats establishing their territory. The warm water of the Gulf Stream also cuts across the Bermuda Triangle and contributes to its abnormalities.

Sailors who know the area well report the mysterious electrical phenomena frequently seen on the masts and yards of sailing ships generally referred to as "St. Elmo's Fire." Travellers through the Bermuda Triangle also report frequent and dynamic bolts of lightning accompanied by a strange, burnt, ozone-like, hot-metal smell. Ball lightning has also been reported there.

Other Bermuda Triangle mariners have reported disturbances in the sea itself so severe that a ship can suddenly be faced by an unpredictable wave the size of a house. The area is also notorious for waterspouts, when tornadoes wrench huge columns of water hundreds of metres up into the air. Those who've experienced these vast waterspouts have no doubt that they present a formidable challenge to ships of almost any size.

From causes that would gladden the heart of science fiction and fantasy enthusiasts at one end of the scale, to oceanographers' and meteorologists' scientific hypotheses and analytical records at the other, the Bermuda Triangle poses its sinister riddles as persistently as the legendary Sphinx once did. It is undeniable that a great many ships and aircraft have been lost there. How *natural* were their disappearances?

In addition to the unpredictable foul weather and electromagnetic anomalies in the Bermuda Triangle, there are still a few raiders and pirates around. They no longer favour cutlasses and pistols, or parrots and tri-corned hats, but their motives and modus operandi remain largely unchanged. At least *some* of the losses in the Bermuda Triangle can be explained as piracy.

Does the sea floor below the sinister triangle offer any theoretical answers to the riddle? Most of that sea floor is well over six thousand metres down and covered with fine sand. The U.S.'s neighbouring continental shelf, in comparison, has a depth of a mere thirty metres. The vast depth beyond the shallows of the continental shelf is exceeded significantly by the Puerto Rican Trench at the southern tip of the Bermuda Triangle, which has a depth of over nine thousand metres and is one of the deepest parts of the whole Atlantic Ocean. Historians speculate that it must almost certainly be the last resting place of many Spanish conquistadores and their treasure-filled galleons.

Another interesting piece of data is that longitude 80° passes through the Bermuda Triangle. Longitude 80° is particularly interesting because it is the agonic line where magnetic north and true north are the same. It is usually necessary for a navigator to allow for the variation between *magnetic* north as shown by the compass and *true* north. On the agonic line no such variation occurs.

Points on a ship's compass.

This agonic line goes on over to the far side of the North Pole and proceeds through the Pacific to the east of Japan, where it is interesting to consider the area that Japanese and Filipino sailors refer to as "the Devil's Sea." As in the Bermuda Triangle, there seem to be statistically more disappearances there than in other areas. The problem the agonic line creates for navigators is that when you *normally* allow for a compass variation of as much as twenty degrees between true north and magnetic north *and then there is no variation*, even the most expert and experienced navigators can make mistakes.

Psychologists refer to this error-inducing mental factor as *perseveration*: the inadvertent persistence of a familiar and well-practised behaviour pattern that is no longer applicable. Try taking a newspaper paragraph and crossing out every letter *e* with a vertical stroke as fast as you can. Then, immediately, take another paragraph and cross out every letter *o* with a horizontal stroke. Individual responses differ, but we are all vulnerable to perseveration to a greater or lesser degree. The tendency to cross out an *e* or two with a vertical stroke will persist even though the new target and response is *o* with a horizontal stroke. When you've allowed for magnetic variations for weeks of sailing, it's difficult not to go on doing it along the agonic line, which your ship has just reached.

This Devil's Sea is also notorious for tsunamis. Similar to tidal waves, but much bigger and faster, these are huge water movements caused by earthquakes and similar disturbances on the seabed. Tsunamis have very long wavelengths. If they have plenty of room to spread out in wide-open water in mid ocean, they may be less than half a metre high and relatively innocuous. When they get closer to a continental shelf they change dramatically and can engulf entire islands.

There's also the human error factor to consider when studying the individual tragedies of the numerous lost ships and planes in the Bermuda Triangle. Florida, Barbados, and Puerto Rico are popular sailing destinations. Some enthusiastic amateurs with insufficient experience, inadequate seamanship, and scant knowledge of the dangers sail blithely into the Bermuda Triangle in a vessel that isn't big enough, seaworthy enough, or well enough equipped technically. Their chances of disappearing are significantly above the risk factors for experienced professionals in big, well-equipped, seaworthy ships.

While analyzing the mysteries of the two infamous triangles — one near Bermuda and the other near Japan — there is another notorious area, called the "Welsh Triangle," that deserves to be considered. The base of this Welsh Triangle runs roughly from northeast to southwest, and includes Pembroke Dock — the town where we investigated the recent, well-authenticated sea serpent sightings. The apex of the Welsh Triangle is out in St. George's Channel between Wales and Ireland.

Close examination of the geology of the landward side of the Welsh Triangle, which includes St. Bride's Bay, shows a number of sea caves, some of them very large, and many of them interconnected, so forming a natural labyrinth occupying several levels. There is also considerable evidence in the area of the activities of our prehistoric ancestors, who were once working industriously in that location.

Welsh Triangle theorists cite the extraordinary reports that emerged from the Milford Haven district in 1977. Strange, chromium-coloured aerial objects were described by many local pupils in the Haverfordwest area. At the height of the phenomena, witnesses claimed to have seen a curious silver-coloured, egg-shaped craft land in a field. They also claimed to have seen unusually tall humanoids wearing what looked like shiny plastic overalls. There were more detailed versions of these reports that included an inspection of a subterranean nuclear shelter. Theories were advanced about Stack Rock, one of a chain of forts dating back to the 1860s that were originally built to protect west Wales from attacks by the forces of Napoleon III of France. With a garrison of 168 men and 23 formidable guns, the chain of forts that included the one on Stack Rock were designed to offer protection to one another and to pour continuous fire on any invading vessels. The main responsibility of the Stack Rock fort was to protect the Royal Naval Dockyard at Pembroke Dock.

During the 1977 Welsh Triangle crisis, several local residents began to suspect that Stack Rock and its historic fortress had somehow become a base for extraterrestrial beings, who were blamed for causing everything from car breakdowns to teleported bovines and exploding TV sets. There are many sensible and logical people living in the vicinity of Stack Rock who still have their suspicions about the place, and who also have vivid memories of the events of 1977. The Welsh Triangle offers a very different set of enigmas from those associated with the Bermuda Triangle and the Japanese Triangle — but the riddles of all three may yet prove to be connected, and all of them can chronicle inexplicable events from the past as well as relatively recent ones.

The tragic disappearances in the Bermuda Triangle certainly go back a lot further than is popularly imagined. Columbus allegedly reported odd compass behaviour in that location — but fifteenth-century ships' compasses were hardly miracles of precise, sophisticated navigational technology. The USS *Pickering* vanished there in 1800. The British ship *Bella* was lost there in 1854 on her way from Rio de Janeiro to Jamaica, and another British vessel, a frigate named *Atalanta*, disappeared there in 1880. The Italian schooner *Miramon* was mysteriously lost in the Triangle in 1884. The USS *Cyclops*, a substantial collier, went missing there in 1918 with several hundred people aboard her. Although *Cyclops* was equipped with radio, she sent no distress signal before vanishing — unlike the ill-fated Japanese freighter *Raifuku Maru*, which vanished in 1925 but reportedly managed to send an SOS: "Danger like dagger now. Come quick." Was a radio operator with language problems trying to signal the word "danger," which actually came out as "dagger" because of a technical malfunction? Or did he see *something* that he could only describe as resembling a dagger threatening the *Raifuku Maru*? The *Cotopaxi* also vanished without trace in 1925. In 1938 — with the advantages of calm weather and a cloudless sky — the steamer *Anglo-Australian* sent a traditional "All's well" message before she sailed into the Triangle never to emerge again. The *Sandra* disappeared in 1950 under equally mysterious circumstances. The *Marine Sulphur Queen* left Beaumont in Texas in 1963 on her way to Norfolk, Virginia. After entering the Bermuda Triangle she was never heard from again. In the same year a fishing boat named *Sno'Boy* left Kingston, Jamaica, and vanished as suddenly, as mysteriously, and as completely as the *Marine Sulphur Queen* had done. In the seventies *Ixtapa, Anita, Saba Bank, Sylvia L. Ossa,* and *King Cobra* all vanished in that area. In the eighties, *Sea Quest* got off a last signal that her navigational kit wasn't functioning properly and then vanished into oblivion, taking eleven people with her. The nineties saw the end of three good, stout ships: *Mae Doris, Intrepid,* and *Genesis.* That relatively long list of unsolved marine tragedies is scarcely the tip of the Bermuda Triangle's sinister iceberg: there were many, *many* more. To say that five hundred ships were lost there would be a very cautious understatement.

On top of the scores of vanished ships, there are the unsolved mysteries of abandoned derelicts like the *Mary Celeste.* In 1840 — thirty-two years before the *Mary Celeste* sailed into legend — something sinister happened to the complement of the *Rosalie,* an elegant but sturdy little French vessel sailing towards Havana. She was found abandoned inside the fateful triangle. Something similarly odd happened to the captain and crew of the *Freya,* which left Cuba and was found with no one aboard her the day after she had sailed on October 3, 1902. The *Gloria Colite* left St. Vincent in good order and with a full complement in 1940. She was found derelict a few hundred miles south of Mobile, Alabama. Her people are still missing. The totally empty yacht *Vagabond* turned up on the edge of the Sargasso Sea in 1969 — none of her missing personnel were ever traced.

Moving from ships to aircraft, the best known of the Bermuda Triangle air tragedies is the fate of Flight 19. On the afternoon of December 5, 1945, five Grumman TBM Avengers took off from Fort Lauderdale in Florida on a run-of-the-mill training mission. They never returned. Wreckage discovered in 1992 was originally thought to be that of the five missing Avengers from Flight 19, but turned out not to be theirs after all. A big Martin Mariner seaplane set out to look for the five missing Avengers and also failed to return. Bermuda Triangle mystery enthusiasts like to argue that the Mariner fell victim to whatever strange paranormal or extraterrestrial interference may have destroyed the Avengers. There is evidence, however, that she exploded in mid-air. Witnesses on a ship, the *Gaines Mills,* in the area at the time the Mariner vanished, maintained that they saw a flash of light in the sky that could have been an exploding aircraft. The commander of the USS *Solomons,* an aircraft carrier taking part in the search for the five missing Avengers, confirmed what had been reported from the *Gaines Mills.* In his opinion, the seaplane had exploded in mid-air.

The controversy surrounding the loss of Flight 19 continues as fiercely as it reverberated throughout the 1940s. There are strong arguments among the researchers and investigators as to how experienced the aircrew were when they set off on that fatal training flight from the Naval Air Station at Fort Lauderdale in Florida. Lieutenant Charles C. Taylor was credited with long and unblemished flying and instructing experience according to most accounts. There were suspicions in other versions that he was drunk or badly hungover from heavy drinking the previous night. That seems extremely unlikely in view of Naval Air Station discipline in the 1940s. Although Flight 19 was acknowledged to be a training mission, it was very clearly *advanced* training, indicating that the aircrew concerned were knowledgeable and experienced men. Efficient and skilful pilots — like any other highly qualified professionals — regularly take part in training seminars and updates, as well as familiarization courses for new procedures or modifications to equipment and techniques. It is incorrect to assume that the title "training flight" implies that those taking part were not experienced flying experts.

Another mystery surrounds the *purported* conversations between Taylor, his accompanying pilots, and the Fort Lauderdale control tower. Just when Flight 19 should have been close to returning to base about an hour and forty-five minutes after takeoff, Taylor is alleged to have radioed in: "Cannot see land; we seem to be off course." The tower then asked for their position and received the answer: "We cannot be sure where we are. Repeat: we cannot see land." Further reports of Flight 19's communications then included phrases such as: "We can't find west. We can't be sure of any directions. Everything is wrong. Everything looks strange — even the ocean." It was very difficult to make anything clearly intelligible out of these alleged signals, as some reports suggest that several of the pilots were transmitting simultaneously.

There is evidence that the conversations actually took place between the men of Flight 19 and Lieutenant Robert Cox, the senior flight instructor at Fort Lauderdale in 1945. Cox overheard someone asking Captain Powers (one of the Flight 19 pilots) what his compass reading was. Powers replied: "I don't know where we are. We must have got lost after that last turn." Cox then signalled to Flight 19: "What's the trouble?" and it was Taylor who answered: "Both my compasses are out. I'm trying to find Fort Lauderdale. I'm over broken land. I'm sure it's the Florida Keys, but I don't know how far down."

It seems possible that Taylor and his men had mistaken Great Sale Cay in the Bahamas for the Florida Keys. The big question the lost pilots had to answer was whether they were on the Atlantic (eastern) side of Florida or over the Gulf of Mexico on the western side. With limited amounts of fuel, their lives depended on getting that answer right.

Whether we prefer the adventurous and imaginative explanations, ranging from UFOs to time travel via extra-dimensional gateways, or the prosaic, scientific, oceanographic and meteorological ones, the Bermuda Triangle remains an intriguing unsolved mystery of the sea.

Though not as mysterious as the Bermuda Triangle, the notorious Goodwin Sands, six miles out into the English Channel — just off Deal as you round the North Foreland — are roughly eighteen kilometres long and ten wide. The Goodwins are as mobile as piglets because of the strong winds and currents that beset them. Although semi-submerged and fatally dangerous in autumn and winter, a hot, dry, calm summer makes it possible to ride bikes and play cricket on the Goodwins at low tide.

It is no exaggeration to say that the Goodwins have probably destroyed more than one thousand ships over the centuries. The great storm of 1703 destroyed many vessels there, including the *Stirling Castle*, a very well built and seaworthy man-of-war. In 1954, the South Goodwin lightship sank with tragic loss of life. It was essential to use a lightship there because it was utterly impossible to find any firm foundation on which to build a lighthouse.

Co-author Lionel's paternal grandmother, Eliza Ann Holmes Cuthbert, of King's Lynn, Norfolk, U.K., was herself the daughter of Captain Cuthbert of King's Lynn, who was master of a sloop of the kind known then as Billy Boys. Lloyd's List of Shipping for April 15, 1859, records that a Billy Boy was discovered at daybreak on the Goodwins: her hull was underwater, and her crew were clinging desperately to the rigging. The valiantly unselfish crew of the Walmer lifeboat went out to save her, regardless of their own safety, as did volunteers on board a Deal registered lugger. Incredibly, despite awesome seas, one of the Billy Boy's crew was saved, although two were lost, including the master.

Co-author Lionel's great-grandfather, Captain Cuthbert, was also drowned when his Billy Boy sank at around the same period in the mid-nineteenth century. Life is full of curious coincidences.

Another unsolved mystery is the weird Sargasso Sea, named after the curious seaweed, called *sargassum*, that floats close to its surface. Mariners have known about it for a long time — certainly since the days of Columbus, who mistakenly regarded it as a sign that he wasn't far from land. When he tried to sound the depth, however, he was surprised to find that the Sargasso was "bottom-less" — at least with the unsophisticated measuring gear at his disposal in the fifteenth century.

In broad terms, the Sargasso Sea can be located between 20° to 35° north and 30° to 70° west. Within that area there are very few marine currents, yet the Sargasso is at the centre of some of the fastest and most persistent streams known to oceanographers. The Gulf Stream goes around part of the Sargasso, and so do the following: the Caribbean, the North Equatorial, the Florida, the Canary, and the Antilles currents. The coming together of these powerful, grand-scale water movements seems to have an isolating effect on the Sargasso. Its own limited currents, such as are they are, are described by expert oceanographers as *entropious* — a specialist term derived from the better known and understood concept of *entropy* — roughly meaning "wasted energy," or signifying "misdirected energy," together with the degree of uncertainty and randomness within the energy system concerned.

As far as research into the Sargasso is concerned, the strong external currents and the internal entropious currents seem to create a very strange water trap: many things are induced to drift *in* — but very little ever drifts *out* again!

A disturbing and dangerous feature that the Sargasso shares with the Goodwins is its ability to move and shift around — slightly, but unpredictably. A model is always useful. Imagine spilling a bucket of fairly gooey, gelatinous seaweed into a bathtub full of water and then taking a large wooden spoon and stirring vigorously all *around* it, but not *through* it. The track of your spoon creates the powerful currents (miniatures of the Gulf Stream and the Antilles Current) surrounding and isolating your miniature Sargasso. Such disturbances as occur within the gooey seaweed are entropious. It also changes its position slightly relative to the bathtub — and within its own random boundaries. These changes are influenced to a major extent by the speed, power, and positioning of your wooden spoon.

Early oceanographic theories, and the suggestions of marine biologists in the past, centred on the hypothesis that the massive quantities of weed in the Sargasso had been swept in from distant coastal regions by the powerful ocean currents surrounding it. Later hypotheses, however, tend in the direction of the adaptation and evolution of the weed *to adjust and modify itself to survival within its curious environment.*

There were legends and myths — as well as some historically verifiable accounts — of lost ships and weird, derelict craft in the Sargasso, centuries before tales of the Bermuda Triangle began to take the world's attention. One gruesome example was the sighting of a slaver *with skeletons as her only complement.* Other strange finds and sightings included the adventure of the *Ellen Austin* in 1881, which had curious parallels with the *Mary Celeste* mystery of 1872. The *Ellen Austin* reportedly found a derelict and sent a prize crew over to it. Just as the *Mary Celeste* had sailed with the *Dei Gratia* towards Gibraltar until the storm had separated them, so the *Ellen Austin* sailed in sight of the rescued derelict they'd found in the Sargasso. Observing that something odd seemed to be happening to the rescued ship, the *Ellen Austin* drew alongside and re-investigated their supposed salvage prize. *It was derelict again, and the prize crew had vanished.* It's interesting to speculate what might have happened had that prize crew been led by the awesomely powerful Oliver Deveau, first mate of the *Dei Gratia,* who fought against dangerous odds to get the *Mary Celeste* safely into Gibraltar with a skeleton crew.

When the derelict *James B. Chester* was found in the Sargasso in 1857, there were overturned chairs and a meal laid out on the mess-room table. The mysteries of the Sargasso extend into comparatively recent times as well. The *Connemara IV* was found derelict there, for example, as recently as 1952, and the *Poet,* all of seventy metres in length, vanished in the Sargasso in 1980.

Like the Bermuda Triangle, the Sargasso remains one of the great enigmas of the sea.

CHAPTER TEN

Lost Lands: Slipped and Sunken Continents

One of the major unsolved mysteries of the sea is the Legend of Lost Atlantis: at its most challenging, the theory suggests that an advanced culture flourished on a large island, or subcontinent, millennia ago and was lost when it sank beneath the Atlantic Ocean — or *moved sideways.*

Pioneering researchers Rand and Rose Flem-Ath came up with a thoroughly analyzed and daring new suggestion in their excellent 1995 work *When the Sky Fell: In Search of Atlantis.* They concluded that rather than submerging, Atlantis had glided across the surface of the Earth to become the present Antarctica, buried beneath the deep ice surrounding the South Pole. In discussing this theory, leading unsolved mysteries investigator Colin Wilson uses the homely but effective analogy of something like the skin on cold soup: it doesn't require much force to make the skin slide over the liquid soup beneath it. The Flem-Aths have proposed one of the best argued Atlantis theories around, one that's definitely worth serious consideration.

The search for Atlantis begins with two of the dialogues of Plato (427–347 BC), *Timaeus* and *Critias*. *Timaeus* gets its name from Timaeus the Pythagorean, and *Critias* is named after Critias the Younger, who was Plato's uncle on his mother's side. In Plato's most famous work, *The Republic,* Atlantis is seen neither as a mystery nor an allegory, but a simple piece of historical fact. Plato learned what he knew of Atlantis from Socrates (469–399 BC), who apparently regarded it not only as real, but the site of an ideal community with an exemplary form of government and a high level of culture. The difficulty is to determine whether Socrates "created" Atlantis as a setting, or model, for a utopian society, or whether he was using something he believed to be historical to defend his utopian theories about the nature and function of abstract justice.

Critias told Socrates, Plato, Glaucus, Adimantus, and Hermocrates that Solon, the great Athenian statesman, had visited Egypt and met a wise old priest at Sais, a city on the Nile delta. (Solon flourished circa 600 BC.) This wise old Egyptian had a great knowledge of history and apparently had access to secret, ancient Egyptian records that told the story of Atlantis and its destruction some ten thousand years before he spoke to Solon of Athens.

According to this wise old priest from Sais, the proto-Athenians from millennia ago had excelled all other races in the arts of civilization and in military prowess. At that time, there had existed beyond the Pillars of Hercules — the modern Straits of Gibraltar — a huge island called Atlantis, said to be larger than Libya and Asia combined.

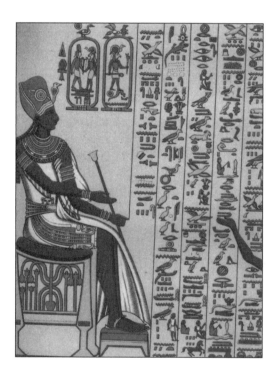

The ancient Egyptian wisdom of Sais would have been recorded in symbols like these.

138

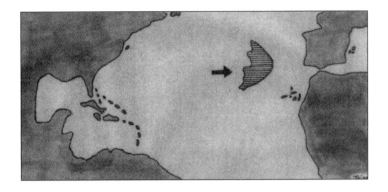

Map of possible location of Atlantis drawn by Theo Fanthorpe.

The Atlanteans were also a very advanced and cultured people with a high level of technology. Their empire contained many North African states and large parts of Europe, but in attempting to conquer the proto-Athenians they met more than their match. The war between them took a terrible toll of both armies, but the valour and military prowess of the Greeks finally beat the Atlanteans, whereupon the magnanimous proto-Athenians liberated the former tributaries of their Atlantean foes and granted them their independence.

The victory had scarcely been celebrated before a series of unprecedented natural disasters overwhelmed Athens and the area around it. Earthquakes and floods also smashed the Atlanteans, and their entire land mass vanished beneath the mighty waters of the Atlantic in a day and a night.

Several scholarly experts in both folklore and mythology have tentatively suggested that at least some of the ancient gods in elaborate old pantheons may well have been real, prehistoric kings and war lords. There is evidence to support the notion that this was probably the case for several members of the Greek and Roman pantheons. Assuming that Neptune-Poseidon was once a powerful historical sea king, his traditional connections with Atlantis become significant. One of the earliest Atlantean creation legends featured a man named Euenor and his wife, Leucippe. Their daughter, Cleito, attracted Poseidon's favours, and, after they became lovers, he built her a wonderfully fortified domain, protected by concentric circles of land and water — the traditional Atlantean layout.

Very ancient traditional Atlantean design drawn by Theo Fanthorpe.

Curious old circular labyrinth design carved on the stone of Rocky Valley, Tintagel, Cornwall. Could these ancient labyrinth designs be connected with the layout of Atlantis?

Having thus made very generous and secure provision for his beautiful and nubile Cleito, the amorous Poseidon fathered five sets of boy twins with her. These all grew up and became kings and governors of the various areas of Atlantis — and of the subsequent Atlantean Empire, which was finally defeated by the determined proto-Athenians before both it and they succumbed to catastrophic earthquakes and floods.

The old Egyptian priest provided Solon with extensive details of Atlantis. There were rich mineral sources that the inhabitants mined, including orichalc, probably a very high grade copper ore, second only to gold in their scale of values. There was an abundance of timber — Atlantis was as renowned for great quantities of high-quality wood as Lebanon was for its biblical cedars. Atlantis abounded in a rich variety of wildlife — including elephants — that found abundant food supplies on its rich pastures. There were lakes, ponds, and rivers that contained an abundance of fish and other flora and fauna. Atlantis was also rich in spices, aromatic flowers, gums, resins, and many medicinal herbs. The description given by the old Egyptian priest included references to fruit trees, and some others that provided the Atlanteans with oil and highly palatable juice drinks. There were wonderful irrigation systems, and both hot and cold springs supplied excellent water of the highest purity.

Bridges crossed the great canals and waterways. A resplendent castle and holy place honoured Poseidon and Cleito — within which the holiest place of all, where the ten princes of Atlantis had been born, was encircled with a golden fence. No human being was ever allowed inside that sacred enclosure.

A formidable army, including indomitable cavalry and lancers, guarded the princes, and the Atlantean ships filled the busy harbours bringing trade from all over the known world. In addition to these busy mercantile marine vessels, there were hundreds of powerful warships, making invasion of Atlantis next to impossible.

Taken as a whole, the description given by the old priest of Sais is so detailed and comprehensive that it seems to go beyond fiction. Could all this have been imagined? How much of it was history, and how much of it was embroidery? Stripping his account to Solon to its barest essentials, we are confronted by a high culture with massive civil engineering capabilities, prosperous overseas trade, and huge natural resources of minerals, timber, and agricultural potential. How did such a great empire vanish beneath the Atlantic?

There are other, stranger records than the words that allegedly passed between the old priest of Sais and Solon of Athens. The rock of Gávea stands on the eight-hundred-metre summit of a steep Brazilian mountain between São Conrado and Barra da Tijuca, not far from Rio de Janeiro. The statue is Sphinx-like, with what looks like a vast human face sculpted at one end. One side of the precipitous monument carries a strange inscription, which some researchers attribute to a Phoenician sea king who lived some three thousand years ago. According to Pedro Lacaz do Amaral, who has climbed in the area many times, this is the memorial to Badezir of Tyre in Phoenicia, the eldest son of Jeth-Baal. This Badezir is reckoned to have succeeded to his father's throne in 856 BC. If he's buried in Brazil, it suggests that ancient seafaring men from Phoenicia knew about the New World millennia before Columbus crossed the Atlantic. Other ruins in the vicinity look to some expert archaeologists as if they might have been Phoenician in origin. According to local news reports, rare Phoenician pottery was discovered in the 1970s in Guanabara Bay.

What is of greatest interest to Atlantean theorists in connection with the Gávea rock, however, is the possibility that the ancient

Phoenicians knew that sea route so well *because they also knew about the destruction of Atlantis.*

Apart from the challenging evidence of the controversial Gàvea rock and its possibly Phoenician inscription to commemorate King Badezir, there is a great deal of additional, and more substantial, American evidence to suggest that people with a high level of culture and technology were there in the remotely distant past. The Aztecs were remarkably capable and sophisticated by the generally accepted standards of their time: they had cities, well-developed systems of properly paved roads, and the administrative skills necessary to control an expanding empire. Their capital city, Tenochtitlan, was almost as big as modern Cardiff and had a population of well over a quarter of a million people.

Founded in 1325 amid the clear waters of the Lake of the Moon, the Aztec capital was expertly laid out and enriched with palaces, pyramids, and temples. As skilfully as the great civil engineers of the Netherlands battled against the North Sea with the construction of their dikes and polders, so the Aztec civil engineers battled with the water in the Lake of the Moon. Artificial islands were built and turned into small holdings and gardens to supply food for the citizens of Tenochtitlan. Causeways and bridges connected the great central city to the surrounding islands. All of this sounds remarkably similar to Solon's account of the wisdom he received from the old priest of Sais.

The Aztec engineering feats were reinforced by their advanced mathematical knowledge, which also underlay their exceptional knowledge of astronomy. Their delight in huge monumental artifacts is shown in one of their gigantic calendars. This consists of a round stone four metres across with a mass of well over twenty tons. Its mathematical accuracy and precision is even more noteworthy than its ponderous size.

For Atlantean researchers, the crucial question is where the Aztecs came from. Could they once have been Atlantean colonists? Or were they even survivors of the cataclysm that destroyed their original, highly cultured homeland? Most orthodox thought among traditional historians places the Aztec ancestors in northern Mexico. There are, however, no traces there of the kind of work they accomplished later. In their own ancient traditions, the Aztecs maintained that they came in the beginning from Aztlan. They said that this was a land to the *east* of America. This ties in with Plato's assertions, based on Solon's testimony derived from the old priest of Sais, that the Atlantean Empire established colonies to their *west* as well as making

142

eastward incursions into the lands on the Mediterranean side of the Pillars of Hercules.

An even more remarkable *possible* connection linking America with Atlantis is the Great Pyramid of Cuicuilco. American archaeologist Byron Cummins made some strange discoveries when he excavated there in the 1920s. It was found that volcanic Mount Xitli had disgorged lava around the pyramid on numerous occasions for several millennia, and this had hardened to form pedrigal. Seven metres of debris had been covered by these volcanic layers.

Diagram of section through a volcano.

Cummins and his colleagues were able to ascertain that these succeeding lava flows had spared the pyramid *because it was already covered with protective rock, soil, and pumice when they occurred.* The only possible conclusion was that it was very old indeed. By studying the solidified lava and other materials covering the Cuicuilco Pyramid, Cummins and his associates concluded that it dated from *at least ten thousand years ago* — a date that fitted well with the account of Atlantis given to Solon by the old priest of Sais.

The riddle of the Pyramid of Cuicuilco is as exciting and intriguing today as it was when the Cummins team revealed it in the 1920s, yet the enigma of Tiahuanaco in Bolivia is, if anything, even more puzzling. There is a great deal of uncertainty and ongoing debate about the age of Tiahuanaco. Many traditional scholars date it to a century or two before Christ. Dr. Rolf Müller, a German astronomer quoted in Herbie Brennan's brilliantly written and superbly researched work *The Atlantis Enigma* (Piatkus, 1999), was of the opinion that Tiahuanaco was at least as old as the Atlantis of Solon's account, and possibly much older. Was Tiahuanaco the centre of a culture contemporary with — and perhaps in regular contact with — Atlantis? Was it possibly an Atlantean colony?

In essence, its impressive structures surpass the great works of the Aztecs. Some of the vast stone blocks of its huge buildings weigh up to seventy tonnes, and were brought from more than one quarry. Quite how they were cut and put into place remains a mystery; there are no obvious tool marks on them, so how were they excavated? The skill with which they were integrated into buildings of colossal strength — able to withstand earthquakes — remains a mystery today. Most curious of all is that Tiahuanaco is more than four thousand metres above sea level and stands a long, long way from any navigable water — *yet it was clearly designed and built as a seaport.* In view of the obsessive religious devotion of many ancient peoples, it was often suggested by earlier scholars that Tiahuanaco was a mysterious holy place, a harbour of souls from which the spirits of the dead sailed mystically to the Lands Beyond the Grave. More recent work has revealed that far from being a remote shrine, Tiahuanaco was a thriving city, the headquarters of an empire that ran as far as Argentina, Chile, and Peru. The great harbours that once flourished there were practical rather than mystical.

The agricultural skills that flourished in Tiahuanaco and in parts of its ancient empire seem to have been as great as their feats of civil engineering and architecture — all of which appear to reflect the accounts of Atlantis originating with the old priest of Sais. The heart of this system was a reticulation of elevated growing areas, irrigated by small water channels. The water channels appear to have served two purposes: irrigation and temperature enhancement. Contemporary Bolivian agriculturalists seem to have seen the value of these dual purpose growing structures and to have employed them with great effect to increase productivity significantly.

Several of the mysteries of prehistoric America may point in the direction of an Atlantis that existed ten millennia before Christ; an examination of ancient Egyptian prehistory produces similar conclusions. Stranger than the Sphinx and the famous pyramids in the Valley of the Kings is the curious Well of Abydos, a vast subterranean reservoir that the best modern civil engineers, armed with all our newest twenty-first-century power and technology, would find it very difficult to emulate today. The great ancient Egyptian questions — like the questions from Tiahuanaco and Cuicuilco — are: who built this vast and complex subterranean structure and *why?*

If the technology attributed to Atlantis really existed, it apparently included certain advanced manufacturing processes that we don't seem to be able to duplicate today. There are reports of diorite jars in the mastabas tombs at Saqqara, in Egypt, hollowed out with a technique that seems almost miraculous to our twenty-first-century manufacturing technology. Diorite is an exceptionally hard metamorphic rock with a typically salt-and-pepper appearance. It is a mixture of hornblende, feldspar, plagioclase, and orthoclase. If quartz is also present in the diorite it is usually referred to as granodiorite. Diorite usually appears in the same geological locations as granite and gabbro, and can frequently be found merged and blended with them. How anything that hard could have been delicately hollowed out using only the limited technology thought to have been available thousands of years BC is yet another enigma contributing to the Atlantean riddle.

A further technological miracle from ancient Egypt was their apparent ability to manufacture copper coated with a very thin layer of antimony. One professor of chemistry working back in the 1930s suggested that they'd discovered an electro-plating technique — something we thought our society had done for the first time in the 1800s. Egypt's mysterious, anachronistic, technological wonders, like those of prehistoric America, all suggest that somewhere between the two — and in contact with them — was a highly advanced culture that knew how to build vast stone structures, create impressive subterranean reservoirs, hollow out amazing diorite containers, and plate copper with antimony. Does Atlantis fit that profile?

The question then goes back to where the Atlanteans themselves came from — assuming that they and their doomed continent ever really existed. Persistent legends of highly intelligent and massively powerful amphibian sea gods, going back to the most ancient of prehistoric times, suggest that they may have been extraterrestrials from a planet in another star system, perhaps near Orion. The Atlanteans of Solon's version were definitely humanoid, although their devotion to Poseidon the Amphibian King of the Sea may be significant in this context. Supposing that aquatic extraterrestrials were involved in founding Atlantis, couldn't they have taught some of their technology to indigenous terrestrial humanoids, who then founded and populated Atlantis with the help of their mentors, the amphibian extraterrestrials?

Where else might the Atlanteans have originated? Simple, old-fashioned Darwinism and associated evolutionary theories may have something to offer here. If the great island, or miniature continent, in what is now the Atlantic Ocean, had developed largely in isolation — as Australia did — its flora and fauna (including its humanoid fauna) might have been very different from those in other parts of the world where they were readily accessible to predatory species. Ferocity, big muscles, and fast reflexes were very useful for a hunter-gatherer competing hard to survive. The open and frequently bloodstained arena of mainland Earth didn't encourage contemplative philosophers, theologians, astronomers, and abstract artists. You fought for your food most of your waking time — or you became food.

What if things were different on isolated Atlantis? If food was plentiful and your neighbours were peaceful and amiable, you'd have the time to develop your intelligence along abstract paths rather than pragmatic ones. It is pure thought, pure research, and ample time for contemplation that produces the greatest cultural and technological progress for a society. The best survivors in a dangerous hunter-gatherer environment were not likely to be the best thinkers: they were too busy surviving and subsisting. But what if the gentler climate of uncompetitive Atlantis in its earliest days allowed its thinkers, dreamers, poets, and philosophers to survive? Given a few thousand years, they could well have come up with weaponry that would keep their great land safe from aggressive hunter-gatherers. By the time they made contact — long before Atlantis went down in the Great Catastrophe that affected many other parts of the Earth as well — the Atlanteans were more than able to hold their own in battles with the hunter-gatherers. They were far better organized than their opponents — and in early warfare the ability to organize and deploy your warriors scientifically was a very significant plus factor. If this theory is correct, the Atlanteans came from nowhere except the inside of a growing and developing human brain — given a few peaceful millennia to *think* without constant violent interruptions.

There are also theories about visitors from other dimensions and time travellers. Neither scenario is impossible — but both have rather low probabilities.

Second only to the persistent and plausible legends of Atlantis is the legend of Lemuria, another great, water-bounded island or sub-continent that is said to have vanished below the Pacific, much as Atlantis allegedly disappeared beneath the Atlantic — or glided across the Earth's surface to become present-day Antarctica, as the Flem-Aths argue most convincingly. The name *Lemuria* seems to have arisen from the efforts of enthusiastic nineteenth-century Darwinian naturalists anxious to find the original homelands of the lemurs, from whom, according to a hypothesis widely accepted by evolutionary theorists at that time, the human race had descended. Ernst Haeckel, an outstanding German naturalist of the time, was convinced that Lemuria not only existed but had been "the cradle of civilization."

Is this what Haeckel was looking for?

Madame Elena Petrovna Blavatsky, born Helena Hahn, lived from 1831 until 1891. She was co-founder of the Theosophical Society, and was convinced by what she described as psychic means that Lemuria had once existed and that it had been the home of one of what she described as "root races" in her book *The Secret Doctrine*, published in 1888. Madame Blavatsky sited her Lemuria in the Indian Ocean, probably because she was aware of ancient Sanskrit accounts of a sunken land there that had once been called *Rutas*. Blavatsky's Lemurians laid eggs and possessed a third eye that was responsible for their great psychic powers. Blavatsky also said that she had learned of the existence of Lemuria after studying the incredibly ancient and mysterious Book of Dzyan.

Mysterious Madame Blavatsky as drawn by Theo Fanthorpe.

According to her revelations, the Book of Dzyan had been translated into Ancient Egyptian to become the Book of Thoth, also known as Hermes Trismegistus, the scribe of the Ancient Egyptian pantheon of gods. If this is the case, then the *very, very old* truths in the Book of Dzyan may also have been inscribed or encoded into the mysterious Emerald Tablets associated with Hermes Trismegistus. At least one of the Book of Dzyan's mystical teachings is compatible with the higher teachings of all the great world religions: "Sow kindly acts and thou shalt reap their fruition. Inaction when a goodly deed is required is tantamount to an evil act ... To reach Nirvana, the seeker needs self-knowledge, and true self-knowledge comes from deeds of love and compassion."

Not surprisingly, this vital moral wisdom can not only be found in Ancient Egyptian texts, but with slight variations of syntax and emphasis it appears to underpin many of the other old, sacred writings.

Rudolf Steiner was another mystic who was certain that he had psychic information about Lemuria. The most plausible of the Lemurian theories is that the Hawaiian archipelago is all that is left of its ancient mountain peaks.

Citizens of many Pacific Islands have closely allied versions of a lost land that they refer to as either *Mu* or *Lemuria*. Where these accounts differ from the accounts of Atlantis is in the *strangeness* of the Lemurians. They are seen almost as a distinct and separate race, differing qualitatively from other ancient human beings who would be acknowledged and recognized as normal brothers and sisters by twenty-first-century *Homo sapiens*.

Another submerged land theory centres on the mysterious Oera Linda Book and its enigmatic references to Atland or Aldland, a large land mass said to have existed in the North Sea between the U.K. and the Netherlands. Published in 1876 by Trubners of London, who were well known and widely respected in the profession, the Oera Linda Book claimed to be a translation of a work originally compiled in the thirteenth century. This early manuscript was written in Frisian and told (among other things) of how a Frisian king named Inka had sailed away towards the setting sun and founded a new kingdom in a great land far to the west of Europe. If this was Atlantis to which Inka sailed, some theorists have wondered whether the word Inca (Peruvian for *king*) came from there. Was the implication in the Oera Linda Book that King Inka of Frisia was the founder of the Inca Empire? Many scholars regard the Oera Linda Book as a complete fabrication, partly because a prehistoric Frisian would have been thousands of years wrong for the founder of the Inca Empire in South America. But if the supposed — and widely accepted — thirteenth-century date for the rise to power of the Inca Empire inadvertently overlooks a much *earlier* founding date, then there may be a link between the supposed North Sea kingdom of Atland, Atlantis, and the early civilizations of South America, with their high technology and culture.

It is postulated by some researchers that the Oera Linda Book was the property of the Oera Linda family for many centuries. A shipwright named Andreas Oera Linda, who worked for the Netherlands Navy in the early 1800s, allegedly had charge of it then. His heir, Cornelius, was still a child when Andreas died around 1820, so the vitally important original manuscript passed into the custody of Andreas's daughter, Aafje. Years later there was a quarrel between Aafje and Cornelius, and the Oera Linda Book eventually went to Dr. Verwijs of Leeuwarden Library. He translated it into Dutch in the early 1870s, and William Sandbach translated it into English for the Trubner version of 1876. Despite the doubts and controversies hovering around it, the Oera Linda Book may yet be justified by sophisticated twenty-first-century marine archaeology.

As recently as September 2003, Dr. Penny Spikins of Newcastle University was examining the seabed near Tynemouth, Northumberland, U.K., when she came across Mesolithic artifacts that were many thousands of years old. David Miles, chief archaeologist for English Heritage, regards Dr. Spikins's seabed discoveries as highly significant.

Other submarine explorers, including Viatscheslav Koudriavtsev from Moscow's prestigious Institute of Metahistory, are very interested in the Lost Land of Lyonesse, said to have been submerged millennia ago off the coast of Cornwall, U.K.

Many researchers attempt to offer these overlapping — but sometimes contradictory — legends of Atland, Lyonesse, and Lemuria with persistent ancient religious accounts of a great flood that devastated the Earth millennia ago.

There is no smoke without fire, and there are very few myths and legends that do not have some connection — however tenuous — with historical reality. There are real probabilities that at least one of these great-sunken-land legends will turn out to have a substantial basis in prehistoric fact.

CHAPTER ELEVEN

Mysteries of the Circumnavigators

Drake's great voyage in the *Golden Hinde* (originally called *The Pelican*) created almost as many mysteries as his magnificent feat of circumnavigation solved. Born in Devon in 1540, he was the son of a Protestant preacher in what was then Catholic England. Young Drake grew up to become one of the greatest seamen of his day. In 1577 there was a semi-secret negotiation between Drake and Elizabeth I that enabled him to set sail for the Pacific. Ostensibly, Drake and his five ships were looking for the elusive Northwest Passage. In fact, they had a covert commission from the queen to see what they could carve out of the Spanish Empire for her. There were some very secret whispers that Drake had actually met Elizabeth before — in a somewhat clandestine romantic mode — and that might have helped to persuade her to accede to his request in 1577.

Because of the political necessity to keep Drake's great adventure camouflaged from Spain, accounts of the circumnavigation are less than accurate in places, while the great secret of Drake's "missing history" has never been satisfactorily solved. All that can be said with any reasonable certainty is that there are significant, unexplained gaps in the chronicle of his reckless, adventurous, swashbuckling life.

It is even possible that Drake's Devonshire lads made it all the way up to Nova Scotia — to give any observant Spanish ships the idea that he really was going off to find the Northwest Passage. If he had, in fact, visited Nova Scotia, it is even possible that he and his sturdy, efficient crewmen from Devon and Cornwall — especially those with unique Cornish tin-mining skills — might have been the creators of the Oak Island Money Pit, just off Chester, a few miles south of Halifax. But if Drake and his men had created that amazing structure — what had they done it for? Had they *already* taken Spanish treasure to hide there, as a sort of mariners' pension fund? Or was Drake's wealth following his buccaneering work up the Pacific coast of America and Canada not entirely from pillaging Spanish settlements and Spanish treasure galleons? Was he, like George Anson — a later circumnavigator who also came home fabulously rich — possibly aware of the ancient secret of the legendary prehistoric Arcadian Treasure?

Tragically, Drake's excitingly adventurous career ended far too soon. He died — possibly of dysentery — on January 28, 1596, when he was still only in his mid-fifties and commanding his ship off the coast of Panama.

The legend of Drake's drum is another unsolved mystery of the sea. Drums are an integral part of many magical rituals; the beat of a drum links human beings with the rhythms of nature. The sound of waves beating against the shore is the ocean's own great drum. It's possible that thoughts of the sea's drumming passed through the great buccaneer's mind as he lay dying. He told his men to take the famous drum that had accompanied him all around the world back to his home in Buckland Abbey near Plymouth. His orders were duly obeyed and the drum can still be seen there.

Legends tend to change over the years. Drake's original instructions were that the drum should be beaten to call him when England was in danger; he would then come back and defend his homeland until the enemy had been defeated. The modern version is that the drum beats on its own when England is in peril. There are well-authenticated reports that the drum has been heard at least three times over the past century: first in 1914 when World War I started; again aboard the British flagship *Royal Oak* when the German fleet surrendered at Scapa Flow in 1918; and finally at Dunkirk. There is even a semi-legendary account of a young British soldier floundering in the water between Dunkirk and Dover after his rescue ship had been sunk by German action. Perhaps the exhausted soldier was delirious or hallucinating because of his ordeal, but he claimed afterwards that he had been picked up by an old British warship of the type that had beaten the Armada centuries before, that his rescuers had been dressed in the sailors' clothes of a bygone age — *and had spoken with strong west country accents!*

Whether it was Drake and his men who saved the young soldier from Dunkirk, and whether his drum ever sounded that day, are unsolved mysteries of the sea. What is certain, and fully authenticated, is that Drake's great feat of circumnavigation was destined to be emulated almost two hundred years later by Admiral George Anson.

Beautiful but mysterious Shugborough Hall in Staffordshire, U.K., birthplace of Admiral Anson, who circumnavigated the world and came back with vast wealth in 1744.

Baron Anson, Admiral of the Fleet, was born in mysterious Shugborough Hall in Staffordshire, U.K., on April 23 (St. George's Day) in 1697. He joined the navy in 1712, commanded a Pacific Squadron in 1740, circumnavigated the world, and returned safely in 1744. Raised to the peerage in 1747, he became first lord of the admiralty in 1751 and admiral of the fleet in 1761 — a richly deserved promotion for a superb sailor and an expert, humane commander. He lived barely a year to enjoy it; he died on June 6, 1762, at the age of sixty-five.

The Admiral's ancestor, William Anson, a successful and prosperous lawyer from Dunston, bought Shugborough Hall in 1624. As a lawyer, Anson, born in the 1580s, was almost certainly an acquaintance, and probably a friend, of his brilliant — but controversial — older contemporary, Sir Francis Bacon, the leading lawyer of his day. Bacon himself was born in 1561 and died in 1626, two years after Anson acquired Shugborough.

Although Francis was *reputedly* the son of Sir Nicolas and Lady Bacon, his parents were known to be fanatically devoted to Queen

Elizabeth I, and there were politically dangerous rumours at the time suggesting that Francis was, in fact, *the queen's own son*, secretly smuggled out of the palace and entrusted to the care of the totally loyal Bacons. If there was any truth in those rumours, then who was the brilliant Francis Bacon's real biological father?

One of the most sensational suggestions was that Elizabeth had had a clandestine affair with the dashing young Francis Drake — later to become one of England's greatest maritime heroes. Drake was a handsome and virile twenty-one-year-old when Francis Bacon was born. Bacon might have been hinting at this hidden truth when he wrote the cryptic phrase "Knowledge is power" — *Nam et ipsa scientia potestas est* — in his *Meditationes Sacrae, de Haeresibus.* To what strange and secret knowledge did Francis Bacon have access, and what power did it give him? Was it merely the knowledge of his true parentage — or did it concern a source of enormous hidden wealth and knowledge that lay carefully concealed overseas? If Drake was Francis Bacon's father, it has to be remembered that he circumnavigated the world long before Admiral Anson achieved that feat. Did Drake pass secrets to his illegitimate royal son, Francis Bacon, that later went to William Anson of Shugborough? The deepest, most important symbolism behind the Arcadian myth may well be that Arcadia represents some distant and remote place where a vast treasure — of secret knowledge, or of actual wealth — lies waiting for the fearless sailor.

Moving from myth and legend to a scientific and historical appraisal of the original inhabitants of Arcadia, they seem to have been occupying the wild hills of the Greek Peloponnesus since time immemorial — Curtis N. Runnels, for example, writing in the *Scientific American* in March 1995, suggested that the ancestors of the Arcadians might have been there fifty thousand years ago. Local tradition speaks of them colourfully as a tribe "older than the Moon." Might that vivid phrase also hint at their extraterrestrial origin? These ancient and mysterious people were famous for their enviably idyllic, leisurely, and libidinous lifestyle. Were they also guardians of some incomprehensible knowledge? Was their casually simplistic, idyllic, rural lifestyle merely a highly successful cover for their vital duties as keepers of the Arcadian treasure? Was that treasure actual wealth, or was it secret knowledge that produced power and wealth? The knowledge of those arcane Arcadian treasure mysteries is often thought by researchers who specialize in such areas to have been entrusted to very ancient secret societies. Their carefully veiled knowledge may well be close to the heart of the mystery of the circumnavigators and the vast wealth they acquired.

Bacon was known to be a secretive man, one involved in many mysteries. His great friend and admirer, the dramatist, poet, and academic Ben Jonson (1572–1637), wrote of him in a birthday poem: "The fire, the wine, the men! And in the midst / Thou stand'st as if some Mysterie thou did'st!"

Some of those mysteries may well have been transmitted and received via the riddle of the secret watermark codes that were apparently circulating among the leading men of his day. The watermark codes themselves could well be strong links with vast unsolved mysteries lying beyond the sea. Were those who knew the secret of the ancient and mysterious Arcadian treasure symbolizing clues to it in their ship and anchor watermarks?

It was their professional legal work that linked Bacon with William Anson and the intriguing secrets of Shugborough Hall, the most enigmatic of which is the strange Shepherd Monument that stands in the grounds. The authors have studied it in the most minute detail — just as they have studied Poussin's original painting *Bergères d'Arcadie*, on which the Shugborough monument is based.

*These strange old anchor and ship watermarks date back at least to the fif-
teenth century. What curious secret messages did they convey to Drake, Bacon,
and Anson centuries later?*

The authors examining the mysterious Shepherd Monument in the grounds of Shugborough Hall, Staffordshire, U.K. It may link Francis Bacon and the Ansons with the mysterious treasures of Oak Island, Nova Scotia, and Rennes-le-Château in France.

Detail of the inscription at the foot of the Shepherd Monument in the grounds of Shugborough Hall. It has never been satisfactorily deciphered.

The enigmatic Nicolas Poussin was born in Les Andelys, France, in June 1594. He died in Lucina, Italy, on November 19, 1665. This made him a contemporary of William Anson and Francis Bacon, and who better than a professional painter like Poussin to understand and create watermark codes? Although the evidence is tenuous, Poussin seems to have had access to some very important secret of the time. Nicholas Fouquet, the immensely wealthy and powerful minister of finance for King Louis XIV (the so-called Sun King), had a younger brother who was a seventeenth-century version of James Bond. This young man encountered Poussin in Rome and sent a message to his influential elder brother to the effect that Poussin had an amazing secret that he was willing to share with the Fouquets. The young spy's dramatic and sensational letter conveyed the idea that this secret was so well hidden that unless it was deliberately revealed by someone who knew how to decipher it, it would remain hidden until the end of time.

Poussin's secret — whatever it was — seems to have been entwined with the ancient Arcadian myths and legends, and in particular with the cryptic phrase: *Et in Arcadia ego.* This can be traced through Publius Virgilius Maro, better known to classicists as Virgil. Born in 70 BC near Mantua, Virgil visited Rome for the first time in 41 BC, when he was in his thirtieth year. He was a brilliant intellectual who had contacts in the highest Roman circles. If there were strange secrets circulating in the Rome of the first century BC, Virgil would almost certainly have been a party to them. He used the famous *Et in Arcadia ego* phrase as part of his fifth eclogue. Poussin incorporated it into both versions of his *Bergères d'Arcadie* where he depicts three Arcadian shepherds and a shepherdess paused thoughtfully beside a tomb bearing Virgil's solemn words. The superficial meaning seems to be: "Even in the carefree, idyllic, bohemian land of Arcadia, I, Death, am waiting." But some academic folklorists and experts in mythology have put different — and much deeper — interpretations on the inscription. To them the "I" of the Latin "ego" in the Arcadian phrase does not symbolize Death, but rather the arcane power itself, the mystical treasure, the secret, awesome, hidden knowledge.

If, as is strongly suspected by some researchers, these strange secrets behind Virgil's words and Poussin's paintings really exist, then understanding them appears to be the prerogative of deeply secretive and carefully concealed brotherhoods and sisterhoods, skilfully camouflaged cells, societies, and communities of the wise. Such *Illuminati* and

Cognoscenti are thought by some researchers to go a great way back into prehistory: these were the true, ancient, and original Arcadians, people who allegedly *knew* Atlantis and Lemuria.

The mystery of Poussin's *Bergères d'Arcadie* canvases is compounded by a table tomb that once stood in the hamlet of Arques, very close to enigmatic Rennes-le-Château on its miniature mountaintop in the foothills of the Pyrenees. In 1885, the Parish priest of Rennes, Father Bérenger Saunière, inexplicably became one of the richest men in southern France. The secret of his wealth and power has never been satisfactorily explained, but it is believed by some researchers that it was connected with the Arcadian treasure *because the tomb at Arques is identical to the one in Poussin's picture.*

Was the tomb copied from Poussin's Arcadian design, or did Poussin visit Arques and see one that was already there? The tomb the authors examined during one of their many visits to Rennes-le-Château was barely a century old and contained the coffins of two lady

Lionel measuring the tomb of Arques near Rennes-le-Château — identical to the Arcadian tomb in Poussin's painting.

members of the Lawrence family. There is, however, a considerable body of evidence indicating that only the table part was recent, and that the lower excavations of the tomb of Arques went back at least to the Middle Ages. The tomb certainly had a deep interior, going well below the two visible coffins, which were about four metres down when we examined it in the 1970s.

*Two decaying coffins belonging to the Lawrence family about
four metres down in the tomb of Arques.*

Curiously, a later owner of the site demolished the Poussinesque tomb. *Why?* The most intriguing mysteries are the ones that are hardest to verify and authenticate.

One fully authenticated and closely recorded result of Anson's amazing circumnavigation, however, was that he undoubtedly returned with so vast a treasure that it filled thirty-two wagons and was guarded by nearly 150 of his loyal and trusted shipmates on its way from Portsmouth to London on Monday, July 2, 1744. But it had not been an easy voyage. A great deal had happened since Anson's good ship *Centurion* had weighed anchor when she left England in 1740.

Extracts from Anson's own journal include: "1741, 8th May. Heavy flaws and dangerous gusts, expecting every moment to have my masts carried away, having very little succour, from the standing rigging, every shroud knotted, and not men able to keep the deck sufficient to take in a topsail, all being violently afflicted with the scurvy and every day lessening our number by six, eight and ten."

Anson's difficulties can be understood, when the problem of controlling a large sailing ship in such conditions are made clear. Another entry reads: "1741, 1st September. I mustered my ship's company, the number of men I brought out of England, being five hundred, are now reduced by mortality to two hundred and thirteen, and many of them in a weak and low condition."

Seamen weighing anchor with the capstan prior to sailing.

*Taking in sail was difficult enough in fine weather.
In a storm it was a formidable problem.*

On November 12, they had great success against the town of Payta. Anson's men occupied it for three days, while his ship's boats were busy plundering it. But by December 7, the original force of 1,872 men had been reduced to fewer than five hundred.

There was great treasure taken on June 21, 1743. Anson reported looting the following items:

> 112 bags of silver,
> 6 chests of silver,
> 11 bags of virgin silver,
> 72 chests of dollars,
> various bags of dollars,
> 114 chests of dollars,
> 100 bags of dollars, and
> 4 bags of wrought plate and virgin silver.

That was, in fact, the supposed *tactical* reason for his Pacific Squadron being deployed against Spain and her allies. In 1739, the British Admiralty felt that war with Spain was inevitable. They also realized that Spain needed the income from Latin America to finance that war. Sir Charles Wager at the Admiralty devised a tactical plan to send two squadrons to the Pacific to rob Spain of her essential war chest, and so weaken her war effort to a point where it could not continue because of lack of money. Anson was one of the two squadron commanders that Wager chose.

In the summer of 1744, at the end of Anson's four-year adventure, he returned triumphant with his bare handful of survivors and his thirty-two wagon loads of treasure. It was widely accepted at the time that the bulk of the treasure had indeed come from his raids on Spain's allies by land and sea.

Yet there may well have been quiet speculation among those who shared certain secret, arcane knowledge that not *all* of Anson's vast treasure had come from Latin America or from prizes like the *Nuestra Senora de Cobodonga*, a Spanish treasure galleon that he had encountered. Anson's *Centurion* had outgunned the *Nuestra Senora de Cobodonga*, and his cannons had raked her again and again with a combination of ball and grapeshot.

A high-ranking naval adventurer who had been legitimately scouring the Spanish Main and beyond could find it an attractive and convincing cover for a little private money-laundering. But what form of wealth was it that was so secret that it had to be laundered?

Admiral Anson's gunners were experts with cannons like this one.

The essence of those unvoiced speculations undoubtedly lay in Anson's close connections with the enigma of Shugborough Hall and the mysteries of the legendary Arcadian treasure.

Johann Nepomuk Salvator (1852–91) was a Habsburg, a son of Leopold II of Tuscany. He enjoyed a successful military career, but in the difficult, reactionary, ultra-conservative political world of the Austro-Hungarian Empire, he unwisely made it plain that he was a liberal and a radical reformer. Johann was intelligent, sensitive, artistic, musical, and anti-clerical. He made an unsuccessful bid for the throne of Bulgaria in 1887, which predictably upset the hard, cantankerous, and unforgiving old Franz Joseph.

Johann was a close friend of Franz Joseph's son, the tragic Crown Prince Rudolf, another radical liberal, who was almost certainly murdered. In 1889, his body and that of his teenaged mistress, Mary Vetsera, were found in their bedroom in the hunting lodge at Mayerling in a highly compromising situation with their brains blown out and the gun in Rudolf's dead hand. Politically sophisticated readers will be highly suspicious of the official "lovers' suicide" version of their deaths.

It is highly likely that Johann and Rudolf had been involved together in a number of political intrigues, which put Johann in great danger now that Rudolf was dead. Johann renounced his title, calling himself plain Johann Orth instead; married his beloved mistress, Milli Stubel, a beautiful and vivacious ballerina; got himself qualified as a skipper; and sailed away with his wife aboard the *Saint Margaret*. He then provided another unsolved mystery of the sea by vanishing with his lady and his ship somewhere off Cape Horn in July 1890. He was not officially declared dead until 1911.

There is evidence that the two of them had obtained *something* of great importance from Bérenger Saunière of Rennes-le-Château: something connected, perhaps, with the mystery of the Arcadian treasure. Did Johann and Milli escape with it after Mary and Rudolf were murdered? Was the *Saint Margaret*'s appearance in the vicinity of Cape

Horn connected in any way with the circumnavigation mystery of Admiral George Anson over a century earlier? There are persistent rumours that the lovers landed safely at a remote spot in South America, changed their identities, and vanished, as far as Franz Joseph and the Austro-Hungarian secret police were concerned.

Many years later, Milli's sister sold her memoirs to a Viennese newspaper. In them, she testified that there had been a vitally important steel strongbox containing coded documents of the highest significance. She also recorded that just before his death, Rudolf had given this box into the safe custody of Countess Larisch, with strict instructions that it was to be given only to someone using the password *R I O U*. On the day of Rudolf's funeral, Countess Larisch was given a message that included the password. Later in the evening, when a heavily cloaked and muffled Johann came to collect it from her, he said that the documents it contained would have meant certain death if Franz Joseph had seen them. That strongbox was believed by some researchers to have been aboard the *Saint Margaret* when she disappeared off Cape Horn. Is it reasonable to assume that its incriminating contents — whatever they were — went to the bottom of that cold, southern ocean? Or did Milli and Johann keep them as a form of insurance? Did Johann's crew come secretly ashore with him and Milli, after scuttling the *Saint Margaret* in some quiet but deep bay off the coast of South America?

CHAPTER TWELVE

The Baychimo *and Similar Mysteries*

In 1914, the thirteen-hundred-tonne *Baychimo,* product of an excellent Swedish shipbuilder, belonged to the Hudson Bay Company. She was a well-designed, well-constructed, steel-framed cargo vessel built to withstand the pressures and problems of the dangerous ice in the perilous northwestern waters. Her single funnel, her long, high prow, and her specially devised bridge made her a welcome and familiar sight among the fur traders and other residents of the Beaufort Sea coast, Victoria Island, and the Northwest Territories. Her regular two-thousand-mile round trips carried vital food and other essential supplies in one direction and furs in the other. The Canadian mariners who commanded and worked the *Baychimo* ranked among the toughest and most skilful sailors in the world. They knew each time they set out that the voyage was going to be difficult and demanding, and July 6, 1931, did not seem to hold any different prospects as the *Baychimo* weighed anchor in Vancouver, British Columbia. Captain John Cornwell had thirty-six excellent men at his command when they sailed that day.

By the time they reached Victoria Island, most of their essential supplies had been unloaded, and the holds were packed with pelts. Cornwell and his men completed their Victoria Island business and headed the *Baychimo* back towards Vancouver. The winter of 1931 was a bad one, and it came earlier than usual that year in the lonely lands of the north. The whole area froze very quickly, and the pack ice closed in on the *Baychimo* like hounds surrounding an exhausted stag. By the end of September there was barely any space to steer her through, and by the start of October the encircling ice had done its worst: the *Baychimo* was trapped.

The nearest habitation was an Alaskan settlement called Barrow. The Hudson Bay Company maintained several strong shelters there for emergency use. Captain Cornwell's seasoned eyes knew that severe blizzards were on the way. He told his men to get off the *Baychimo* and find what shelter they could in the Company's buildings. They made it safely to the life-saving huts, but were trapped there for two or three days while the blizzards raged on.

Unexpectedly, the *Baychimo* somehow freed herself from the encircling ice — that event alone seemed almost supernatural in view of the prevailing weather — and her complement boarded her again with all speed. With the full power of her sturdy engine, the *Baychimo* throbbed away to the west as fast as the hazardous ice would allow. Then, after only a few hours, the gallant little steamer was again trapped in the ubiquitous ice.

There was a major problem on October 8, while some of the *Baychimo*'s crew were playing football on the ice. The ice cracked in entirely the wrong place for the trapped ship, and she began moving irrevocably landwards. The experienced mariners were certain that she would be crushed. Urgent SOS messages brought two rescue aircraft from Nome and twenty-two of the crew went home aboard them. This left the fearless Captain Cornwell and fourteen of his toughest and most resolute Canadian sailors to handle the *Baychimo* — if, miraculously, she ever broke free of the encircling ice. There was no knowing how long they would have to wait: at the worst it could be a year! Accordingly, they constructed a well-insulated shelter and settled down on the pack-ice to play a waiting game with the deadly ice.

November 24 brought another crisis. As her stalwart crew sheltered in their hut, the *Baychimo* disappeared under nearly thirty metres of ice! They searched everywhere for her without success, and decided that the ice had finally done her in. As they began the long trek home over the frozen mainland, they met a friendly and helpful Eskimo seal hunter. When he heard their story, he told them that he'd seen the *Baychimo* about seventy kilometres to the southwest! Cornwell and his implacable men slogged to the spot their informant had described — and found the missing ship! They took what few furs they could transport, and with heavy hearts left the indomitable old *Baychimo* to her fate in the ice. The captain and crew were finally flown safely home.

Reports came in regularly from Eskimo hunters that the *Baychimo* had been sighted repeatedly, and in 1932 an explorer named Les Melvin came across her as he travelled from Herschel Island to Nome with his dog team. Les actually got aboard and checked out the furs — most were still in excellent condition — but there was no way that one man on his own could sail her to safety.

In 1934 a botanist from Scotland, Isobel Hutchinson, found the *Baychimo* and got aboard her as Les had done two years before. The ship was seen again in Alaska in 1935. In 1939, just after the outbreak of World War II, Captain Hugh Polson encountered the *Baychimo*, but was unable to rescue her from the ice — despite his best efforts. Eskimo fishermen saw her in 1962, floating a few kilometres out into the Beaufort Sea, and again in 1969 when she was reported trapped in the ice between Icy Cape and Point Barrow.

Is she still around? She may well be! Her designers and builders can feel justifiably proud of their creation, which has defied the ice and polar storms for so many decades.

Sightings of the ill-fated *Erebus* and *Terror* have been far rarer and less well substantiated than the many sightings of the *Baychimo*. Nevertheless, there have been tenuous reports that both vessels have been occasionally sighted over the years since they vanished in 1845 along with the whole team who accompanied Sir John Franklin's fatal quest for the elusive Northwest Passage. Named after the legendary gateway to the nether regions of Greek mythology, the *Erebus* was officially rated as a Hecla-class bomb ship. She had three masts and measured over thirty metres in length, with a breadth of nine metres and a draft of four metres. Her stout wooden hull gave her a displacement of nearly four hundred tonnes. Designed by Sir Henry Peake, the *Erebus* was built in the Pembroke Dockyard in Wales, U.K., in 1826. Her companion on her final, tragic voyage was the *Terror:* very similar to the *Erebus* in design, but nearly fifty tonnes lighter. Also designed by Sir Henry Peake, the *Terror* was built at Topsham, England, in 1813, while the threat from Napoleon still lingered in English minds. Bomb ships of that period carried heavy mortars and were intended to bombard enemy coastal towns from the sea. The heavy mortars they carried weighed up to three tons each and had a ponderous recoil. Any ship firing them had to be powerfully reinforced — which was what made the *Erebus* and *Terror* particularly appropriate for expeditions to the northern and southern zones of ice.

Both ships, therefore, had been powerfully reinforced with these transverse timbers, first to withstand the recoil of their own deadly mortars in time of war, and now, in peace, to defend them against the anaconda-like dangers of the crushing, encircling polar ice. Having just returned from James Clark Ross's expedition to the Antarctic, where they had ventured only with sail, the two ships were now fitted with massive twenty-horsepower steam engines. These had been acquired from London Railways and modified to drive propellers. It was felt that propellers, rather than paddle wheels, would be much more useful when forcing the ship's passage through the encircling ice that so frequently blocked the way through the elusive Northwest Passage. This was the vital route for which Sir John and his men were now so diligently searching.

Without realizing that it might be construed as a sinister omen of impending death by a superstitious sailor, Sir John's devoted wife, Lady Jane, had draped a Union Jack over him for warmth as he lay asleep a few days before the expedition sailed. In view of his worries over the portentous Union Jack, Sir John was particularly happy when a London pigeon alighted in the rigging of the *Erebus* shortly before they weighed anchor. The dove, or pigeon, the bird of peace, always meant good luck to a seafaring man when it landed on his ship.

Sir John Franklin and his men sailed from the Thames in London on May 19, 1845. *Erebus* and *Terror*, identified by their black and yellow paintwork, carried provisions for at least three years, and those provisions could be augmented by hunting and fishing in the traditional manner. As becomes evident later, it may have been Sir John's provisions that doomed him and his men. They headed up to the Orkneys first, then on to the Whalefish Islands west of Greenland. It was here that the *Barretto Junior,* a small but efficient supply ship, brought fresh meat for them. This encounter with the *Barretto* also provided an opportunity for officers and crew to send letters home. One of these contained a glowing tribute to Franklin from Lieutenant Fairholme. He wrote: "He has such experience and judgement that we all look on his decisions with the greatest respect." The lieutenant went on to praise Franklin's great human qualities as a shipmate and companion. In view of Lieutenant Fairholme's richly deserved praise for Franklin, there is an undercurrent of mystery as to why a number of crewmen left the expedition at this point and sailed home on board the *Barretto.* Could it have been anything to do with the food, even at that early stage? Had they become ill because of something ominously wrong with the vast stores of provisions aboard the *Erebus* and *Terror?* For whatever reason, they were on board the *Barretto* when Franklin's two vessels sailed away towards Baffin Bay on July 12, 1845.

On July 26, 1845, barely two months after Franklin's expedition had left London, two whalers, the *Prince of Wales* and the *Enterprise,* sighted the *Erebus* and *Terror* in Baffin Bay, not far from the entrance to

Lancaster Sound. The weather was reasonable, and Captain Dannet, in command of the *Prince of Wales*, invited Franklin on board. Captain Robert Martin, who was in charge of the *Enterprise*, was also there, and he made several significant notes about their meeting that were of great importance to later investigators. In Martin's opinion, Sir John was confident and optimistic. Referring to his expedition's provisions, Franklin was sure that they had enough for as much as seven years — if it was sensibly augmented with good hunting and fishing. It was much in Sir John's mind to invite both whaling captains back to the *Erebus* to return their hospitality, but the weather took a sudden severe turn and the ships were driven away from one another. Apart from their later controversial "ghostly" appearances, neither the *Erebus* nor the *Terror* — nor any of their ill-starred crews (over 130 men altogether) — was ever seen alive again.

By the standards of their day, the men of Franklin's expedition were exceptionally well provided for, which makes their subsequent failure all the more mysterious. Knowing that boredom was almost as big a threat as the ice to expeditions of this kind, Franklin had arranged for more than three thousand books to be carried on board his two ships, and there were teaching sessions for crewmen who had not had the same educational advantages as their officers. There were practical physical comforts in addition to the mental ones provided by the lessons and the ships' libraries: an ingenious system of pipes below the floors carried water to warm the berths — it was as well thought out and as effective as the Roman hypocausts had been eighteen hundred years earlier.

Erebus and *Terror* headed north from Baffin Bay, but the ice presented so formidable an obstacle that they had to steer south again. A note in a cairn found years later by search parties reported that Sir John Franklin had died aboard the *Erebus* on June 11, 1847, while they were locked in the ice in Victoria Strait, which lies between Victoria Island and King William Island — and within a year, more than twenty more men had died. The hundred-plus survivors, under the command of Captain Francis Crozier from the *Terror*, then decided to leave *Erebus* and *Terror* to the mercy of the ice and attempt the almost impossibly difficult trek southwest to Fort Resolution — *nine hundred kilometres away!* Not one of them ever got there.

By 1847 — having heard no news of Franklin's expedition — the British Admiralty decided that help was probably needed. Consequently, they sent three rescue parties under the leadership of Dr. John Rae, James Ross, and Captain Henry Kellett. These three expeditions all searched long and diligently — but found no trace of Franklin's men, nor his ships.

Lady Jane Franklin and the British government offered huge rewards, and one search party after another ventured out by land and sea looking for Franklin's men and his missing ships. In 1850, near the mouth of Wellington Channel on Beechey Island, the searchers found hundreds of empty and abandoned tins, the ashes of old fires, and other remains — including three graves. Franklin's men had evidently wintered there in 1845. The full facts did not emerge, however, until 1859, when Captain Leopold McClintock, commanding one of Lady Franklin's own rescue ships, found artifacts and records that had been left on King William Island. Lieutenant William Hobson, McClintock's second-in-command, also made significant discoveries — including human remains. Captain Erasmus Ommanney of the *Assistance* found other important evidence at Cape Riley on Devon Island, close to Beechey Island. Evidence gleaned by these determined searchers from local Inuit hunters and fishermen filled out more details of the Franklin tragedy. There were eyewitness Inuit accounts of men dragging sledges over the ice, falling, and dying where they fell from starvation and exhaustion. Why *starvation* when they had brought so much food with them? The clues seemed to lie in the heaps of abandoned tins, and in the suggestions made by the pathologists who later examined some of the bodies from Devon Island.

Franklin's provisions had included generous quantities of food sealed inside airtight tins: still very much an innovation in the early 1800s. Tragically, the tins supplied to the Franklin expedition seem to have been lined with lead solder, and the pathologists who investigated the tragedy much later strongly suspected lead poisoning. Its symptoms were similar to those of scurvy, and Franklin's own marine medical experts on board the *Erebus* and the *Terror* would have been unlikely to consider lead poisoning as a possibility — until it was far too late. Lead poisoning may have been a major contributing factor, but the expedition's failure still remains one of the great unsolved mysteries of the sea.

The history of food canning begins with a gifted French inventor named Nicolas Appert. During the Napoleonic Wars, Appert found that food could be preserved if sealed and heated in an airtight glass jar. He worked on the process for a long time, then wrote a book about it in 1810. He also set up his own factory where foods were processed and preserved. The French government gave him an award of twelve thousand francs in appreciation of his achievements. His method was highly successful, although nobody at the time really knew why; it wasn't until much later that medical science realized that it was bacteria that caused food to decompose, and that heating killed the bacteria inside Appert's sealed glass containers.

Meanwhile, in England, John Hall, founder of Dartford Iron Works, and his friend, Bryan Donkin, took up Appert's ideas in 1811. They used metal cylinders constructed from tinned iron to store the food. Unlike Appert's glass containers, Hall and Donkin's tin cans were almost unbreakable. They set up a canned food factory in Bermondsey, London, and the navy was among their biggest customers. What militates somewhat *against* the theory that Franklin's expedition may have been destroyed by lead poisoning are the excellent reports that came back from officers and sailors alike, when they were asked to comment on Hall and Donkin's canned foods. It's interesting to note, however, that Franklin actually sailed from London, not far from the Bermondsey works of Hall and Donkin.

It's also interesting to note that in 1824 — more than twenty years before the ill-fated Franklin Expedition — Captain Sir Edward Parry went in search of the Northwest Passage for the third time. He took canned foods with him on this voyage, one of which was a tin of roasted veal in gravy. Opened by scientists and subjected to stringent laboratory tests in 1939 — 115 years after it was processed — *it was found to be still in good condition.* If canning was as good as that in 1824, what was wrong with the canned foods that Franklin purchased for his expedition twenty years later? It would be reasonable to suppose that the science of canning had improved over those twenty years.

The other unsolved mystery associated with the tragedy of the Franklin Expedition is what really became of his two sturdy ships after their crews were forced to abandon them? How can the many mysterious supposed sightings of the *Erebus* and *Terror* be explained? Those reports shift the whole story from courageous, tragic history into the realm of unsolved mysteries and anomalous phenomena. Ever since the tragedy occurred there have been persistent reports of sightings of ships *closely resembling* Franklin's missing vessels among the ice of the tantalizing Northwest Passage. The Inuit evidence suggested that the ships had vanished *into* the deadly ice blocking the Northwest Passage — but did they re-emerge, as the *Baychimo* did?

The most intriguing report of all concerning the fate of the *Erebus* and the *Terror* is as recent as 1937. A pilot flying over the area where

Franklin's expedition had come to grief was certain that he could see the remains of a large timber vessel lying on top of the ice. Being short of fuel, the aviator had to return to base to refuel before going back to make a proper search for the ship he was certain he had seen. When he got back it had totally vanished.

Researchers who are prepared to consider a *psychic* explanation have put forward intriguing theories about a curse. They argue that both the *Erebus* and the *Terror* were devastatingly powerful bomb ships, capable of throwing deadly mortar missiles into coastal towns being attacked by the British navy in the early years of the nineteenth century. The horror of such mortars is that they are indiscriminate: fighting men, farmers and fishermen, civilians, women and children, innocent bystanders, the frail, the sick, and the elderly are all equally likely to die, or suffer appalling injuries, when the mortar rounds fall on their homes. The psychic scenario is that a horrendously wounded witch or wizard, shaman or magician, put his, or her, dying curse on the ships that had fired their mortars into his, or her, particular little coastal town. We still understand very little of the true powers lurking deep within the human mind. Used benignly, there are many astoundingly *good* things that mindpower can achieve. Used negatively, it may also be able to generate dangerous *evil*.

CHAPTER THIRTEEN

Pirates, Slavers, Buccaneers, Privateers, Wreckers, and Smugglers

The unsolved mysteries of the sea are often associated with the perplexing mysteries of the human mind and the depths to which it can sink. The callous cruelty and greed of wreckers, willing to lure ships onto treacherous rocks and then murder any survivors who struggled ashore merely for the sake of stealing what survived of their cargo is almost impossible to fathom. One of the most poignant of all wrecker stories is associated with lovely old Chambercombe Manor, which nestles in a secluded valley close to Ilfracombe, Devonshire, England. Northwest of the rugged Trayne Hills and northeast of Shield Tor, ancient Chambercombe Manor is listed in the Domesday Book. Less than a mile from the manor are the sands of Hele Beach, and at one time a secret tunnel connected the ancient house to them. Sir Henry Champernon was lord of the manor of Ilfracombe in 1162, and Chambercombe was part of his estate, but there are records of a certain Robert of Chambercombe who was in possession a century or so earlier. It later went to the Duke of Suffolk.

In 1865, a tenant of Chambercombe Manor discovered a small window, high up near the roof, to which there was no corresponding room or doorway. He eventually broke down the plaster coverings of a bricked up doorway and found the missing room. In the centre was a four-poster bed, its rotting curtains still in place. The intrepid farmer pulled them down and found a skeleton lying there — in some accounts, *chained* there. Medical examination concluded that it was the skeleton of a teenaged girl from the seventeenth century.

Some local traditions and legends recalled that there had been a smuggler and wrecker named Alexander Oatway, whose son William had been a far more pleasant man than his father. One night, hearing cries for help following a wrecking adventure along the dangerous rocky coast, young William rescued a beautiful Spanish girl, whom he subsequently married. They had a daughter, Kate, who grew up to be as lovely as her mother. In the course of time, young Kate married a dashing Irish buccaneer captain named Wallace and went off to live with him in Dublin, promising her parents that she would return to visit them whenever possible. Some time later there was another wreck and William went out to see if he could help any survivors. He found a girl battered beyond recognition by the rocks and pounding waves, still clinging to life by a thread. He carried her home where he and his wife did what they could for her, but she died during the night. The Oatways had always wanted to buy Chambercombe, but had never made enough money. Now, on the dead girl's body they found a money belt full of gold coins and jewels — far more than the price of Chambercombe. They drew the bed curtains around the unknown dead girl and bricked up the room.

The next day, a shipping agent called to enquire about a missing passenger from the wreck whose body had not been accounted for. He showed the Oatways the passenger list: the dead girl they had just bricked up in what was to become the infamous sealed room of Chambercombe was *their own daughter: Mrs. Kate Wallace.* The money they had stolen from her body had been intended as a gift from her and her Irish buccaneer husband to enable them to buy Chambercombe and live there in peace and security for the rest of their lives.

There were several other versions of the legend, most of which took in the detail of the sinister chain said to have been found attached to the girl's skeleton in 1865. According to one such variant, Alexander Oatway, the smuggler and wrecker, had also been a vicious white-slaver, procurer, and pimp. Any attractive women who struggled ashore after his wrecking activities were sent off to work in various London brothels in which Alexander had a financial interest. The notorious sealed room at Chambercombe was said to have been used by Alexander and his men to get such captives ready for clients before sending them off to London. One determined woman put up such brave and prolonged resistance that Alexander and his thugs spitefully bricked her up alive to die of thirst and starvation. Yet another grim possibility is that the victim who died in that sealed room was part of a large-scale white-slaving operation that extended from Europe — including Devonshire — down to the Barbary Coast.

The outstanding recent work of the heroic Salcombe divers and the South West Maritime Archaeological Group provides ample proof that Barbary corsairs were operating near Gara Rock off the South Devon coast in the mid-seventeenth century. Were those Barbary pirates and slave traders connected with Alexander Oatway and the hidden skeleton at Chambercombe?

Whatever the truth behind the skeleton on the bed in the sealed room of Chambercombe Manor, there is another unsolved mystery of the sea linking Chambercombe and Hele Beach — just as the subterranean passage does. Many psychic investigators and mediums over the years have seen the famous Grey Lady of Chambercombe — but who is she? The bravely rebellious prisoner who wouldn't surrender to Oatway's henchmen? Oatway's own daughter, Mrs. Kate Wallace? Or could the phantom be connected with Lady Jane Grey, so cruelly and unjustly executed as a helpless pawn in a desperately complicated but wildly stupid and greedy bid for the Tudor throne? Certainly Lady Jane Grey once stayed at Chambercombe, and her room was adjacent to the sinister sealed room with its unidentified woman's skeleton. In addition to many sightings of the mysterious Grey Lady, visitors have often heard strange cries and groans of pain.

At some time during the earlier part of the 1600s a ship went down near Gara Rock in the Salcombe Estuary. Almost four centuries later a group of courageous and determined divers found what was left of it — and their amazing discoveries created yet another strange and sinister unsolved mystery of the sea. The mystery centred on gold — huge quantities of it — and raised the question of the identity of the ship that had gone down. The second question concerned the gold itself: why had that mystery ship been carrying such wealth? The first thought must be that if expensive purchases had to be made in a period when there were no credit cards and no electronic banking systems, gold was the most widely accepted international medium of exchange. Someone had come to a lonely part of England's southwest coast in order to make a major purchase with all that gold — but who had manned that ship, and what had they come to buy?

The ship now appears to have strong connections with North Africa, and the most likely possibility is that she had come to buy European slaves. The gold itself was from North African or Middle Eastern sources, and tests on the ship's remaining piece of timber also pointed that way. But Dutch artifacts were also found among the wreckage. Does this suggest a Dutch vessel, chartered by North African merchants, or a Barbary corsair commanded by a skilful Dutch captain? During their long period of ascendancy, many of the Barbary corsairs were content to sail under the guidance of experienced European mariners.

To understand the mystery more deeply, it's necessary to delve into the history of the Barbary Coast pirates. In medieval times the four traditional Barbary States of the North African coast were listed as: Algiers, Morocco, Tunis, and Tripoli. Their main source of income was derived from officially (and *unofficially!*) selling foreign ships the right to pass through Barbary waters to trade with local ports. Those who didn't pay promptly, regularly, and generously were likely to be abducted and held for ransom or sold as slaves.

During the twelfth and thirteenth centuries many European ships ventured into Barbary waters carrying pilgrims and crusaders. Those who were protected by the indomitable Knights Templar usually got through: even the hardest and most aggressive Barbary corsairs were reluctant to tangle with any ship of the Templar fleet, or with any vessel carrying a significant number of the formidable Templar warrior-priests as guardians. But many pilgrims and would-be crusaders were not so fortunate and were consequently sold into slavery.

Ottoman Turkey and Habsburg Spain were locked in a long, bitter struggle for supremacy in the Mediterranean. Piracy was a richly rewarding dimension of this struggle, and it lured many a red-blooded adventurer into the long-drawn-out war. One such adventurer was the Turkish corsair Khair ad Din, who had a beard that matched his wild blood and was accordingly known as Barbarossa. (No connection with the famous twelfth-century Holy Roman emperor, Frederick, who was also called Barbarossa for the same reason!) Khair ad Din was born circa 1483 and died in 1546. He and his equally able brother, Aruj, took Algiers from Spain and put it under Turkish control. Barbarossa then went on to conquer the rest of the Barbary States, which subsequently took their name from their conqueror's red beard. Such men were typical of the later Barbary Coast pirates.

As a result of the American War of Independence, American merchant ships no longer came under the protection of the British navy when sailing in Barbary waters, and, consequently, a great many Americans were captured and sold as slaves in the Barbary States. Joseph Hoffman's screenplay *Yankee Pasha* was based on Edison Marshall's excellent historical novel, and although the details of the story were fictional, they could well have been based on fact. Jeff Chandler and Rhonda Fleming starred in Joseph Pevney and Howard Christie's highly acclaimed 1954 production, which told the story of a daring

American adventurer who risked everything to go to the Barbary Coast to rescue his beautiful fiancée, Roxana, who'd been white-slaved while on her way to France.

Outraged by so many real-life incidents on which the fictional Roxana's ordeal was based, the United States navy sailed in force to the Mediterranean and blasted the Barbary Coast ports from which the pirates came. They also engaged them in devastating bombardments and fierce hand-to-hand battles at sea. Gunboat squadrons under the overall command of Commodores Preble and Dale shattered the pirates.

The famous British admiral Lord Nelson praised one superb piece of American action led by Lieutenant Steve Decatur on February 16, 1804. Seventy-four volunteers under his command raided Tripoli harbour to burn the American frigate *Philadelphia*, which had recently been captured by the Barbary corsairs. Tough, all-action hero Ruben James was serving as a bosun's mate at the time he joined Decatur's raiding party. Badly wounded in the hand-to-hand skirmishing, James nevertheless flung himself between Decatur and a savage pirate during their next piece of action. Thanks to his unselfish bravery, Decatur remained unscathed. Rock-hard Ruben James recovered from his wounds and served valiantly in the U.S. navy for over thirty years.

A year later, the triumphant American marines stormed the Barbary pirates' stronghold at Derna in Tripoli, and apart from a further visit to the Mediterranean by Commodores Decatur and Bainbridge in 1812, the centuries-old menace of the Barbary Coast pirates had been qualitatively and quantitatively reduced. Yet, like strange and eerie whisperings of the wind in a derelict graveyard, vestigial traces of them lingered on — such corsair remnants might even have been responsible for the mystery of the *Mary Celeste* more than half a century after Decatur and Bainbridge did their highly effective work.

Once Napoleon had been finally defeated, the European naval powers also had time and energy to devote to keeping down the Barbary corsairs.

The hypothetical "slavers' gold" found with the Barbary wreck near Gara Rock in Devonshire was intriguing enough, but it represents only a minute fraction of the hidden treasure associated with piracy worldwide over the centuries.

Piracy is almost as old as history itself, going back at least three or four millennia. The Roman historian Polybius seems to have been one of the first to use the word *pierato* to describe pirates well over a century before Christ. The young Julius Caesar — long before he came to power — was once captured by pirates and held to ransom. His first act on getting home was to organize a formidable band of his contemporaries, track the pirates down, and execute them. There was also a sense in which some Anglo-Saxon chroniclers regarded the Norse sea kings and Viking raiders as pirates.

A semi-legendary fifth-century adventuress, a character not unlike Robin Hood's famous Maid Marian of Sherwood, was Princess Alwilda from Gotland in Sweden. Alwilda turned to piracy in order to stay free when her royal father attempted to arrange a marriage for her with Alf, Prince of Denmark, which she didn't want. The romantic twist to the story came about when Alf, whom she had hitherto been trying to avoid, defeated her pirates in a sea battle. As he had risked his life during the fierce fighting in order to marry her, Alwilda decided that he was the right kind of man after all and changed her mind about him. The rest of their history fades into the mists of time — but tradition says that they lived long and happily together, and Alwilda ended her days as queen of Denmark. If only Shakespeare had known about her, she might have featured as one of Hamlet's ancestors!

Other highly successful and courageous women who were pirates in the Alwilda tradition included an Irish girl, Grace O'Malley, born in 1530. She was also known as "Granuaile" (meaning bald) because she cut her hair short so it didn't get in the way when she was fighting. After a long and adventurous career at sea, Grace fell foul of Sir Richard Bingham, who was governor at the time. He impounded her fleet and arrested her son. Grace — never lacking in audacious courage — went to present her case to Queen Elizabeth herself. Elizabeth ordered Bingham to release Grace's ships and granted her an annual pension so that she did not have to resort to piracy any longer. In return Grace and her son — who became her fleet commander — remained loyal to Britain and fought the Queen's enemies at sea whenever necessary.

Grace was a successful enough pirate in British and Irish waters, but even her exploits were eclipsed by the amazing Madame Cheng, who took over her husband's fleet when he died in 1807.

Time after time the authorities attacked her Red Flag Pirate Fleet — and came off second best. When all else had failed, they declared a general amnesty, and Madame Cheng accepted it — on condition that her second husband, Chang Pao, who had been Cheng's deputy, was given an officer's commission in the Chinese army!

Typical Chinese junk with shallow draft of the type used by Madame Cheng's Red Flag Pirate Fleet.

Mary Read was another well-known female pirate, and a companion of Ann Bonny, also spelled Bonnie. They sailed with Calico Jack Rackham until he and most of his crew were captured and hanged. Both women were spared because they were pregnant, but Mary died of fever shortly afterwards, and Ann vanished from pirate history — either she escaped, or her rich family paid some heavy bribes to get her safely back home to Ireland.

Among other famous pirates who almost certainly left their hidden treasure somewhere in the world were Henry Avery (Long Ben), a particularly cruel and savage English pirate who took delight in wreaking havoc on Mogul ships in the Arabian Sea; Jean Bart from Dunkirk, who may well have buried his treasure near Plymouth; Roche Brasiliano, a Dutch pirate based in Brazil who preyed on Spanish treasure galleons and may well have hidden his loot in Jamaica when he turned up there in 1670; Nick Brown, who enjoyed a great reputation among other pirates, but whose head was pickled and taken back to the authorities so that his captor could claim his reward. There was also the highly successful and widely travelled Chris Condent, who retired in peace and luxury to St. Malo, France, after plundering ships from Africa, Arabia, Madagascar, and Mauritius.

Bartholomew Roberts — Black Bart to his friends — flourished in the early years of the eighteenth century. A wild, fearless, adventurous Welshman like Morgan, Black Bart captured at least 350 ships during his many piratical operations in the Caribbean and off the coast of West Africa. One of his greatest successes was taking the Portuguese treasure ship *Sagrada Familia*, which was carrying a vast fortune in diamonds when he captured her.

There were also well-educated and highly intelligent men among the pirates, like Dr. Basil Ringrose, an English surgeon who sailed with Bartholomew Sharp and his crew. Ringrose was killed in action in Mexico in 1686. Another highly intelligent pirate was Bill Dampier from Somerset. He was a brilliant navigator who escaped in a canoe after being set down on the Nicobar Islands in the Indian Ocean, like poor old Ben Gunn in Stevenson's *Treasure Island.* Dampier proved that he had the survival skills of Daniel Defoe's Robinson Crusoe, a character based on the real-life desert island survivor Alexander Selkirk — with whom Dampier was not on the best of terms. Despite his high intelligence and brilliance as a navigator, there were a lot of important interpersonal skills that were a closed book to Dampier.

Selkirk was born in Fife in Scotland in 1676, son of the village cobbler and tanner in Largo. Alexander had no intention of joining the family business and went to sea instead. At the age of twenty-seven, he joined Dampier as first mate on the *Cinque Ports.* They struggled around Cape Horn and reached an island in the Juan Fernandez archipelago. Dampier and Selkirk quarrelled over whether the *Cinque Ports* was seaworthy enough to continue, and Selkirk decided to stay on his island until another, sounder ship called there. He had a lonely four-year wait — during which time he almost lost the power of speech — but he was eventually rescued by Captain Woodes Rodgers of the *Duke.* By an odd coincidence, Dampier was sailing with Rodgers as the *Duke's* pilot and navigator.

But piracy is far from confined to ancient history, or to the so-called Golden Age of Piracy with characters like Teach, Morgan, Kidd, and Ann Bonnie. It is still flourishing dangerously today. The International Maritime Bureau based in London, England, still receives hundreds of contemporary reports of pirate activity. As recently as 1996, a British couple were attacked with grenades and assault rifles while cruising near the Greek Island of Corfu. Contemporary pirates operate in the South China Seas, where entire ships and their cargos are likely to vanish. The waters off the coast of Brazil are also vulnerable to pirate activity, as are the seas off West Africa. Today's pirates use a wide variety of armaments and equipment: dugout canoes and bladed weapons in one area, and the latest automatic machine pistols in another.

It remains a political unsolved mystery of the sea why modern governments — and the especially the United Nations — with all the latest air power, naval technology, and hardware cannot make piracy obsolete.

In the Golden Age of Piracy, which began in the sixteenth century, there was high-level government involvement. English privateers (pirates with licences) were encouraged (overtly or covertly) to attack Spanish treasure galleons. North African pirates were licensed to attack the English. Pirates from Madagascar were operating for the benefit of France. There were so many wheels within wheels and so many changing allegiances that at times it was almost impossible to distinguish friend from foe on the high seas.

It was the War of the Spanish Succession, fought over the first decade of the eighteenth century, that brought the concept of the buccaneer to the fore. Hired by various governments of the day to fight their rivals, their name came from the French word *boucan*, which was a device used to smoke the dried meat used on board ships. The buccaneers had a safe refuge in Tortuga for a while and then in Jamaica. The great swashbuckling Welshman Sir Henry Morgan, Deputy Governor of Jamaica, had started his career as a buccaneer, a field in which his outstanding organizing abilities had enabled his followers to capture not only Portobello, but Panama as well.

Less well known in the western world were the outstanding Chinese pirate leaders who flourished at broadly the same time as Morgan. Pinyin made the most of his opportunities during the power vacuum that separated the Ming and Ch'ing emperors. Piracy always exploits a power vacuum. Another outstanding Far Eastern pirate named Cheng captured Formosa and defended it vigorously for several years. His wife, Madame Cheng, took over his Chinese Red Flag Pirate Fleet when he died and became even more successful and powerful than he had been. The power vacuums that favoured the pirates there ended with the rise of Tokugawa in Japan and the firm establishment of the Ch'ing Dynasty in China.

What did the pirates of golden ages of piracy do with their ill-gotten gains? Where did they hide their treasure? And how much of it is still lying around waiting to be dug up? No matter how hard they tried to keep their treasure locations secret, there were often strangely persistent rumours about their hiding places. Connecticut River runs through Northfield Massachusetts. Clarke Island, which occupies a significant place in that river, not far from Pine Meadow, is steeped in legends of pirate gold. According to one legend, Kidd and his men made their way upstream searching for somewhere to hide their loot. The place had to be so distinctive that they would always remember it and recognize it again easily — even if it was years before they could get back there to collect it. Their chosen site had to be a spot that would be unlikely to change, somewhere that was also unlikely to have a road driven across it or buildings raised on it. It had to be well hidden, well clear of the beaten track, not *too* conspicuous — but just conspicuous enough for them to recognize it again with absolute certainty.

Kidd and his men lived at a time when most minds were bedevilled by superstitions of various kinds; seafaring men were often highly superstitious, and pirates seem to have been the most superstitious of all. It was widely believed that treasures needed watchful, vengeful guardian spirits to protect them. The ghost of a murdered man was regarded as ideal for the purpose. According to the legend of Clarke's Island, Kidd's men drew straws to see who was going to be killed and buried with the treasure to keep it safe until the others returned to share it out. Wherever there's a protective guardian spell, there's also a counter-spell in such legends. If three men came together to the treasure site at midnight when there was a full moon and stood around their excavation like the legs of a tripod, they would be able to retrieve the treasure — *provided that no one spoke.*

It was said that a determined treasure hunter named Abner Field and two staunch companions attempted to follow the counter-spell and dig for Kidd's gold. After hours of heavy, silent excavation, they saw one corner of an old sea chest. A spade struck the chest as they dug harder and faster, and just as it made contact, one of the three excited hunters forgot that silence was essential. He cried out exultantly, "We've hit it!" Then all three watched in horror as the chest sank out of reach.

An interesting parallel legend of an elusive buried treasure centres on the village of Southwood in Norfolk, England, where a thatcher and his friend risked all to extract a treasure from the centre of Callow Pit, a deep pool that legend said was guarded by a powerful evil spirit. In demonic legend, Asmodeus is the evil spirit that protects such treasures. Just as the two friends were lifting the chest from the deep mud, one of them shouted triumphantly, "We've got it now! Not even the Spirit of the Pit could take it from us!" A huge black claw came up out of the mud and seized the chest. To give the thatcher and his friend their due, they clung grimly to one handle of the treasure chest, which finally came off in their hands. The chest itself vanished down into the mud — never to be seen again by mortal eyes. The handle was for many years on the door of the local church, which, itself, eventually fell into ivy-covered dereliction.

In order to analyze whether or not Kidd had anything worth burying anywhere — let alone on Clarke's Island — it's necessary to consider the links between politics, economics, and piracy. When pirates, privateers, and buccaneers in the era of Drake, Jean Fleury, and Morgan, for example, were sent out with letters of authority from their respective governments, it was in the interests of those governments to protect their adventurers in return for a large share of their loot.

Jean Fleury sported a wide range of names and aliases. He was a dare-devil Italian swashbuckler in charge of a squadron of French privateers and buccaneers who referred to him as El Francés, Juan Florentino, and Giovanni da Verrazano. He and his French crew were legally working for the King of France when they captured and looted the Aztec treasures that Cortes had sent to Madrid. Despite his unassailable legality, however, he was arbitrarily executed for piracy when the Spanish caught him in 1527.

There may be much more to Fleury, however, than piracy and privateering alone. He *could* tie in with the mysterious Arcadian treasure associated with Rennes-le-Château and Shugborough Hall and the mystery of circumnavigators like Admiral Anson. On the wall of the Church of Saint Mary Magdalene, which the enigmatic priest Bérenger Saunière refurbished and filled with strange, cryptic clues, there is a very puzzling painting showing Christ and the disciples standing on a hill covered with flowers: the *terrain fleury*. Is Saunière hinting at a connection with Jean Fleury and the treasure that supposedly came from his piratical adventures, but may have come — at least in part — from something far older and stranger?

Great as Fleury's exploits were, they were overshadowed a century later by those of an outstanding Dutch seaman, Piet Heyn. In 1628, not far from Cuba, Piet captured *the entire Spanish treasure fleet*. It took a week to unload what he'd captured, and tradition says that one thousand cartloads of treasure followed his triumphant entry into Amsterdam. Not surprisingly, he was promoted to admiral of the fleet, but died soon afterwards while fighting pirates who were raiding the coast of Holland. History sometimes seems to enjoy its ironic moments.

An interface between Eastern and Western piracy followed the Spanish occupation of Manila in the Philippines in 1571. Spanish and Chinese traders dealt in pearls, jade, spices, silk, ivory, and other expensive luxuries — while pirates in their turn preyed on the treasure ships that carried such rich merchandise.

When it became more profitable for kings, queens, princes, and influential politicians to take the lions' share of the profits of organized and legitimate trade instead of goods stolen at sea, pirates, privateers, and buccaneers were no longer encouraged and protected. It was William Kidd's fatal misfortune to be an anachronism in the history of piracy. He set out to be a privateer just when licensed piracy had passed its sell-by date.

In 1696, Kidd, in charge of the *Adventure Galley,* headed for Madagascar — then the proverbial pirate paradise for those working in the Indian Ocean. Kidd eventually captured the *Quedah Merchant,* which was carrying money, iron, opium, sugar, and silk. That was a ghastly mistake: she belonged to Muklis Khan, who had great influence with the East India Company and demanded that the Company should compensate him for Kidd's theft of his ship and its cargo. Because the politico-economic climate had changed so much and pirates were now more or less *persona non grata,* Kidd was flying for his life. It was at this time that he might *just* have had time and opportunity to hide his treasure on Clarke Island.

He was captured and tried in England, used as a political pawn in an attempt to incriminate and drag down some of the influential people who had allegedly sponsored his doomed trip on the *Adventure Galley,* and duly hanged on May 23, 1701.

Kidd's treasure — if he had anything worth burying — may or may not still lie somewhere on Clarke Island, or it may have got as far north as Oak Island, Nova Scotia, where it may have been hidden in the depths of the mysterious money pit. That strange, elaborate, cunningly protected labyrinth, however, seems to be far more complex than anything a pirate in a hurry could have constructed. It would have taken a skilled and disciplined force of well-organized and carefully directed men to create the Oak Island structures. Templars might have done it; Drake's men could have achieved it — as could Morgan's — but it would have been far beyond the capabilities of harassed, hurried pirates like Kidd's rather dubious and untrustworthy crew.

Another unsolved piratical mystery of the sea is what became of Störtebeker's vast treasure hoard. He was a medieval pirate, skipper of the *Red Devil,* who raided Bergen and other ports and got away with huge quantities of gold and silver. He was finally captured and executed in 1401, leaving his lost treasure concealed somewhere near Marienhafe, not far from the Frisian shore, in Haven near Lubeck, or perhaps on the island of Bornholm, Denmark.

Some of Henry Morgan's hidden treasure was discovered on the island of Providencia in the San Andrès archipelago by a young English couple named Seward, who were shipwrecked there in 1734 while on their honeymoon. While exploring a cave they came across almost a million pounds' worth of gold, silver, and jewels that had been hidden there by Morgan and his men. It was only a small part of what Morgan and his men had captured: most experts on buried treasure believe that far bigger hoards are still hidden somewhere on Providencia.

Edward Teach, known as Blackbeard, one of the most famous pirates of all time, was almost certainly clinically insane. He braided coloured ribbons into the huge black beard that gave him his nickname, and also wove slow fuses into that and his hair. It gave him the appearance of a demon emerging from hell when he went into battle surrounded by smoke. Anthony de Sylvestre was an eyewitness to Blackbeard's death, and in his opinion Blackbeard's vast fortune in doubloons and pieces of eight was hidden not far from Maryland, U.S.A., on a small island called Mulberry.

One of the most interesting and tantalizing accounts of hidden treasure concerns a hoard of Spanish wealth taken by an English pirate named Bennet Graham, who was better known in piratical circles as Benito. According to some versions of the Benito story, he escaped from a battle with the Spanish navy in 1819 in one of their own treasure ships, the *Relampago*. He made it as far as Wafer Bay on Cocos Island and hid his treasure there before being caught and hanged. His cabin boy escaped and eventually made his way to Tasmania, where there was a prison settlement in those days. One of the inmates of that penal colony was a woman named Mary Welch. On being released she married and went to San Francisco. According to Mary's account, she had been Benito's mistress when she was much younger, and had actually gone with him to Cocos Island to help him bury one load of treasure after another. She also claimed that just before he was hanged he had given her a vital plan of where the various treasures were buried on Cocos. A company was formed — much like the various treasure hunting companies that searched Oak Island, Nova Scotia, throughout most of the nineteenth and twentieth centuries — and Cocos Island was duly searched from end to end in 1854. According to Mary, everything had changed so much since she was there with Benito that she could not now reconcile his map with the site at all. Nothing was found by that 1854 expedition — but that certainly doesn't mean that there's nothing still hidden there today.

Other treasure hunters have frequently visited Cocos looking for different treasures. The daring English pirate Eddie Davis was believed to have gone ashore on Cocos during the seventeenth century with no fewer than seven boatloads of treasure. Yet another semi-legendary Cocos treasure cache was believed to have come from the *Mary Dear*. Lima, capital of Peru, was under siege in 1821. It looked like the rebels were winning, and the leading citizens decided to load all their valuables onto the *Mary Dear*. Captain Thompson had other ideas. He sailed the ship to Cocos where he and his mate, Jim Forbes, hid its cargo somewhere. They were later captured and forced to go back to Cocos to reveal where the treasures were hidden. Their captors underestimated their courage and agility: Forbes and Thompson vanished into the jungle. The Lima treasures were not recovered.

Years later, in 1844, a carpenter named Keating obtained a Cocos treasure map from a sailor named Thompson. With his partner, Boag, Keating went to Cocos and came back alone — but very rich. According to him, Boag had drowned in a local river because he was overloaded with gold from the Lima hoard. In 1929, another treasure hunter called Bergmans found a Cocos cave full of treasure — plus a skeleton that he assumed had once been the missing Boag!

The Seychelles hold the key to the unsolved mystery of Olivier le Vasseur's treasure. Olivier, known as *La Buze*, meaning the vulture, or the buzzard, was a French buccaneer who was hanged for piracy in 1730. His last words were reputedly, "Let him who can find my treasure!" The challenge was accompanied by several sheets of paper that he threw down derisively among the avid spectators who had come to watch him die.

At least one of Olivier's strange cryptic messages fell into the hands of the Savy family, from Mahé Island in the Seychelles, who found that Olivier's clues — if they *were* clues, and not just his final macabre joke — were extremely difficult to unravel. Determined and highly able Reg Cruise-Wilkins became interested in the Olivier treasure mystery in 1949 when he met one of the Savy family while on holiday on Mahé. He spent decades working on the problem and finally came up with the theory that the enigmatic hints Olivier had left involved the Twelve Labours of Hercules from Greek mythology: so le Vasseur had been an intelligent man, and a versatile cryptographer with a classical mind — as well as a pirate. Although the energetic and determined Cruise-Wilkins found many curious buried things that fit his Labours of Hercules theory, he never found the treasure itself.

The mystery of treasures hidden close to or even *below* the sea was not by any means confined to the activities of such pirates and privateers as le Vasseur. Among his many other misfortunes, for example, King John of England (born December 24, 1167, reigned from 1199 to 1216) lost a great deal of treasure in the Wash, the great, shallow inlet of the North Sea that has King's Lynn as its main seaport. John had been on his way to London when the disaster happened, but retired to Newark, where he died, according to some accounts, in Swinestead Abbey. His reign had caused such suffering and discontent in England that it was widely rumoured that one of the Swinestead monks had poisoned him in the belief that to kill so evil a man was a righteous act. By whatever means John met his end, there can be no doubt that a thirteenth-century fortune still lies under the waters of the Wash as they separate Norfolk from Lincolnshire.

The sea mysteries connected with smugglers frequently refer to alleged hauntings in buildings close to the shore: stories that the smugglers enthusiastically encouraged, as these were the bleak and lonely places in which their contraband goods were hidden until they could be safely dispersed and sold. One such legend from Norfolk, England, concerns the so-called "Shrieking Pits" of Aylmerton, which were believed to be "haunted" by nothing more paranormal than a smuggler trying to discourage people from prying into the area.

The pits themselves are very old — probably Mesolithic — and like all such unexplained prehistoric sites tended to acquire folk names associated with devils and demons or fairies during the Middle Ages. Norfolk also has a famous ghost known as the Brown Lady, seen and photographed at Raynham Hall. Dauntless Captain Marryat, the author of many stirring marine adventure stories, actually stayed at Raynham Hall, encountered the apparition, and boldly fired a pistol ball through her! Fortunately, it was a genuinely inexplicable phenomenon and not, as Marryat suspected, a smuggler in disguise to frighten people away from the area.

Herstmonceaux in East Sussex, England, just fifteen kilometres west of Hastings, has a castle that is credited with numerous ghostly apparitions. Old Lord Dacre was unduly anxious in case younger lovers tempted his beautiful young wife, and, being somewhat eccentric as well as groundlessly jealous, he would parade around beating a drum as a warning to them. A huge, weird, glowing figure of a ghostly drummer was seen on the battlements when the castle was semi-derelict in the eighteenth century — the heyday of smuggling activity in that area. The most likely explanation of the uncanny apparition is that it was a smugglers' trick to keep the inquisitive away from the castle when the smugglers were using it as a store for contraband.

The unsolved mysteries of the sea are awesome and innumerable, but the mysteries of the human mind are wider and deeper still. When the devious, aberrant, and unpredictable behaviour of pirates, wreckers, buccaneers, slavers, privateers, and smugglers is interwoven with the unanswered riddles of the ocean, the complexity of the fabled Gordian Knot seems as simple as undoing a shoelace.

CHAPTER FOURTEEN

Mysterious Maps and Ancient Sea Kings

One of the most awesome and challenging unsolved mysteries of the sea is the possibility that a civilization with an advanced level of culture and technology existed on Earth millennia ago — many thousands of years earlier than the earliest cultures traditional mainstream historians and archaeologists currently accept. If the accuracy of the renowned Piri Reis Map can be confirmed, and if it can be supported by other corroborative evidence of a similar kind, then it looks as if *someone* many thousands of years ago may have had a great deal of uncannily accurate information about the geographical details of Antarctica that are now concealed below a layer of ice a mile thick.

Piri Reis, after whom the famous old map is named, was an admiral in the Turkish navy. He was born sometime during the period 1465–1470, with the later date being the more probable one, in Gallipoli (also called Gelibolu), which was then strategically important as a naval base. The Turkish historian Ibni Kemal wrote colourfully that children born in Gallipoli had boats for cradles: there was, in fact, a proud and lengthy tradition of seafaring people there.

Piri's uncle was another famous Turkish admiral, Kemal Reis, and young Piri had gone voyaging with him from the age of twelve. Despite (or perhaps because of) starting his adult life as a pirate, Uncle Kemal had been appointed admiral in 1494. Young Piri was a keen observer as well as a quick learner when it came to navigational and seafaring skills. During his eye-opening travels with Kemal, he wrote parts of his book, *On Navigation,* in which he vividly describes the places they visited together and the actions in which they were engaged.

Turkish admiral Piri Reis.

Uncle Kemal was appointed first admiral during the battles between the Turks and Venetians in 1500–1502. He gave Piri command of part of the Turkish fleet, and his nephew more than justified the confidence that Kemal had placed in him. Shortly afterwards, Kemal was killed in a sea battle — and Piri lost his powerful and influential protector. Mediterranean politics were particularly volatile at the start of the sixteenth century, and Piri understandably decided to quit the unpredictable adventures of the open sea for a while and return to Gallipoli to work on his book and his maps.

The end of Piri's adventurous life is clouded by battle failure — and a woeful retreat that led to his execution. In 1554, having captured Muscat from the Portuguese, he failed to capture Hormuz. Hearing that a vastly superior European force was now sailing towards him, Piri escaped with three ships, abandoning the rest to their fate. By the time Piri docked in Cairo, news had reached the authorities there of his retreat from Hormuz and the loss of the ships he had left behind. He was promptly arrested, imprisoned, and beheaded.

During his long, adventurous career at sea, Piri had learned many things in many places. It may be sensibly surmised that as a writer on navigation, and an expert cartographer in his own right, he had assiduously questioned other navigators and studied older maps in their possession. The ancient libraries of Istanbul (once Constantinople) and Egypt were well known to him — and who can even begin to guess at the lost knowledge that was once stored there? There are good reasons for believing that the Piri Reis Map is based on far older works.

The fierce controversy that rages around the Piri Reis Map and its massive implications often generates more heat than light, and that's a great pity. The free, open-minded, scientific investigation of evidence in any field of knowledge is hindered by insults, ridicule, and attacks on the intelligence and integrity of the theorist. Attacks on personalities do nothing to prove or disprove a challenging new hypothesis. Facts and logic are the only acceptable weapons in the great war of ideas. Every new theory — however different from the currently accepted view — is entitled to the courtesy of interested, objective examination and evaluation. The suggestion that the Earth was spherical once met a great deal of hostility. Darwin's ideas about evolution encountered similar vituperative opposition. Energy expended in vicious internecine warfare among scientists, researchers, and investigators creates huge obstacles to progress. All that's necessary is a polite, "I think your ideas may be wrong — and these are my reasons for doubting your theory. Do you have any stronger evidence or arguments with which you'd like to support and reinforce it?"

The Piri Reis Map is not particularly clear or easy to follow, but it does seem to show with remarkable accuracy — an accuracy that appears rather more than coincidental — the northern coast of Antarctica. Professor Charles H. Hapgood began his academic career as a historian whose students asked him to look into the theories of Atlantis. His researches led him to the ideas put forward by Hugh Brown, who thought that the entire planet could be realigned to rotate around a new axis. Hapgood's progress based on Brown's thoughts was that it wasn't necessary to make such a major and radical terrestrial shift. Hapgood wondered whether it was more probable that the outer crust could move around on a soft, molten layer of rock just beneath it. He put these ideas forward in 1958 while working with James H. Campbell. There is also clear evidence that a high-ranking USAF commander, Harold Z. Ohlmeyer, wrote to Professor Hapgood about the Piri Reis Map in July 1960. That lieutenant colonel then said: "The claim that the lower part of the map portrays the Princess Martha coast of Queen Maud Land, Antarctic and Palma Peninsula, is reasonable. We find that this is the most logical and in all probability the correct interpretation of the map."

Back in the 1950s, the Piri Reis Map was sent to the U.S. navy to be evaluated. The chief of the navy's Hydrographic Office then was an engineer named Walters, and he consulted Arlington Mallery, who was widely acknowledged at that time as an expert cartographer.

There is evidence that Mallery painstakingly worked out the finer details of the projection technique that Piri Reis had apparently used, and once he cracked that, Mallery was able to make a spherical version of the map. According to some researchers, this had a degree of accuracy that both delighted and amazed the expert staff at the navy's Hydrographic Office.

As though the remarkable evidence of the Piri Reis Map wasn't enough, Professor Hapgood also examined the mysterious old Oronteus Finaeus Map, which was made in 1531 or 1532 and is now carefully preserved in the map room of the Library of Congress in the U.S. Hapgood said at the time, "I had the instant conviction that I had found here a truly authentic map of the real Antarctica."

Who exactly *was* the Oronteus Finaeus who drew the mysterious and controversial map? Research shows that his name could be varied in several ways: Oronce Fine (or Finé), Orontius, and even Orotius. But despite the numerous name variants, he's the same man. Born in Briançon in 1494 or 1495, he managed to upset the law in 1518 and found himself in jail as a consequence. After being released, Oronce took a medical degree at the Collège de Navarre in 1522 and then decided to specialize in maths rather than medicine. He designed and built many things, from scientifically accurate sundials to the very effective city defences of Milan. He even calculated π to 22 and 7/9 divided by 7. That gives a figure of 3.174603174. He later recalculated and came up with 47/15, which works out to 3.133333. His third and final attempt at π was 3 and 11/78, which works out at 3.141025641, whereas the real value of π is 3.141592654. Even allowing for the fact that Oronce was then professor of mathematics at the Collège Royal, his calculations were remarkably good for a man working with sixteenth-century equipment. That kind of mathematical skill encourages confidence in his cartography.

Another very interesting piece of evidence Professor Hapgood unearthed and studied was the map made by Philip Buache, perhaps as early as 1737, but certainly not later than 1739. This Buache map appears to be based on a report of a voyage made by two French ships, the *Aigle* and the *Marie*, which left Port de l'Orient on July 19, 1738, and sailed down to examine as much of Northern Antarctica as they could. There is a degree of controversy and disagreement about the importance of this map: a great many details of Antarctica are shown — far more than the *Aigle* and the *Marie* could have found out, according to some expert researchers. On the other hand, it is only fair to accept that a map drawn after their epic voyage of 1738 probably owed more to keen eyewitness observation from the valiant crews of those two French ships than to the ancient cartographical traditions linking the maps of the prehistoric sea kings to an ice-free Antarctica that shifted mysteriously when the moving lithosphere slid it towards the South Pole.

Interesting and puzzling as these old maps are, they are reinforced by several other enigmatic charts and portulans (medieval maps that showed the route from one port to another) that lend credence to Hapgood's theories and the researches of Graham Hancock and the Flem-Aths. These pioneering examples of the early cartographers' skills include the work of the Majorcan Cartographic School. The oldest known maritime charts, which not surprisingly came into existence at about the same time as the first known nautical compass, date from the late 1200s and are concerned mainly with the Mediterranean — affectionately referred to on the charts as "Mare Nostrum," meaning "our sea." In the middle of the twelfth century, Aragon and Catalonia were part of the same kingdom to which the Balearic Islands were added nearly a century later. There was a flourishing trade with North Africa at the time, because Africa was believed by all the more adventurous medieval merchants to be the most lucrative source of gold and ivory. Arabian and Jewish cartographers were acknowledged to be outstandingly good at that time, and were accordingly admired by mariners and merchants alike. Majorcan maps were highly prized; Ramon Llull, a renowned Catalonian academic, maintained that his contemporaries should never venture out to sea without both a map and a compass. In the middle of the fourteenth century, Peter, then king of Aragon, decreed that every ship under his royal aegis must carry two sea charts.

Angelino Dulcert created a superb map as early as 1339 when he worked in Palma on Majorca. Dulcert carefully incorporated details of mountains, lakes, and rivers — in the same way they were shown on the puzzling old maps of the Antarctic landmass. The Catalan Atlas made in 1375 goes further afield than Dulcert's work. It even shows parts of the Orient, and Marco Polo's travels made an important contribution to it.

Another great contributor to the fascinating world of early maps and the mystery of their ancient sources was Martin Behaim from Nuremberg. Born in 1459, Behaim created what he described as his *Erdapfel,* his globe of the Earth. But long before Behaim's work, the great Italian mathematician Giovanni Campani from

Novara, working in the thirteenth century, described with great accuracy how to construct a globe in his *Tractus de Sphera solida*. Behaim found great success in Portugal, was knighted by King John, and made a number of voyages to the African coast. He later returned to Nuremberg, where he constructed his *Erdapfel*. It showed the Antarctic Circle right enough, but the space where the tantalizing details of the land below the ice might have been depicted was used instead to show the names of three prominent citizens of Nuremberg who had been instrumental in commissioning Behaim's globe. Behaim himself acknowledged that his geographical work was based on Ptolemy's *Cosmography*.

Claudius Ptolemaeus, widely known as Ptolemy, was a brilliant Greek astronomer and geographer who did most of his scholarly work in Alexandria in Egypt. Born in 85, Ptolemy lived until 165. His works were regarded by most cartographers for twelve or thirteen centuries after his death as a sound basis for their own maps.

Another very unusual feature — perhaps the most significant and mysterious feature of the entire Behaim Globe — was his inclusion of the *supposedly mythical* Isle of Antilia. It was otherwise referred to as *Septa Citade*, meaning the Island of Seven Cities. There was a legend to the effect that in the year 734 a Portuguese archbishop from Porto, assisted by six other bishops, had taken care of their respective refugee flocks and fled with them to escape from the Moorish expansion into Spain. Complete with their essential household goods and domestic cattle, the refugees had landed on the Isle of Antilia, somewhere far across the Atlantic, and prospered there.

One of the best theories ever offered as an explanation of the Oak Island Money Pit mystery was put forward by the authors' great Nova Scotian friend George Young, now sadly deceased. George's hypothesis was that the Money Pit had been created by religious refugees from across the Atlantic, who had created the pit to house the mortal remains of their esteemed leader — or leaders. If the allegedly mythical Isle of Antilia portrayed on Behaim's Globe was really Nova Scotia, it would fit very well with George's excellent theory. Religious refugees arriving there in the eighth century would have been welcomed and hospitably treated by the friendly indigenous Canadians, who would, over the course of centuries, have absorbed them into their own Micmac Nation.

Many of the mysterious and controversial old maps indicate that at one time there were rivers flowing over an apparently ice-free Antarctic continent. Rivers inevitably carry materials down to the sea, and they create characteristic sediment where they reach the coast. Various tests carried out by reputable and prestigious academic teams have indicated stratification and sedimentation of types usually associated with rivers around parts of the Antarctic coast. Experts have also dated those sediments as being up to nine thousand years old. Allowing for reasonable margins, doesn't this agree with the possibility of an ice-free Antarctica close to the dates suggested for the loss of Plato's Atlantis?

A united expedition of Norwegian, Swedish, and British academics, researchers, and explorers carried out sonar and seismic investigations of what lay below the Antarctic ice cap in 1949. Their findings were known to Ohlmeyer, who included them in his correspondence with Hapgood in 1960. These investigations appeared to confirm that the rivers and general topography below the Antarctic ice were largely in accord with the Piri Reis Map and Hapgood's fascinating theories about it.

Further enthusiastic support for Hapgood's ideas about a mobile lithosphere came from no less an intellectual giant than Albert Einstein. He felt that there was considerable mileage in the theory that as the vast masses of ice around the poles were by no means symmetrical or evenly distributed, the Earth's rotation could produce a centrifugal momentum that would encourage the Earth's lithosphere to move.

Was there really an ancient, technologically advanced culture of ancient sea kings who spread their knowledge over most of the world? One of the most powerful pieces of evidence in favour of Hapgood's thoughts about just such a prehistoric culture comes from medieval China. A carved rock column there dates from the middle of the twelfth century. According to Hapgood, it demonstrates the same grid system, the same knowledge of spherical trigonometry, and the same very advanced technology found in the Piri Reis Map and the other old charts and maps known in the West. If Hapgood was correct about the mysterious Chinese sea chart carved on the old pillar, it would seem to be a very powerful argument in favour of the worldwide dissemination of the knowledge held by the hypothetical ancient sea kings.

To give a fair balance to the argument, however, it needs to be accepted that when Hapgood, Mallery, and other cartographers carried out their detailed examinations of the ancient maps, they seem to have made certain modifications and adjustments in an attempt to get back as closely as possible to the information that *appeared* to be the prerogative of the ancient sea kings — if they and their hypothetical culture ever existed.

The academic processes involved are broadly parallel to techniques used by some Bible scholars: if errors are found in, say, a thirteenth-century copy, the researchers go back to an earlier fifth-century draft and give the older data priority. If part of the Piri Reis Map doesn't fit the modern Antarctic coastline too well, an assumption could be made that the originals — from which Piri Reis *supposedly* copied his map — were better than the copy that he made.

The most honest and objective researchers can sometimes be carried off course by the powerful currents of their own enthusiasm. There is a cautionary tale that every investigator should ponder while weighing the evidence for and against his, or her, favourite theories.

A pyramidologist had spent half a lifetime working out his theories about the Great Pyramid. He had convinced himself by many years of complex mathematical calculations that the measurements of the Great Pyramid were a code to the future, an enigmatic prophecy in stone. Finally, he was able to visit the huge monument and study it firsthand. Things went well for a while; then he encountered a stone that contradicted his cherished calculations. A watchful attendant observed the distraught pyramidologist attempting to saw a piece of stone away so that the pyramid would fit his beloved hypothesis. There are times when we are all tempted to cut away the stones of fact if they endanger our preconceived ideas. It's a widespread human weakness.

When the famous western gunfighter Wyatt Earp was old, frail, and dying, a young journalist begged him for the truth about the gunfight at the OK Corral. Earp smiled gamely and said, "Hell with the truth, kid. Print my legend!"

CHAPTER FIFTEEN

Legendary Voyages: Odysseus, Sinbad, Jason and the Argonauts

Academic experts in folklore, myth, and legend have a natural curiosity about how *real* some of their heroes and locations might actually be. To say that there is no smoke without fire is proverbial, almost clichéd, but it is a truism nevertheless. Myths, legends, and folklore had to come from somewhere. Exaggeration has a lot to do with their genesis; misunderstanding of causality also plays a major part; and yet, in the final analysis, myths, legends, and folktales can usually be traced back to a real time, a real place, and real people.

What does the Homeric legend say about Odysseus, alias Ulysses? He was the son of Laertes and ruler of the little island kingdom of Ithaca. Renowned like Robin Hood and Brer Rabbit for his ability to outwit his enemies by superior cunning, Odysseus played a major part in the Trojan War. In addition to his cunning, he was as great an orator as Shakespeare's Antony — and this combination of intelligence and verbal persuasiveness made him a formidable opponent. Before his marriage to the faithful and fearless Penelope, Odysseus was one of the suitors who competed for the hand of Helen, who was ostensibly the cause of the Trojan War. The real reason was far more likely to have been trade rivalry — but Homer (or the Homeric Writers' Co-operative) decided that going to war over the most beautiful woman in the world made a far more exciting storyline than fighting over who sold olive oil and wine in the best overseas markets.

When Menelaus won the contest to marry Helen, Odysseus, camouflaging his personal disappointment, suggested that it would be a wise move for Menelaus to ask the other suitors to swear to defend his exclusive rights to the lady. That was how Odysseus found himself in the ironic position of trying to get Helen back from Paris, Prince of Troy, in order to return her to the man who had beaten him to it in the marriage competition!

Odysseus was physically heroic as well as cunning. When the Trojans were getting the better of things in a pitched battle with Menelaus's Greeks, it was Odysseus who stood like a granite boulder and held the field; it was Diomedes and Odysseus who led an audacious night raid on the Trojans; and it was the cunning mind of Odysseus that thought up the Trojan Horse ruse that won the war for the Greeks.

Odysseus's powers of oratory came to the fore when he and Ajax were competing for the magnificent armour that had become available when Achilles was slain. Odysseus's speech won the armour for him — and the frustrated Ajax went insane and committed suicide.

His return to Ithaca after the Trojan War was a ten-year catalogue of problems and misadventures. This was explained to the satisfaction of the Greek theologians by the concept of a pantheon of rival gods and goddesses, some of whom were determined to destroy Odysseus, while others were equally determined to help him. In the Homeric view he was a pawn on the divine chess board, or a puppet whose strings were alternately in friendly and unfriendly divine hands. He saved his men from the hungry Cyclops, from Circe's magic, and from the mind-eroding pleasure drugs available from the Lotus-Eaters. Pluto, Ruler of the Underworld, allowed Odysseus to get useful advice from his dead mother and from Ajax that proved helpful on later adventures.

Odysseus then encountered the Sirens and the monsters, Scylla and Charybdis. Charybdis had started life as a nymph. The daughter of Poseidon and Gaia, she had a habit of flooding lands for her father's underwater kingdom — the opposite of Dutch land reclamation work. Zeus finally turned her into a monster and gave her the job of sucking water in and out three times a day. Charybdis lived in a huge cave at one side of the dangerous Strait of Messina. Opposite her was an even less friendly monster called Scylla, who, like Charybdis, had once been a beautiful nymph, daughter of Phorcys, himself a sea god and the son of Pontus and Gaia. Sailing between Scylla and Charybdis has become as proverbial as being jammed between a rock and a hard place, or being between the devil and the deep blue sea.

Because of jealousy over the handsome Glaucon, Circe the enchantress — never renowned for her placid nature and generous inclination to forgiveness — had poured some rather nasty magical toxins into the pool where the lovely Scylla regularly bathed. What came out of the water had six heads, twelve feet, and a body that consisted mainly of howling, barking dogs. Each time a ship came too close, every head seized a sailor, whose fate was swift and certain because each head had three rows of teeth.

As a punishment for eating sacred cattle that belonged to the sun god, a bolt of lightning destroyed the ship and Odysseus alone was saved. He found himself next on the island of the deliciously nubile nymph Calypso, and wasn't entirely inconsolable for the next seven years — during which she insisted on keeping him there as her lover. Zeus, whose sense of justice and fair play probably made him intervene for brave and loyal Penelope's sake, finally rescued Odysseus from the deliciously insatiable Calypso and popped him into a small boat. In this, Odysseus reached the island inhabited by the Phaeaceans, who treated him extremely well and then took him home to Ithaca.

Once home again, he disguised himself as a beggar to reconnoitre; he saw that his brave and faithful Penelope was holding off an army of unpleasant suitors who were trying to force her to marry one of them in order to take over the kingdom. With a little help from his father and his son, Odysseus used his famous bow to take out the suitors, rescue Penelope, and live more or less happily ever after as the restored king of Ithaca.

There are many theories about where these voyages *really* took Odysseus, and these theories create yet another intriguing unsolved mystery of the sea. Most hypotheses centre on the Mediterranean coasts and islands, which seems logical enough, but there are a number of scholars and researchers who look further afield. One such bold theory put forward very convincingly by E.J. de Meester even takes Odysseus as far as Scotland and Ireland!

It is clear from most theories of where Odysseus really went that the first part of his trip is comparatively easy to pin over a real map of the Mediterranean. He left Troy intending to head home to Ithaca. That would have been approximately southwest, not far from Cephalonia (Kefallinia in contemporary Greek), which is the largest of the Ionian islands and lies to the west of the Gulf of Patraikos. Along with Ithaca and some smaller islands in the vicinity, Kefallinia is a department, or administrative district, of modern Greece. It was once an important centre of Mycenaean civilization, and Homer almost certainly referred to the island as Same. Some classics scholars think that Odysseus was actually based in Kefallinia rather than on Ithaca itself.

The Romans added it to their Empire in 189. The Normans were there in the eleventh century. Then the Neapolitans and Venetians were in charge until the Turks drove them out towards the end of the fifteenth century. The Turkish occupation wasn't a long one, however, because the Venetians recaptured it in 1499. All of the Ionian Islands were a British Protectorate until 1864, when they went back to Greece. Despite the terrible earthquake damage of 1953, several important Mycenaean tombs can still be seen on the island.

The size of Kefallinia makes it a useful signpost for today's researchers hoping to find the one hundred square miles that make up Ithaca itself. It was not only the home of Odysseus, but perhaps the island of Homer as well — or of one or two talented and influential authors who served on the Homeric Writers' Co-operative. The island is thought to have taken its name from Ithacis, a Cephalonian prince, who settled there with his brother and built a fountain that provided the islanders with good, clear, clean spring water. Inhabited for at least four thousand years — possibly much longer — Ithaca could well have been the capital of the Cephalonian State during the Mycenaean era when the Trojan War was raging and Odysseus was the king of Ithaca. The Cave of the Nymphs is situated very close to Vathy, Ithaca's capital city, which also boasts one of the largest natural harbours in the world. There are also some interesting ruins at Stavros that are well worth a research visit.

Odysseus was clearly setting out for Ithaca in what he'd intended to be a southwesterly direction when the storm hit him and drove him badly off course. He reached the coast of North Africa and encountered the Lotus-Eaters and the Cyclops there. The islands of Jerba and Kerkenna are strong candidates for real places either visited, or approached very closely, during Odysseus' journey home from Troy.

Meester, among other researchers, considers the view that in the original shorter version of the story, Odysseus was still in command of ten or twelve ships and several hundred sailors and warriors when he left the North African coast.

Was the island of the god of the winds, who was friendly and helpful to them, really Malta, or Pantelleria in the Sicilian Channel? Pantelleria is certainly closer to the coast of Africa than to the coast of Italy. In either case, Odysseus and his men were well received and helped there — and were not far from Ithaca and Kefallinia.

Leaving out the romantic embroidery about being disguised as a beggar, not being recognized, and then almost single-handedly killing all the evil suitors who were pestering Penelope, the original version might well have ended when Odysseus, at the head of nearly one thousand loyal, battle-hardened warriors, turned up like the Seventh Cavalry and massacred the suitors along with any household traitors who'd been collaborating with them.

A number of thoughtful researchers have considered the idea that Homer (or the co-operative that wrote under his name) had got hold of *another* adventure story about a Mediterranean merchant who had sailed to Cornwall to buy tin and got badly blown off course by a storm. The two stories, according to this theory, were then *welded together* to form the long, popular version of Odysseus's return from Troy to Ithaca.

In this second part of the adventure, Odysseus has only one ship with a small crew, and is later totally alone. He goes to Telepylus, where there is a narrow bay with high, steep cliffs on each side. Timmerman, a Dutch translator of Homer, suggested that this was an acceptable description of a Scandinavian fiord. Could Telepylus have been a Greek form of Telemark in Norway? Place names can often provide useful signals to historians. The inclusion of *By*, *Thorpe*, or *Toft* in the name of any East Anglian town or village in the U.K. is a strong indication that it was once a Scandinavian settlement. The authors' own East Anglian surname, *Fanthorpe*, suggests Viking genes from the remote past. Over a century ago, Théophile Cailleux wrote *Poesies D'Homere: Faites en Iberie et Decrivant non la Mediterranee mais L'Atlantique Theorie Nouvelle* — which translates broadly as his new theory that Homer's poetry describes adventures in the Atlantic, not in the Mediterranean. Iman Wilkens said much the same thing in *Where Troy Once Stood*. Wilkens argues that Troy was actually in England and Mycenae was across the Channel in France. His theory is based on geography, archaeology, and place names, which he claims are more likely to be Celtic than Greek or Turkish. The point is also made that when Schliemann excavated Troy, the walls were not big enough to encircle a city of fifty thousand people, which was the population credited to it.

Another factor that favours Europe rather than Asia Minor in Wilkens's argument is the number of rivers and waterways in the landscape near Troy. Iman reckons that these are more likely to be European than part of Asia Minor. In fact, the fourteen rivers mentioned as being near Troy are, according to Wilkens, near Cambridge in England. He presses the point further: when Troy (Cambridge?) was destroyed, the survivors founded a new city on a great river not very far away. According to Wilkens's theory, that new city was London! He argues that the Celts referred to it as Caer Troia, and the Romans called it Londinium Troia Nova. As for the River Temese, surely, argues Wilkens, that has to be the River Thames.

Wilkens's theory begins as something so wild and way out that it has an almost fantastic, dream-like quality — but it's full of remarkably clear, sensible, and well-written arguments that leave the open-minded student of prehistory admiring the writer and seriously re-examining all previous ideas about the travels of Odysseus.

What if Homer (or a member of the Homeric team), visiting Spain, heard the story from one of the Phaeaceans living in the Gibraltar area and then Hellenized the adventure to meet the expectations of a Greek audience?

Imagine that the second part — the Odysseus-fighting-on-alone part — started with the trip to Cornwall to obtain tin, and then went northwest to Ireland. The Bay of Shannon in Ireland has almost everything needed to match the Homeric description — and it's even better than a Scandinavian fiord in some ways. Looking carefully at place names again, Homer's Limus with an Irish *ick* suffix becomes *Limerick*, which is right at the end of the Bay of Shannon. In the original Irish Gaelic language Limerick is *Luimneach*, which is also close to Homer's Limus. Tipperary is only a few miles east of Limerick, and again, the place name analysis comes close to the Homeric Telepylus.

Leaving Ireland, our hero (the Greek Odysseus, King of Ithaca, or the anonymous, adventurous tin merchant) sails north as far as Scotland, then east to the Orkney island of Hoy. The Greeks undoubtedly knew about the Orkneys by the time Pytheas the explorer returned from his voyage there in the fourth century BC.

Pytheas was brought to public attention in the U.K. in 1893, when Sir Clement Markham, then a noted historian, published an article about him. Pytheas came from the Greek colony of Massalia, known in our own century as Marseilles. He explored Britain thoroughly, and then tried to sail north as far as he could. He described encountering a sea of slush, fog, and ice that prevented any further progress, and reluctantly turned back. There is no knowing quite how far north he managed to go: that's yet another of the sea's unsolved mysteries.

In the sixth century BC, Pythagoras had already recorded his firm belief that both the planet Earth and the universe we occupy are spherical. Babylonian astronomers had reached similar conclusions before Pythagoras did. Pytheas would have been well aware of their ideas, and, as an educated man, would have shared them. Ostensibly, his business instincts would have taken him in search of tin, which the Bronze Age Greeks valued highly and referred to as *kassiteros*. The U.K. was known to them as the Kasiterides Islands because it was the source of their vitally important *kassiteros*. The Phoenician sailors and merchants also knew it well. But over and above his mercantile purposes, Pytheas had the heart and soul of a real explorer, a true seeker of new knowledge for its own sake. He had two significant advantages over other merchant adventurers who were primarily concerned with the tin trade: Pytheas was an expert astronomer and mathematician; he had also mastered the use of the strange navigational gadget called the *Gnomon*. This was a Phoenician instrument that worked on a shadow principle that the Greeks had acquired via Anaximander of Miletus, who lived and worked in the sixth century BC. The tireless historian Herodotus described it. Anaximander also drew a map of the world as far as it was known in his day — a great credit to him, as his map showed it to be spherical!

Pytheas also recorded seeing "fish the size of boats which blew water into the air" while he was up to the northeast of Scotland among the Orkneys. These were almost certainly the Orkas Islands, or Islands of the Seals, which Pytheas also recorded. Whales are still seen in the area today, and must have been much more numerous when Pytheas saw them — long before the modern whaling industry reduced their numbers so drastically.

Returning to the Odysseus-in-Scotland theory, the Orkney name Kirkwall might even be stretched to sound a bit like Circe. Was it possible — however remotely — that Circe's island was in the Orkneys? She lived, according to Homer, in a high stone house, or tower. Elpenor suffered a fatal fall from the top of it. The Orkney *broch* is a tall stone tower. There are hundreds of them in the area. If it's possible for these ancient stone towers to have been there long enough for Homer to have known about them, was Circe's tall stone house really an Orkney broch?

Where did our adventurous tin merchant go next after leaving the Orkneys? Some researchers who accept this Scottish theory of his travels consider that he sailed westwards again, then south between England and Ireland. As far as Odysseus' communications with the departed are concerned, there are plenty of Mesolithic and Neolithic burial mounds he might well have regarded as gateways to the underworld. And assuming that he was in that area, was beautiful Calypso's island really the Isle of Man?

Another tantalizing unsolved mystery of the sea that links with Pytheas and the Homeric voyage of Odysseus is the location of Ultima Thule. To the ancient Greeks and Romans, it simply meant the most remote of the northern lands — literally as far as you could travel before the ice got in your way and prevented all further movement north. It might have been Greenland, Iceland, or one of the northern islands. Going back to place names and their importance to historians, the tiny island of Foula in the Shetland group may be a reasonable candidate. *F* and *Th* sound very similar indeed — especially when the speakers and listeners have different linguistic codes as their first languages. Could Foula have been Thule? It's not impossible.

The unsolved sea mysteries surrounding Odysseus and the marvels he supposedly encountered on his fateful voyage home from Troy are matched by the equally intriguing sea mysteries that involved Jason and the Argonauts and their quest for the Golden Fleece. The story begins with the infant Jason being smuggled away to be reared by a wise old centaur because of various court intrigues to usurp the throne of Jason's father, Aeson. Jason's evil uncle, Pelias, was now in power in Iolcus, a city in Thessaly in northeastern Greece. After learning all that wise old Chiron the Centaur could teach him, Jason set out to regain his father's kingdom.

Greek theology almost invariably sets out to explain human sufferings, setbacks, and disasters in terms of quarrels between the gods or some offence a mortal had knowingly, or inadvertently, committed that had angered the gods. In the case of bad King Pelias, it was Hera, the wife of Zeus, who was angry with him. His sin was to have paid tributes to every god and goddess but her. In New Testament times, when Paul spoke to the Athenians he observed their altar "To the Unknown God" and used it as a basis for his sermon. It had more than likely been erected by a prudent, but superstitious, Greek worshipper who was anxious not to follow Pelias's road to ruin.

On his way to Iolcus, Jason assisted what seemed to be a frail old woman across a flooded river. The feeble, but surprisingly heavy, crone turned out to be the goddess Hera in disguise. In his battle with the torrent, Jason lost a sandal — a vital ingredient in a prophecy to Pelias to beware of a man with only one sandal. When Jason and Pelias met, Pelias asked what Jason would do if he was the king and someone was causing him difficulties. Jason replied that he would send the man on a quest to recover the Golden Fleece. Pelias prompt-ly gave him the job!

There was no shortage of volunteers to help him: Greece's bravest, noblest, wisest, fittest, and strongest heroes flocked to join Jason's crew. Argus, the famous craftsman and shipwright, built the *Argo* for him, and the elite crew, according to some accounts, includ-ed the great Greek woman athlete, Atalanta. She was the same lady who could easily have defeated Melanion in the famous race to win her hand in marriage had not the cunning Melanion thrown down three Golden Apples to distract her. This is especially interesting in view of Atalanta's connections with Arcadia and the semi-mythical Arcadian treasure. According to some versions of her history, Atalanta was the daughter of Iasus and Clymene of Arcadia. Cutting through the romantic mythology and ornamentation of the story, a possible connection can be made between Atalanta as an adventurous Argonaut in quest of the Golden Fleece and Atalanta of Arcadia — with inside knowledge of the very ancient and mysterious Arcadian treasure. Are there links with Admiral Anson's long voyage, the *Argo*'s long voyage, and the curious Arcadian Shepherd Monument in the grounds of the Ansons' Shugborough Hall in Staffordshire, U.K.? Is it even remotely possible that there's a tenuous linguistic link between Arcadia and the Argonauts?

Another strange mystery connected with Jason, the Argonauts, and their ship is its legendary talking prow, or figurehead. Compare this with the accusations levelled against the noble and indomitable Templar Order. The odious Philip IV of France, ironically called Philip le Belle, treacherously attacked the great Templar Order in 1307. Part of the propaganda he levelled against them was that they worshipped a magical talking head and took orders from it. The Templars, as is well known, are linked with Rennes-le-Château, and Rennes is linked with the Arcadian treasure mystery. In the famous Harrison Ford epic *Raiders of the Lost Ark*, the suggestion was made that the Ark of the Covenant was "a radio for talking to God." The biblical account of one important episode in the life of the boy Samuel suggests that he heard a voice calling his name while he slept in the vicinity of the Ark in the biblical holy place known as Shiloh. Taken together, the ancient stories of talking heads, talking prows, and the voice that Samuel heard at Shiloh all suggest that there *may* have been some sort of highly advanced communication technology in those far-off times. Does that link, perhaps, with legends of the advanced technology reputedly available in Atlantis and Lemuria?

Unsolved mysteries are rarely individual strands — they are more like the complexities of spiders' webs.

The Argonauts reached Salmydessus to find that King Phineus was being persecuted by harpies. These creatures were described by the early Greek writers as half-woman, half-bird, and all bad. Two of the Argonauts claimed the North Wind as an ancestor — consequently they were blessed with the gift of flight. They drove the harpies so far from Salmydessus that the starving King Phineus, whose table had been a favourite target of the harpies, was never troubled by them again. Phineus was more than grateful and warned the Argonauts about a peril that lay in their way as a very serious — perhaps fatal — obstacle to their quest: the Clashing Rocks.

These Clashing Rocks, known to the ancient Greek navigators and sea adventurers as the Symplegades, stood near the Bosporus entrance to the Black Sea, which was known as the Euxine to the ancient Greeks. Pliny, the famous Roman writer who died when Vesuvius erupted in 79, had an interesting theory about the Symplegades. He said that they were actually the precipitous Fanari Islands, and, because they were so close together, they appeared sometimes as two, sometimes as one, depending upon the course of the approaching ship and the angle from which the mariners saw them. This gave rise to the belief that they actually moved and clashed together.

Phineus advised the Argonauts to send a bird through the gap between the rocks ahead of the *Argo*. The plan was that the rocks would try to crush the bird and would then need time to get back into position ready for their next clashing together. While they were thus imperfectly prepared to crush their next victim, the *Argo* would have a chance to get through. The plan was duly put into operation: the bird survived, apart from the loss of a few tail feathers; the *Argo* received some minor damage to her stern, but was otherwise unscathed.

It's necessary to go back earlier than Jason's visit to find out where the magical Ram with the Golden Fleece had originated. Phrixus was the son of Athamas, King of Boeotia, and his first wife, Nephele. They also had a daughter, Helle. Tiring of Nephele, Athamas took a second bride, Princess Ino, who was the daughter of Cadmus, King of Thebes. They also had two children, but Ino realized that Nephele's son, Phrixus, would become king eventually, as he was older than her boy. The wicked and cunning Ino deliberately interfered with the vitally important seed corn so that it wouldn't grow. Boeotia was verging on starvation when

Athamas sent messengers to the Delphic Oracle for help and advice. Evil Ino waylaid them on their return and bribed them to tell the King that unless Phrixus was sacrificed the corn wouldn't grow. The next part of the story is so close to the biblical account of Abraham and his intention to sacrifice his much loved son, Isaac — who is saved by the ram — that there is almost certainly a link between these ancient Greek and Hebrew traditions. Athamas was on the point of sacrificing Phrixus to save his people from starving when a golden ram flew towards them. Phrixus and his sister Helle climbed onto the golden ram's back and it soared away with them. Tragically, Helle fell off and was killed, but she was immortalized when her name became part of the word *Hellespont*, the name of the narrow straits separating Europe from Asia, the strait that is known today as the Dardanelles.

Phrixus arrived safely in Colchis, the kingdom beyond the eastern shore of the Black Sea, or Euxine. The ram was sacrificed to Zeus and its magnificent Golden Fleece was presented to Aeetes, King of Colchis. Its magical powers were such that Colchis was destined to enjoy safety and prosperity *as long as the Fleece was kept there*. Prudently, Aeetes had it hung in a huge oak tree with a vigilant, insomniac dragon to guard it. So much for the origin of the Fleece, but what was the origin of the Golden Ram that saved Phrixus? (He, incidentally, married one of Aeetes' daughters, had several children with her, and lived a long, happy life in Colchis with his princess.)

Poseidon, god of the sea, features in many of the sea's unsolved mysteries — and the origins of the Golden Ram come into that category. A highly desirable Greek girl named Theophane was understandably being pursued by half the eligible Greek heroes, who all wanted to marry her. Poseidon wanted her for himself and used his divine powers to hide her on the Isle of Crumissa. The disappointed suitors discovered where she was and set off in hot pursuit. Poseidon then disguised all the inhabitants of Crumissa by turning them into cattle, and Theophane into a ewe. The angry suitors arrived and began to kill the cattle — whereupon Poseidon changed them all into wolves. Then, still lusting after the beautiful Theophane, he changed himself into a ram so that they could mate. The Golden Ram that was born as a result of their union became the magical flying ram that saved Phrixus and ended its earthly days as the Golden Fleece in the giant oak tree of Colchis. Zeus, however, transformed it after it had been sacrificed to him, making it into the constellation of Aries the Ram.

Aeetes was not in the least happy about letting Jason have the Golden Fleece, but Aeetes' enchantress daughter, Medea, intervened to help Jason carry out one or two of the seemingly impossible tasks that Greek heroes were inevitably asked to perform: these just went with the territory! Having coped with the bulls that breathed fire and kicked opponents to death with their brazen hooves, Jason took on the warriors who sprang from the dragon's teeth. Medea's next piece of assistance was to lead Jason to the Golden Fleece and give the dragon a powerful, magical narcotic while Jason seized the object of his quest.

Jason's dramatically successful voyage is more than mythology and legend: it's a genuine and intriguing unsolved mystery of the sea. The Argonauts' mythological twigs and branches grow from a sturdy historical main trunk. In ancient times, fleeces were placed in rivers in Crete to collect the gold dust from the water: hence the existence of more than one golden fleece. Some of these fleeces were probably exported from Crete to Colchis. There are some expert researchers who hypothesize that the epic voyage actually took Jason and his men along a number of Eastern European *rivers*, using what the Vikings were later to refer to as the *Great Portage*. It has also been conjectured that Jason got as far as the Baltic, where merchants would have become involved in the lucrative amber trade. The Argonauts could then have steered west and south, through the English Channel and back through the Pillars of Hercules into their own familiar Mediterranean waters.

In Jason's time the waters of the Black Sea were believed to have been much lower than those of the Mediterranean, but a number of contemporary oceanographers and marine geologists have put forward the theory that some kind of major seismic trauma allowed the waters of the Mediterranean to break through and lift the level of the Black Sea by ten or twelve meters. A number of underwater explorers have reported finding the remains of ancient settlements and many shipwrecks from classical times piled with ancient amphora that once held oil, wine, or rare perfumes. Many different seafaring cultures from the old world have left their traces there: Greeks, Romans, Byzantines, Scythians, Goths, and Genoese, as well as early Turks, Russians, and Ukrainians. To the fearless and adventurous ancient Greek mariners the Black Sea was known as *Pontos Axienos:* the "Inhospitable Sea." The Underwater Archaeology Research and Training Centre at Kiev University, together with the Institute of Nautical Archaeology, produced a great many exciting and intriguing results when they conducted surveys of the Crimean coast as recently as 1997.

Both Odysseus and Jason undertook memorable, audacious, and exhausting voyages that leave their actual historicity an intriguing unsolved mystery of the sea. Great as they were, however, the life and adventures of Sinbad — the famed sailor of *The Arabian Nights* — surpassed them both. Who was the historical Sinbad, and where did he *really* sail?

Just as Chaucer set some remarkably accurate cameos of life in the fourteenth century into his *Canterbury Tales,* so *The Arabian Nights* contains at least as much fact as fiction. Its setting is as cleverly contrived as Chaucer's pilgrimage, during which his wonderfully assorted characters — the Knight, the Miller, and the Wife of Bath — tell one another stories as they jog along to Canterbury.

Scheherazade is the beautiful and highly intelligent young daughter of the Grand Vizier who serves King Shahryar. Having been bitterly disappointed and unhappy in a number of earlier matrimonial relationships, Shahryar has instituted a new policy of one-night nuptials followed by the queen's execution in the morning. In spite of his reputation, Scheherazade marries him, but begs to have her younger sister, Dunyazade, with them in the royal bridal chamber. The girls had arranged that shortly after midnight Dunyazade would pretend that she was unable to sleep and would beg Scheherazade to entertain her with a story. Shahryar found himself also unable to sleep, and readily granted his royal permission for the story to begin. Scheherazade told the superbly exciting tales preserved in *The Arabian Nights,* and, like every good magazine editor retaining her audience's loyalty with a series of cliff-hanger endings, she always broke off at the most exciting point in the tale. King Shahryar, anxious to hear the next enthralling episode, naturally postponed her execution again and again, day after day, until he finally fell in love with her and happily cancelled the decree concerning executing a new wife every morning. In the best folktale tradition, he and Scheherazade then lived as happily ever after as did Cinderella and Prince Charming. The loyal and helpful Dunyazade was probably recruited into Shahryar's Royal Harem as well!

Scheherazade was as brilliantly creative as Chaucer, and each of them fuelled a fertile imagination with shrewd and perceptive observations of the real life going on around them in the Southwark and Baghdad of their respective eras. Chaucer's Shipman from Dartmouth knew every port from Carthage to Hull on the Humber, and in

Chaucer's eyes: "Hardy he was, and wise to undertake; With many a tempest had his beard been shake."

Scheherazade's Sinbad (frequently spelled Sindbad) was cast in that same basic, realistic, nautical mould: the life-saving chronicles of her serialized Sinbad included the factual adventures of many a real marine adventurer. The mysterious seas that lay south of Asia and east of Africa were the setting for these adventures. In *The Arabian Nights* the stories are arranged as seven separate voyages — the significance of the numerologists' favoured number seven again being inescapable, as with the old phrase "Seven Seas." Scheherazade drew on her wide knowledge of Indian and Persian collections of ancient myths and legends of the sea, as well as ancient poems of marine adventures such as Homer's works. These, together with the real exploits of contemporary sailors, form the three main strands of her work.

The seven voyages are themselves supported by a sub-frame within the main structure of *The Arabian Nights*. Sinbad is now extremely rich and enjoying the leisure and pleasure of his luxurious home. A poor, very hard-working porter, also named Sinbad, writes a poem about how hard he works for very little reward. This poem reaches Sinbad the Sailor, who generously invites the poor man into his house, treats him kindly, and gives him gifts. Each day for seven days, the wealthy Sinbad tells the impoverished porter the story of one of seven great voyages. Chronologically, the seven voyages all take place during the reign of the magnificent Caliph Harun al-Rashid, meaning Aaron the Just, who richly deserved that title. A brief survey of Harun's background sheds additional light on Sinbad's many mysterious adventures.

Harun was caliph from 786 until his death in 809. While he was young, the Barmakid Viziers ran the empire along with Harun's mother. On the whole, they ran things very well: the state was powerful, prosperous, and tolerant. This was due in part to the flexible religious background of the Barmakids themselves. They had been Buddhists, then Zoroastrians, and had finally converted to Islam. Because of their Persian ancestry, they were regarded as foreigners within the caliphate and were accordingly less than popular with local nationalists and the conservative elite.

As well as his sympathy for the poor, his concern with justice, and his general high level of statesmanship, Harun was a brilliant soldier — another Alexander of Macedon. While his father was still caliph, the young Harun led an army against the Eastern Roman Empire and was within a hair's breadth of capturing Constantinople. He accepted an annual tribute of seventy thousand gold pieces a year instead, which was faithfully and regularly paid during the reign of Empress Irene. Her successor, Nicephorus, reneged on the deal, but discovered to his cost that the justice of a man like Harun cut both ways: Harun invariably kept his word, and expected others to do the same.

It was also vitally important to Harun that his deputies and officers throughout the caliphate were faithfully carrying out his wishes to improve the living conditions of his people — especially the poor. With the same personal courage that made him such an invincible soldier, Harun dressed as an ordinary citizen and went around Baghdad incognito from time to time, chatting and listening perceptively. It was not surprising that such a man became a legend in his lifetime, a role model for others — and, especially in his generosity to the poor, a role model for Sinbad the Sailor, who was also a combination of courage, honesty, ability, and generosity.

The story of Sinbad's First Voyage begins with his own family situation: Sinbad was very much like the Prodigal Son in Christ's parable. Sinbad's father, a wealthy merchant, died while Sinbad was still a young man. Lacking experience, Sinbad spent money like water until there was almost nothing left. He then decided to try to recoup his fortune, sold what little remained of his father's legacy, and took passage on a ship to Basra. He and the other merchants on board travelled from island to island, trading profitably as they went.

Attracted by one particular island, they went across to it, rested, and then began lighting fires and cooking meals. Unfortunately for the merchants and sailors, the apparent island — despite its sandy borders and small palm trees — was a gigantic marine creature. It had been asleep, or in some form of suspended animation, for so long that waterborne sand had drifted around it, and vegetation had followed. The sailors' cooking fires woke the enormous creature. Accounts of sailors mistaking vast, motionless, resting marine creatures for small islands are ubiquitous, and it is possible that it has actually happened on rare occasions. The survivors of such errors would have told and retold their stories in every port in the world. In Scheherazade's account, several of the sailors managed to get back to the ship when the gigantic creature dived — but Sinbad was among those who didn't. He was, however, miraculously saved by a wooden tub that drifted past him. Such tubs were often kept on deck to catch rainwater and to store fish caught by the mariners as they sailed in order to supplement the ship's original supplies. Among religious crewmen, they also would have served for ritual washing. The largest of these deck tubs would have been an excellent buoyancy aid — more than ample to keep a man afloat. Sinbad's emergency float finally drifted with him to an island, where he was very surprised to find a beautiful mare tethered near the beach. Shortly afterwards he discovered her groom, a servant of King Mihrjan. This man explained to Sinbad that the King's finest mares were brought to this particular island in order to be served by the mysterious sea stallions. In Scheherazade's version of Sinbad's First Voyage, these strange horses came up from the water: another unsolved mystery of the sea.

Historically, it seems more probable that they were perfectly normal stallions, kept in secrecy and seclusion on a remote but lush and fertile island within Mihrjan's aegis in order to protect a particularly good bloodline. On the other hand, there is a mysterious echo in this part of the story of the secrecy connected with the birth of King Merovée, founder of the enigmatic Merovingian Dynasty. Myths and legends state that Merovée's mother was either seduced or raped by an inexplicable sea creature referred to as a Quinotaur, which she encountered while swimming. In some versions of the legend she was already pregnant with Merovée at the time, and in some abnormal way the genetic codes of the embryo's human father were augmented by those of the Quinotaur. For whatever reason, he was always known as "Merovée the Twice-born." This particular unsolved mystery of the sea also harks back to chapter three, "Who Were the Water Gods?" in which the possibility of the existence of highly intelligent extraterrestrial amphibian visitors is explored.

Good King Mihrjan welcomed Sinbad with warm hospitality when he and the groom returned to Mihrjan's capital. In order to help Sinbad, the kindly king appointed him harbour master and registrar of shipping.

There follows an episode that parallels the biblical account of Joseph's adventures in Egypt: Sinbad's ship — the one on which he had originally embarked for Basra — turned up in Mihrjan's harbour. Just as Joseph's siblings failed to recognize their brother, Sinbad's old shipmates failed at first to recognize him. When his identity was acknowledged, Sinbad gave kindly King Mihrjan as rich a present as he could muster from the goods aboard the ship, which represented the profits of his trading prior to the problem with the sleeping sea monster. He continued to trade successfully all the way back to Baghdad and ended up far richer than he had been before he squandered what his father had left him.

An interesting pointer to the accuracy and veracity of Scheherazade's version of the Sinbad stories is her hero's honest self-analysis and introversion. Despite his happy and luxurious lifestyle in Baghdad after the great success of his First Voyage, Sinbad becomes aware of his own wanderlust and his overriding need to visit new places, to have fresh adventures, and to trade overseas again — not just to make more money, but for the sheer pleasure of trading.

It was this that set Sinbad afloat on his Second Voyage. After a successful and profitable start aboard a smart new ship, he and his fellow merchants reached a beautiful but uninhabited island. Sinbad ate well and then fell asleep in the warm sun. When he awoke, his friends had sailed without him. The Scheherazade version again reveals Sinbad's humanity and naturalness. He sinks into deep despair, wishing that he had never left his safe and luxurious home in Baghdad. His pragmatism and common sense come to his aid, and he climbs a tall tree in order to get a broad idea of the island's topography. From this vantage point, he sees what he thinks at first is the great white dome of a building in the distance: a temple, a palace, a mosque, perhaps? Action and curiosity now drive out the melancholy and depression; Sinbad sets off to investigate the great white dome.

It turns out to be a vast roc's egg, and within minutes of his arrival, the female roc comes home to cherish her gargantuan egg. The Scheherazade version mentions at this point that the roc is so huge that it eats elephants! Did the roc ever exist? Several interesting hypotheses have been put forward in connection with this unsolved ornithological mystery of the sea. The largest extinct bird of which traces were found on Madagascar was the *Aepyornis maximus* — but it was flightless and stood no more than four metres high.

The famous Venetian adventurer Marco Polo comments on Madagascar and Zanzibar. Writing in the thirteenth century, he says that the people there referred to an enormous eagle-like bird of colossal size that was capable of picking up an elephant in its talons. Its technique was to lift its prey into the air and drop it from a height in order to kill it. There was at one time a species of dwarf hippopotamus on Madagascar. Is it possible that a predatory bird of enormous size might have been able to lift one of these? Is it also possible that a linguistic misunderstanding — and/or a confusion of one pachyderm with another — might have led to the dwarf hippopotamus being mistranslated as *elephant*? Marco Polo's evidence supports Scheherazade's version of Sinbad's adventures with the roc.

According to her account of his Second Voyage, the dauntless hero uses his turban as a safety rope and ties himself to the roc's leg while it covers its ponderous egg with one huge wing. The roc eventually lands on a precipitous mountain peak where Sinbad unties his turban and alights safely. The area is full of dangerous snakes — and diamonds — and when he eventually makes a perilous descent, he has enough precious stones to buy a kingdom. He befriends a merchant — one of many who try to procure the diamonds by using animal carcasses that the eagles pick up and drop among the precious stones. The merchants then frighten away the eagles and — if they're lucky — pick up any diamonds adhering to the sticky meat. Because he has made such a lucrative haul of jewels while he was up among the perilous peaks, Sinbad generously shares them with one of the unlucky merchants, and in return he is taken back to civilization with his new friends, wealthier even than before.

Afflicted by his old, insatiable wanderlust, Sinbad sets out on his Third Voyage. After a prosperous start, the ship is blown off course and reaches the Island of the Zughb where it is attacked by the small, hirsute, ape-like islanders. These fiercely agile opponents finally steal Sinbad's ship and vanish in it, leaving the Baghdad merchants and their crew stranded on the island. After some time has passed, the marooned men explore the island and find a huge castle in the centre. Unfortunately, this is inhabited by an enormous, anthropophagous ogre, who begins devouring Sinbad's companions — just as the Cyclops dealt with Odysseus's men. As in Homer's *Odyssey,* the seafarers blind the cannibalistic giant, who returns with even more dangerous companions. Sinbad and his men take to the sea in a crude, makeshift craft. In Scheherazade's version of this Third Voyage in *The Arabian Nights,* there is a direct reference to the men paddling furiously as the seafarers endeavour to put all the distance they can between themselves and the rock-hurling ogres of Zughb Island. But where was Zughb Island, and why does the Sinbad evidence reinforce the Homeric account so strongly? And why is there this specific reference to *paddling* as distinct from *rowing*?

In the Hawaiian sea mysteries described in the next chapter, the petroglyph of a paddler is the symbol for strength. Although seagoing canoes off the east coast of Africa were paddled, the use of paddles rather than oars is associated very strongly with the Polynesian seafarers of the Pacific. Just how far did Sinbad and his companions sail before they encountered the aggressive, hirsute people of Zughb and the anthropophagous ogres on that island? Had Sinbad and his companions made their way westwards around the Cape of Good Hope, or out through the Straits of Gibraltar — known to them as the Pillars of Hercules? Nothing was impossible to such men.

Their furious paddling eventually brings them to an island, only to find that the peril here is a gigantic serpent: far more deadly than the cannibalistic ogres from whom they just escaped. Sinbad, however, does escape, and is finally rescued by the captain and crew of the ship on which his goods had been left when he was inadvertently abandoned on the Island of the Roc. Before returning to Baghdad, however, he lists all the strange marine creatures he encounters in these wild and unknown waters. Among them he lists gigantic turtles, which — when the paddling references are also given their due significance — *might* indicate that they were in the South Pacific rather than the Indian Ocean or Arabian Sea.

There are also possible tenuous links between Sinbad's Third Voyage encounters with the small, hirsute islanders from Zughb and the legends of the small, ancient Hawaiian race referred to in a number of myths, legends, and ancient traditions as the Menehune. In one particular Hawaiian legend known as "The Maid of the Golden Cloud," the Menehune people make a large seagoing vessel in the forests of Waolani. Scheherazade's version of Sinbad's Third Voyage describes the small people of Zughb as dangerous ship-takers. The Hawaiian version describes them as skilful ship-makers. Could they be one and the same people viewed from different perspectives?

As on his two earlier mysterious voyages, Sinbad finally returns to Baghdad after his Third Voyage richer than ever before.

The Fourth Voyage introduces some elementary but practical sociology, just as psychology found its way into the earlier voyages. This time Sinbad decides to leave the peaceful wealth and luxury of Baghdad as a result of the social pressure from a group of his peers who call to see him and spend their time discussing the joys and excitements of mercantile adventures in distant lands. Predictably, the Fourth Voyage starts well enough, but it is interesting to note while trying to solve the sea mysteries of Sinbad's voyages that Scheherazade's version includes not only the phrase *from island to island* but expressly adds *and from sea to sea*. Sailors of Sinbad's epoch considered the various seas and oceans over which they travelled to be qualitatively discrete. This implies that the phrase *from sea to sea* indicated a long journey encompassing widely separated parts of the world: another small clue to his going as far as the Pacific.

After the vessel is severely damaged in a squall, which causes it to sink, Sinbad and a few fellow merchants drift to the shores of yet another cannibal kingdom, where his companions are duly fattened and eaten. Sinbad escapes and walks to a neighbouring kingdom. The realism of Scheherazade's narrative is now reinforced by basic economic theory to complement her psychology and sociology. The people in this realm ride their horses without saddles and bridles. Sinbad teaches them the basic arts of saddlery, and because of the economic principle of supply and demand, his rare and highly utilitarian leather goods command a high price.

Everything in this kingdom goes well for him, and at the king's insistence, Sinbad marries a rich and beautiful lady. What he doesn't know at the time is that there is an inviolable custom in this culture: when either partner dies, the survivor is placed in the tomb with the dead spouse. To his horror, his wife becomes ill and dies. Sinbad pleads that, as a foreigner, he ought to be exempt from the local burial customs. His argument falls on deaf ears, and he is incarcerated with his dead partner. As each new doomed spouse is sealed up in the vast mausoleum, Sinbad's ruthless piratical streak — his supercharged survival instinct — comes to the fore. Reasoning with himself that the survivors will soon die anyway, Sinbad clubs them to death with a hefty femur he's found lying around in this dismal Cave of the Dead. In his ethical code, it seems to be a form of euthanasia. He then subsists on the food and water that each had brought to extend their last hours in this gloomy burial cave. It is customary in this strange land to bury the dead with all their possessions — especially their money and jewellery — and as well as stealing the scant provisions of food and water from the doomed surviving spouses, Sinbad helps himself to the valuables surrounding those who were dead when they were deposited in the cave.

Finally, hearing a scavenging animal at work among the bones, Sinbad realizes that it must have found its way into the dismal cavern-tomb somehow. Following it reveals to him a light in the distance, which he discovers is another way out on the far side. He eventually scrambles out through a rock fissure and settles down to wait for a passing ship. A vessel duly arrives, rescues him, and eventually ensures his safe return to Baghdad. The proceeds of his grave-robbing activities ensure that — as on all his earlier excursions — the wily and ruthless Sinbad comes home richer than he was when he left.

This ruthless, grave-robbing, murdering Sinbad is far less admirable than the hero of the first three voyages — yet he is, if anything, more bluntly honest and grimly realistic than the character revealed to the reader in the earlier adventures. His determination to *survive* regardless of moral scruples and ethical prohibitions makes him clearly discernible as a genuine historical character. This is no jovial pantomime hero: this is a strong, flesh and blood human being driven to his limits by adverse circumstances.

The most memorable and significant component of the Fifth Voyage is Sinbad's encounter with the Old Man of the Sea. This strange, parasitic creature seems to be a distorted representation of one of the mysterious divine, semi-divine, or demonic characters analyzed in chapter three, "Who were the Water Gods?" Taking Greek and Roman pantheons into account, the Old Man of the Sea may be an indistinct recollection of some enemy of Bacchus, the god of wine — because it was by using wine that Sinbad was able to get the fatal parasite off his shoulders and kill it. Here in this Fifth Voyage, Sinbad's realistic ruthlessness and determination are effective, but there is far more moral justification for them when he fights the Old Man of the Sea than in his treatment of the doomed spouses in the mausoleum cavern.

Having returned in triumph from his Fifth Voyage, Sinbad resolves to remain in the secure and comfortable luxury of his magnificent home in Baghdad. This resolve lasts only until he meets up with another party of loquacious merchant friends and sets off on his Sixth Voyage. Scheherazade's effective and dependable narrative formula is clearly evident once again as this mystery of the sea unfolds.

The ship is blown off course into what the captain describes as a strange, unknown sea of which he has no previous experience. The vessel is eventually wrecked on a rocky, surf-battered island coast. Sinbad's companions gradually die of hunger and disease, until he is once more the sole survivor. He travels across the island's mountains — which are rich in jewels — and finally reaches a small river. By its banks he constructs a raft, only a little narrower than the walls of the nearby cavernous tunnel into which the river makes its way to unknown, subterranean depths.

Sinbad climbs aboard his makeshift raft and drifts on it into the shadowy gloom of the tunnel. He drifts a long way in the dark, but finally emerges into a pleasant and civilized area, where he is taken to meet the kindly and generous king of the island. Just as things went from bad to worse when the ship was wrecked, everything now goes incredibly right for Sinbad. One stroke of good luck follows another. He learns that the island is called Sarandib, also spelled Serendip, and that it is roughly eighty leagues long by thirty wide. (A league is an anachronistic measure of approximately three miles, about five kilometres.) He also reports that Serendip must be close to the equator because its days and nights are of equal length. Sinbad's attention is also drawn to a very tall, steep mountain on the island, to its delicious fruits and fragrant herbs and spices. He also describes the profusion of jewels and precious stones to be found there.

These factors taken together make a case for the mysterious island of Serendip being Kauai in the Hawaiian archipelago. The captain of the merchants' ship was dismayed to find that he had inadvertently sailed into an ocean he didn't know at all. Had he sailed as far as the Pacific? Kauai is mountainous, with a peak of over five thousand feet. Most significant of all the similarities is the tunnel. We have friends on Kauai who told us while we were working there in 2004 how they had travelled by raft for many hours down one of the long, dark tunnels that carry water below the mountainous island. Kauai is not on the equator, as Serendip was supposed to be, but it is not far north of it, and day and night there are reasonably close to each other in length. Kauai is called the Garden Island with sound justification: its fruits and herbs are excellent, as were those Sinbad found on Serendip.

The English author and politician Horace Walpole (1717–1797) used Serendip as the name of the country in one of his stories, *The Three Princes of Serendip*: the three princes of the title continually made unexpected happy discoveries. The name Serendip may have been derived from the old name for Ceylon, now Sri Lanka. It is perfectly feasible that Sinbad's Sixth Voyage took him up to Sri Lanka in the Indian Ocean — a little closer to the equator than Kauai. What is much less probable is that the ship's captain would have been distressed and anxious there, or thought that he was in a strange ocean. The mariners and merchant adventurers of Sinbad's time were perfectly familiar with the Indian Ocean and its islands. Whether Sinbad and his companions reached Kauai must remain for the time being — until more evidence is available — another unsolved mystery of the sea.

Was this one of the hazardous rocky coasts on which Sinbad's vessel was wrecked?

Did Sinbad climb these mysterious mountains?

Sinbad's Seventh Voyage contains the mystery of the three gigantic sea monsters big enough to swallow an entire ship. This narrative of Scheherazade's can be linked to the detailed descriptions and analyses in chapter four, "Monsters of the Deep." Before any of the huge creatures could destroy the ship, however, it was caught by a sudden storm and driven onto the shoreline, where it was smashed to pieces. Sinbad was rescued by the servants of a kindly and generous old sheik who ruled the territory. He treated Sinbad very well indeed and offered him his beautiful daughter as a bride, on the understanding that the young couple would rule the old sheik's territory after his death. After his earlier marriage — and the horror of being buried alive with his dead bride — Sinbad's hesitation is understandable. But no such morbid burial customs applied in the sheik's territories, and Sinbad duly married the benevolent old man's daughter.

They lived happily together for several years until the old sheik went to his eternal reward. Sinbad — now the ruler of the sheikdom — was intrigued and overwhelmed with curiosity by the strange power that enabled some of his citizens periodically to change into birds and fly. He finally persuaded them to take him with them, and after several of his characteristic hair's-breadth escapes from death and destruction, Sinbad returned safely to his lovely bride. Unlike his first wife, this lady — who was as kind and affectionate as her father had been — continued to live happily with him, and they finally returned to Baghdad together, where they lived in luxury for the rest of their long and happy lives.

Like Jason and Odysseus before him, Sinbad the Sailor occupies a substantial place in factual history — as well as making contributions to myth and legend. These three heroes have left many an unsolved mystery of the sea in their wake.

CHAPTER SIXTEEN

Sea Mysteries of the Hawaiian Islands

The Hawaiian Islands are among the most mysterious places on Earth, as well as the most beautiful. One of their many intriguing sea mysteries is linked with the curious Hawaiian petroglyphs. The word comes from the Greek *petros*, meaning *stone*, and *glyphe*, meaning *sculpting* or *carving*. A petroglyph can, therefore, be defined as a picture or symbol carved into a stone surface.

How did the petroglyph makers reach the islands? Who were they? Where did they come from? And what do the symbols really mean? Some of the petroglyph traditions assert that the Hawaiian volcano goddess, Pele, brought the designs and the methods of making them with her. But who was Pele?

Described as fair-haired and light-skinned, the beautiful, awesomely powerful Pele came from over the sea. How far? And from which direction? The answers to these questions may solve some of the riddles of the petroglyphs. Some of the oldest European petroglyphs are estimated to be at least ten thousand years old — perhaps considerably more. Others, far more recent, date from comparatively modern times.

In the early seventeenth century, an academic named Peder Alfson described petroglyphs he'd discovered in Bohuslan in southwestern Sweden. The designs included animals, means of transport, weapons, and human forms. The Hawaiian petroglyphs are strikingly similar in some ways to the ones from Bohuslan that Alfson described nearly four centuries ago.

Many of the most significant and mysterious Hawaiian petroglyphs can be seen at Pu'uloa, which means *the long hill*. According to some ancient Hawaiian traditions it was to Pu'uloa that Pele came from

Swedish and Hawaiian petroglyph diagram.

over "many great high and curving waves." These petroglyphs are called *kaha ki'i* in Hawaiian. *Kaha* means *to scratch* or *to mark* and *ki'i* is *a design* or *picture.*

There are numerous theories as to whether this Pele, traditionally thought of as the goddess in charge of the great volcano, was a real prehistoric character or simply part of an ancient religious tradition. In several accounts Pele was said to have travelled *vast* distances over seas and oceans, and it is important to remember, as noted already, that she had very fair hair and light skin. Linking Hawaiian and Swedish petroglyphs creates the very real possibility that Pele was a Norse, or Viking, princess.

Theoretically, her voyage would have been via Iceland, Greenland, around the northwestern ice of Canada, then south past Alaska and down the Pacific coast of America. Finally, with favourable winds and currents, her Viking longboats could have reached Hawaii — an incredible journey, but not an impossible one.

Pele is unlikely to have acquired the status of a goddess, especially a very powerful volcanic goddess, unless she had demonstrated unusual powers in that area.

The *post hoc ergo propter hoc* fallacy comes in here. What if coincidence (whatever coincidence, or synchronicity, really *is*) had either just started, or just completed, an eruption at the moment when Pele and her people landed on Hawaii? The "after this, therefore because of this" fallacy might have raised her status dramatically. The fallacy of causation by association is as old as human thought.

A totally different and much more mysterious tradition brings the goddess Pele from Mu and not from Sweden. Mu, largely synonymous with the Lemurian tradition, delves deeply into mysticism, metaphysics, theology, and philosophy, as well as the strangest enigmas of human origins.

A remarkable exposition of these possible human origins comes from *Lemurian Scrolls* by Satguru Sivaya Subramuniyaswami. In a series of what he describes as mystical visions, Sivaya tells how he believes mankind migrated to Earth countless ages ago because they needed what he describes as a "Fire Planet" in order to progress. In Sivaya's view, in what he believes he was taught by the Lemurian Scrolls, our etheric, non-physical human ancestors began to solidify and materialize into something eventually recognizable as contemporary human beings.

Sivaya also refers to a very advanced being, Lord Skanda, whom he describes as the Celestial King of Lemuria.

The essence of Sivaya's mystical descriptions suggests that there was a transition from a non-material state of being to a physical one. The non-material original, however, according to Sivaya, seems to experience a chronic feeling of discontent and of entrapment within the physical body. Modern psychology and psychiatry are well aware of the frequency with which feelings of depression, discontent, futility, and dissatisfaction with life afflict a great many people.

The mystical Lemurian explanation of human origins as put forward by Sivaya in *Lemurian Scrolls* runs in parallel for a mile or two with the experiences of modern psychotherapists.

Sivaya also refers to what he believes to be the mystery of flight still retained by some of the higher souls not heavily materialized or entrapped in physical bodies — human or animal.

One of the greatest mysteries of the beautiful garden island of Kauai is the Lemurian mountaintop monastery where the enigmas of *Lemurian Scrolls* are still taught today to honest, dedicated, and sincere open-minded seekers after truth. It is well worth visiting the monastery's website: http://www.hindu.org/ka. Relating these mystical teachings from *Lemurian Scrolls* to other ancient arcane and esoteric traditions from the remote past, there is an immediate nexus with the four-element theory of the alchemists. *Lemurian Scrolls* emphasizes the migrating entities' need of a fire planet in order to develop further. The complementary, *combinative* powers of fire are one side of the alchemical equation air, earth, and water, but the four traditional elements are also said to be capable of dynamic *conflicts*. When fire and water met, alchemists believed that these conflictual elemental dynamics were capable of releasing vast unknown powers.

These interactions are seen at their most potent, according to ancient alchemical lore, when an enormous volume of water — such as a sea or ocean — is interfaced with an equally awesome amount of fire — such as a volcano.

Volcanic islands such as those in the Hawaiian group are, therefore, according to *both* Lemurian and alchemical tradition, likely to be significant sites of paranormal and anomalous phenomena. Such sea-fire islands are undeniably rich in myths and legends that permeate their ancient cultures. Some of these myths and legends that relate to the lost land of Mu, also known as Lemuria, connect with the volcano goddess Pele. If there is any kind of historical reality behind these lost land versions of her origins, it rests on the existence at one time of a real geographical continent in the Pacific where the volcanic Hawaiian Islands stand today.

This particular unsolved mystery of the sea suggests that the very ancient Lemurian civilization occupied a small continent, or an extremely large island, located in the vicinity of the present Hawaiian archipelago. In these legends, the ancient Lemurians, or Mu-onians, apparently possessed limited powers of levitation, but it was not sufficient to save more than a tiny minority of them when the volcanic trauma destroyed much of their homeland.

They were alleged to have had some degree of telepathic communication, limited powers of telekinesis, and advanced knowledge science, mathematics, and astronomy. They were also believed to have possessed significant healing powers and medical and pharmaceutical skills — especially herbalism.

The legends referring to Lemurian powers of levitation, telepathy, and telekinesis are in harmony with much of what is hinted at in *Lemurian Scrolls.* Their advanced knowledge of maths, science, medicine, and astronomy is also compatible with the information given about Lemurians in those ancient mystical sources.

If Pele was a survivor from the destruction of Mu, and if she was one of the minority of Lemurians, the highly advanced, cultural, and technologic elite, might she have possessed enough telekinetic power to divert one or two lava streams, or to direct some of the dangerous floodwater resulting from the volcanic trauma?

Consider a geological phenomenon in which the continent of Mu is traumatized by earthquakes, volcanoes, or both. Some of the very powerful Mu-onian elite are able to escape, but they can only divert or delay tides of floodwater and blazing lava. Pele and a few others reach the mountaintops and highland areas of what is now the Hawaiian archipelago. Her powers are just about sufficient to play a positive role in saving lives and limiting damage during the chaos.

These interventions are witnessed by other survivors. Their accounts become part of the legend of Pele, goddess and controller of the volcano.

There are numerous other strange unsolved mysteries in Hawaii, a great many of them connected with the sea. Just as bleak inland areas, dark forests, and open wildernesses were the territory of legendary werewolves and vampires, so wild, white, dangerous waters became the habitat of shark-men and shark gods.

One of these legends concerns Kauhuhu, otherwise known to expert folklorists as the Molokai shark god. Sometimes the myth is retold as the story of *Aikanaka* which means *man-eater*. Aikanaka is the old name for Pukoo, a small harbour on Molokai.

One story of Kauhuhu begins with Kamalo, a priest whose temple was situated at Kaluaaha, a small village overlooking the narrow waterway separating Molokai and Maui. The mountain known as Eeke towered above Kaluaaha, and the priest's two brave young sons enjoyed many adventures in the water and on the mountain's steep, red slopes. Unfortunately, their boldness led them to the sacred enclosure — which was strictly taboo — belonging to a great chieftain and magician named Kupa. Kupa's greatest magical skills lay in his "talking drums." While he was away fishing, the two venturesome boys trespassed into his sacred enclosure and played his forbidden drums.

Servants and subjects of Kupa reported the boys to him, and he ordered the servants whose special role it was to provide his temple with sacrifices to kill the boys. They did. Kamalo heard of his sons' deaths and went out to seek vengeance against Kupa. Kamalo's problem was that Kupa was far more powerful than he was. Fear of Kupa prevented other priests, wise men and women, magicians, and prophets from helping Kamalo. They sympathized with his cause, but they were afraid to do anything to help him in case news of their involvement reached the deadly and vengeful Kupa. The most they did was to pass him on to the next wise man or woman.

At last, close to despair, Kamalo made his way down the precipitous slopes to the temple of the shark god, Kauhuhu. Here, the story was the same: the priest of the shark god refused to aid Kamalo because he was afraid of Kupa's retribution — but he did direct Kamalo to a cave called *Anaopuhi*, the *Cave of the Eels*.

In Anaopuhi the legendary sea dragons known as Waka and Mo-o guarded the terrifying shark god, Kauhuhu.

The movements of the waves and surf played a significant role in legends of the shark god. In many western traditions, it is the seventh wave that is the largest or most magically important one. In the Hawaiian myths and legends it is the *eighth* wave that matters most.

According to Vincent Tylor, an expert on Lemuria and on the ancient, mystical art of card reading, the ace of hearts represents Lemuria, but the eight of hearts stands for Mu. Together they equal the nine of hearts, the trinity of trinities, the mystical square of three. This highly significant and symbolic number was also revered by the ancient Pythagoreans. They in turn were recognized by their contemporaries as magicians as well as mathematicians.

In ancient Egypt, the Brotherhood of the Knotted Rope were said to have been in great demand because they had access to the secret of creating a perfect right angle, which was essential for building vast temples, statues, and pyramids. They simply took three — the key to their secret — then added four and five to create a Pythagorean right-angled triangle. The square of three (the symbolic nine) added to the square of four (sixteen) gave the square of five (twenty-five). Nine plus sixteen equalled twenty-five and proved the Pythagorean theorem that the areas of the two small squares of a right-angled triangle equalled the area of the large square, the one constructed on the hypotenuse. It had not escaped these early mathematical explorers that the side of four units added to the side of five units also brought them back to their mysterious nine. Neither did it escape them that the digits two and five (making the twenty-five square units of the largest square) also added to make the mystical, magical seven that was a vital aspect of Pythagorean precepts.

So Vincent Tylor's expert analysis of card symbolism is echoed by the old Pythagorean knowledge.

Co-author Lionel also teaches mathematics and discovered what is published as "Fanthorpe's third constant." This is highly relevant to the importance of three and the square of three.

Finding the length of the diagonal of a cube is normally a two-stage process. The diagonal of a face is found first using traditional Pythagorean geometry. The cube is then turned so that this diagonal of the face (XZ) becomes the base of another right-angled triangle (XYZ), the hypotenuse of which is the diagonal of the whole cube (XY). Fanthorpe's third constant is the square root of three, an irrational number like the Greek π. When the side of the cube is multiplied by this square root of three, the answer is the diagonal of the cube — found by one swift simple calculation using Fanthorpe's third constant.

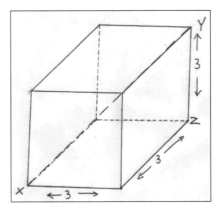

Diagram of cube diagonal.

Back now from Pythagorean mathematics to the significance of the eighth wave in the legend of Kauhuhu, the awesome shark god. The eighth wave was so huge and so high that it broke right inside Anaopuhi, the Eel-cave. From the deluge of its foaming crest strode Kauhuhu in his human form. Despite his terrifying power and raging anger, Kauhuhu was merciful to Kamalo and promised to help him avenge the deaths of his sons.

Once again, curious old number magic enters into this unsolved mystery of the Hawaiian sea. The shark god promised Kamalo that he, the great and terrible Kauhuhu, would be his *kahu,* or guardian, and ensure that Kupa was duly punished for killing Kamalo's sons. Kauhuhu ordered Kamalo to collect four hundred black pigs, four hundred white chickens, and four hundred red fish. If the first four numbers most significant to numerologists are taken as one, three, seven, and nine, these numbers together add to twenty, and twenty squared is four hundred. To a numerologist it would also be significant that there were three groups of four hundred each and the creatures in groups represented air (the birds), water (the fish), and earth (the pigs). When the groups were complete, there were twelve hundred creatures altogether. Numerological technique adds the digits one, two, and the zeros to reach the magical three once more. The more closely this sea mystery of the shark god is analyzed, the more intriguing its numerology becomes.

Numerology is one of the more culturally advanced techniques of prediction and divination. It requires an above average level of number skills. It also requires a sophisticated capacity for abstract thought. The intricate numerology woven throughout the legend of Kamalo and Kauhuhu the shark god suggests that it originated in an advanced culture: Lemuria or Mu?

The shark god kept his promise to Kamalo by appearing one day as a small white cloud of a type Kamalo recognized as supernaturally strange. This white cloud grew alarmingly and huge black clouds soon followed it, like some vast and terrifying army of the sky. Lightning flashed from the black cloud-warriors. The white cloud that was Kauhuhu, the shark god, led his destroyers to the head of the valley where Kupa ruled. From the enormous black clouds rain fell in torrents. Its power was irresistible. The sides of Kupa's valley were devastated and washed down towards him and his doomed people. His sacred place, or *heiau,* was smashed to pieces by the flood, and Kupa and all his people were swept away into the sea by that thundering avalanche of mud and water.

But Kauhuhu had not yet finished with Kupa. The shark god had called all his shark-people to enjoy a memorable feast: they were waiting in the ocean where the avalanche plunged into the Pacific. Kupa, his family, and his disciples were eagerly devoured by Kauhuhu's shark-people.

This event, or something very similar on which it was closely based, almost certainly took place in the area in the remote past. The small harbour near Kupa's region is named *Aikanaka,* meaning *the place of the man-eaters.* The unsolved mystery of the sea associated with Aikanaka is *how* and *why* so many sharks gathered in the same place at the same time. Did they contact one another as whales and dolphins do? Did something *external* call them, or cause them to congregate there in Aikanaka? If so, was that something the same mysterious force the ancient Hawaiian legends call Kauhuhu, the shark god?

In addition to the legends and myths surrounding the shark god himself, other unsolved sea mysteries of the Pacific focus on lesser beings, the were-sharks. One of the most dangerous of these was known as Nanaue. In addition to Kauhuhu, there was another prominent shark leader known as Kamohoalii. Like Kauhuhu, Kamohoalii was able to appear in human form when it suited him. According to the legend of the birth of Nanaue, the were-shark, Kamohoalii saw a beautiful girl, Kalei, bathing in the surf as he swam below her in his shark shape.

That night, he assumed his human form and went in search of Kalei. He was tall, graceful, and powerful in this human form and soon won Kalei's love. Soon after their wedding, she became pregnant with Kamohoalii's son. Sadly he told her that he must go on a very long journey and would never be able to see her again. Then he gave the tearful young expectant mother strict instructions about the care of their son who was soon to be born. He never once let Kalei know that he was really Kamohoalii, King of the Sharks. His main instructions to Kalei were that the boy's body would be unusual in some way and must be kept hidden. He also said that their son should never be allowed to eat meat.

When Nanaue was born, Kalei was anxious about an aperture in her son's back, but she said nothing about it to anyone and kept it carefully covered with a *kapa* cloak. As he grew older, this aperture widened and deepened. Rows of sharp, predatory teeth grew inside it. It came to resemble the mouth of a shark, and Kalei became increasingly worried when Nanaue began to consume small birds, animals, and fish through this gruesome miniature shark's mouth set into his back. His own feelings about his strange abnormality are not recorded in the mythology. It does, however, note that when young Nanaue went into the water, he assumed his full shark form and ate voraciously. Although she watched in horror, Kalei still had natural maternal feelings for her were-shark son.

Things took a fateful turn for the worse when Nanaue reached the age when he was regarded as an adult male. His grandfather, Kalei's father, according to custom, took Nanaue to eat with the other men. Kalei could no longer control his diet, and Nanaue began to gorge him-

Mysterious Wailua Falls on Kauai — the island of the were-shark legends.

self on the meat dishes available in the men's eating house. He was insatiable. There was no limit to his appetite for meat, and the more meat he devoured, the more he resembled his carnivorous aquatic father.

The first climax came when his kapa cape was torn from his back during seasonal work on the taro areas where food was grown by the residents of Waipio. Cries of horror and alarm echoed from the crowd of villagers. Nanaue fought them on all sides, severing a limb here, crushing a skull there. Dealing out mayhem all around him, he fought his way towards the sea. Despite his strength and razor sharp teeth, the villagers trapped him, but he escaped. He was later recaptured and killed.

David Richarde, the bishop of Hawaii for the Interdenominational Templar Church, has a very deep, expert knowledge of cetaceans, and of dolphin intelligence and communication in particular. The authors had the pleasure and privilege of meeting Bishop David and his family when we were carrying out research for this volume and filming in Kauai in January 2004. Dolphins are one of the sea's greatest unsolved mysteries. Just how intelligent are they? And how can their intelligence be measured?

Brain size is positively correlated with intelligence, but size is not the only factor. Dolphins have very large brains — bigger than human brains, in fact. The number of convolutions of the outer cortex of the brain — the structure that gives it its walnut-like appearance — is also positively correlated with intelligence, and dolphins have highly convoluted cerebral cortices.

In order to analyze brain function and intelligence in any depth, it's useful to describe its topography. Mammalian brains — like ours — have a paleocortex as a foundation. This is very similar to the brain of a fish, a reptile, or an amphibian. It's pretty basic, and is usually referred to as the rhinic lobe, because it was once thought to relate primarily to the sense of smell. The Greek word *rhinos* means *nose*. This is more or less encapsulated, or overlaid, by the limbic lobe, named from the Latin word *limbus*, meaning an *edge, fence,* or *border*. Above these two is the supralimbic lobe, and surrounding all three is the neocortex — an immensely complicated net, or canopy, of intertwined brain cells. According to current neurological science, our thoughts, problem-solving intelligence, and emotional feelings are all generated somewhere in here. A few more centuries of research may lead to different conclusions.

Arthur Koestler (1905–1983), the brilliant Hungarian-born writer and philosopher, deservedly captured a hugely enthusiastic readership with *Darkness at Noon* (1940), *The Ghost in the Machine* (1967), and *The Roots of Coincidence* (1972). Koestler was fascinated by unsolved mysteries — especially mysteries of the mind and brain. On one occasion he argued that when a psychiatrist invites a client to lie down on the couch, he is inviting him to lie down beside a horse and a crocodile. There could be no better way to sum up the functions of the three-fold human brain.

When brains and intelligence are being compared among different species, there are researchers who believe that it is possible to observe and measure the relative levels of primary sensory processing — how much of the brain is concerned with what is seen, heard, tasted, smelled, and touched — and associative ability — how much of the brain is used for associative skills, cognition, and problem solving, otherwise known as *general intelligence.* According to some researchers in this field, a rat uses nine-tenths of its brain for sensory processing, and only one-tenth for problem solving. A cat uses approximately one-half for each. The higher anthropoid apes use about one-quarter sensory to three-quarters problem solving. Human beings in these researches averaged one-tenth sensory, which leaves us with nine-tenths for problem solving — an approximate reversal of the rat's ratio. In this set of comparisons, human beings seem well ahead of our mammalian rivals, but the picture is significantly changed when we compete brain-for-brain with cetaceans such as dolphins. Their cetacean brains have an *extra* cortical lobe that we just haven't got!

No IQ tests have yet been devised that would enable the researcher to compare human intelligence with, say, whale or dolphin intelligence, but the incredible fact remains that if we base our assumptions of species intelligence on the relative proportions of how much brain is used for sensory functions and how much is left spare for thinking and problem solving, the cetaceans look as if they might score ten or twenty times our human score! This apparent anomaly has to be balanced by considering the factors we describe as manipulation, technology, and tool-making. Human beings are manipulators. Cetaceans are not.

Yet another factor that suggests high intelligence in association with the brain structure of dolphins is that they have something that appears to be a sense of humour. Dolphins are undeniably playful, and are frequently observed to behave in ways that suggest they possess a well-developed and sophisticated sense of humour. Dr. Sterling Bunnell has been quoted as suggesting that playfulness and humour are indicators of high intelligence.

It was a pleasure and privilege for us to be able to interview Bishop David Richarde on Kauai recently, and we are very grateful to him for his kind permission to include a number of his exciting ideas about the mystery of the cetaceans in this chapter. In addition to his specialized knowledge of cetacean intelligence, Bishop David is an expert on the mysteries associated with the Graal, the enigma of the Arcadian treasure, and what he refers to in one of his deeply moving philosophical poems as "Arcadian Memory." The influence of his communication with the cetaceans he so loves and admires comes through powerfully in his poems:

> … something more than Life's presence takes over.
> Breathless sigh … faint to the threshold …
> Child of the Universe, no more, no less.
> You are returned before all illusion of pain existed,
> All illusion of separation, all illusion of time and space.

Referring to the awesome tones of the cetaceans he has studied and admired for so long, David also writes in "Adonaisai: for and by Cerulean Cetacean":

> By this Tone the Touch of Reception
> May return to All,
> And that Love reside in the Sharing
> Of the Blue Paradise Triune.

When we interviewed Bishop David about his encounters with cetaceans, he said:

> My first encounter with them was off the coast of Florida in 1967. Many years later on my first visit to California in 1978, I began swimming with grey whales near Malibu Beach. Two years later I moved to Hawaii and began regularly swimming with dolphins — many times being surrounded within a ring of them, penetrated with sonar. For those who have not experienced this sonar communication, it can be overwhelming. It encompasses images, vibration, and sound quite different from what human communication is aware of.
>
> In 1980, I met three humpbacks off Poipu, Kauai. This was a radical departure from contact and infor-

mation garnered via dolphins. The encounter was written up in the *Garden Island* paper, as there were many witnesses. It took twenty years to understand what that encounter — the whales surrounding me, rolling above water to look, placing their fins above and around my head — an encounter full of "the touch of tone" comprised. Looking above water to gaze at humans is very rare for whales, an intimacy of great honour. Many other encounters augmented the sharing of the breath of life. The cetacean record (akashic, breath of life) of the "grail" (we use this only as some vague reference to "who is served by it?" or "how does one serve it?") is over 400 million years long.

Bishop David is implying here that the vast cetacean intelligence is more concerned with imprinting and reading the mysterious Akashic, or Akasic, Record (both spellings are acceptable) than human intelligence is — but it seems highly likely that cetacean-human partnership and co-operation would enable the human participants to increase their Akasic literacy significantly. These Akasic Records themselves may best be defined as a concept found in the metaphysics of India. In essence, the Akasic Records theory suggests that they are a gigantic repository of the *total memories* from every incarnation of every intelligent being. Certain gifted individuals (human, cetacean, or otherwise) are thought to be able to extract information from these records. In theory, this could not only provide them with detailed information about past events, but could also enable them to make abnormally accurate predictions about the future, extrapolated from that vast reservoir of data.

It was also pointed out by Bishop David that the mystical connection between the mysteries of the sea and the strange Arcadian treasure could well have another important link with the enigma of the cetaceans. He reminded us that dolphins have five fins, and that the tradition of Merovée the Twice-Born, founder of the Merovingian Dynasty and a highly significant figure in the Arcadian enigma, involved his having a sea father as well as an earthly one. The possession of five fins would qualify a dolphin as a Quinotaur, the *quin* part of the name representing *five*, and the *taur* part being a *bull*. Dolphins are referred to as "bulls of the sea," and David's researches had led him to the parallel case of Princess Aithra, whose experiences had apparently been similar to those of Merovée's mother. Aithra, the mother of the famous Greek hero

Theseus, was said in the legend to have been pregnant by her husband, Aigeus, *and* Poseidon (or one of his aquatic minions such as a Quinotaur) *simultaneously*. Sweeping aside all the other mythical and legendary accretions, is there a suggestion that Theseus's great strength, intelligence, and courage came from non-human, aquatic genes?

David also commented on the similarity between the words *dolphin* and *dauphin* (the title of an historic French royal ruler), a similarity that could owe its origins to the Merovée tradition.

One of the greatest and most beneficial of that category of sea mysteries that is associated with dolphins, as Bishop David explained to us during our interview with him, is their ability to provide communication therapy for autistic children. In his opinion, dolphins are able to exert healing powers in other areas, too. His final comments to us were particularly interesting:

> Encounters of a mystical kind with cetaceans have similar effects on people from around the world — even when these people have never been apprised of what may happen. In other words, something is afoot (afin?) that is beyond our understanding. People who have swum with dolphins may have extraordinary dreams of sacred geometry. The principal forms? Hexagonal crystallography, rhomboid dodecahedrons, etcetera. In a sense they [the cetaceans] are teaching people the essence of spherical space. In fact, some have related that the dolphins will actually create these forms with their own bodies while sharing in the open sea. These effects are so consistent that more research is needed to establish the pattern of very real information hidden in these communications.

And so, on this high, optimistic note of what the future of human-cetacean partnership could yield, our selection of unsolved mysteries of the sea reaches its conclusion.

BIBLIOGRAPHY

Beckwith, Martha. *Hawaiian Mythology.* Hawaii: University of Hawaii Press, 1976.

Blashford-Snell, John. *Mysteries: Encounters with the Unexplained.* London: Bodley Head Ltd., 1983.

Blundell, Nigel. *The World's Greatest Mysteries.* London: Octopus Books Ltd., 1984.

Bord, Janet and Colin. *Mysterious Britain.* London: Granada, 1974.

Brennan, Herbie. *The Atlantis Enigma.* London: Judy Piarkus Publishers Ltd., 1999.

Briggs, Katharine M. *British Folk Tales and Legends: A Sampler.* London: Granada Publishing in Paladin, 1977.

Brookesmith, Peter, (Ed.). *Open Files.* London: Orbis Publishing, 1984.

Brown, Michael, (Ed.). *A Book of Sea Legends.* Harmondsworth: Puffin Books, 1974.

Cavendish, Richard, (Ed.). *Encyclopaedia of the Unexplained.* London: Routledge & Kegan Paul, 1974.

Clark, Jerome. *Unexplained.* United States: Gale Research Inc., 1993.

Childress, David Hatcher. *Lost Cities of Atlantis, Ancient Europe & The Mediterranean*. United States: Adventures Unlimited Press, 1996.

Cohen, Daniel. *Encyclopaedia of Ghosts*. London: Guild Publishing, 1989.

Crosby, Yvette, (Ed.). *Zento Hawaii*. Hawaii: Zento Media Inc, 2003.

Dixon, G. M. *Folktales and Legends of Norfolk*. Peterborough: Minimax Books, 1983.

Dobbs, Horace. *Journey into Dolphin Dreamtime*. London: Jonathan Cape, 1993.

Dyall, Valentine. *Unsolved Mysteries*. London: Hutchinson & Co. Ltd., 1954.

Edwards, Frank. *Stranger Than Science*. New York: Ace Books Inc., 1959.

Eysenck, H. J. and Carl Sargent. *Explaining the Unexplained*. London: BCA, 1993.

Encyclopaedia Britannica. Britannica Online: http://www.eb.com.

Fanthorpe, Patricia & Lionel. *The Holy Grail Revealed*. California: Newcastle Publishing Co. Inc., 1982.

———. *The Oak Island Mystery*. Toronto: Hounslow Press, 1995.

———. *Secrets of Rennes le Château*. Maine: Samuel Weiser Inc., 1992.

———. *The World's Greatest Unsolved Mysteries*. Toronto: Hounslow Press, 1997.

———. *The World's Most Mysterious People*. Toronto: Hounslow Press, 1998.

———. *The World's Most Mysterious Places*. Toronto: Hounslow Press, 1999.

———. *Mysteries of the Bible*. Toronto: Hounslow Press, 1999.

Flem-Ath, Rand & Rose. *In Search of Atlantis*. Toronto: Stoddart Publishing, 1995.

Fowke, Edith. *Canadian Folklore*. Don Mills, Ontario: Oxford University Press, 1988.

Godwin, John. *This Baffling World*. New York: Hart Publishing Company, 1968.

Goldsmith, Oliver. *History of the Earth and Animated Nature*. Edinburgh: Thomas Nelson, 1842.

Graves, Robert. "Introduction." In *Larousse Encyclopaedia of Mythology*. London. Paul Hamlyn, 1959.

Guerber, H. A. *Myths and Legends of the Middle Ages*. London: Studio Editions Ltd., 1994.

Haining, Peter. *The Restless Bones and Other True Mysteries*. London: Armada Books, 1970.

Hapgood, Charles H. *Maps of the Ancient Sea Kings*. United States: Adventures Unlimited Press, 1996.

Hitching, Francis. *The World Atlas of Mysteries*. London: Pan Books, 1979.

Hough, Peter. *Supernatural Britain*. London: BCA, 1994.

Lambert, R. S. *Exploring the Supernatural*. London: Arthur Barker Ltd., 1955.

Lum, Peter. *Fabulous Beasts*. London: Thames & Hudson, 1952.

MacBride, Likeke R. *Petroglyphs of Hawaii*. Hawaii: Petroglyph Press Ltd., 2001.

Mack, Lorrie, et al, (Ed.). *The Unexplained*. London: Orbis, 1984.

Michell, John and Robert J. M. Rickard. *Phenomena a Book of Wonders*. London: Thames & Hudson, 1977.

Morin, Patricia, (Ed.). *Inspiration Journal*. Hawaii: Char Ravelo, 2003.

Muck, Otto. *The Secret of Atlantis*. London: Collins, 1979.

Paget, Peter. *The Welsh Triangle*. London: Granada, 1979.

Pott, Mrs. Henry. *Francis Bacon and his Secret Society*. London: Sampson Low, Marston & Co., 1891.

Pukui, M. K. *The Waters of Kane and Other Legends of the Hawaiian Islands*. Hawaii: Kamehameha Schools Bernice Pauahi Bishop Estate, 1994.

Reader's Digest Association. *Folklore, Myths and Legends of Britain*. London: The Reader's Digest Ass. Ltd., 1973.

Reader's Digest Association. *Strange Stories, Amazing Facts*. London: The Reader's Digest Ass. Ltd., 1975.

Rolleston, T. W. *Celtic Myths and Legends*. London: Studio Editions Ltd., 1994.

Russell, Eric Frank. *Great World Mysteries*. London: Mayflower, 1967.

Saltzman, Pauline. *The Strange and the Supernormal*. New York: Paperback Library, Inc., 1968.

Schutz, Albert J. *Things Hawaiian*. Hawaii: Island Heritage Publishing, 1997.

Snow, Edward Rowe. *Strange Tales from Nova Scotia to Cape Hatteras*. New York: Dodd, Mead & Company, 1946.

Subramunijaswami, Satguru Sivaya. *Lemurian Scrolls: Angelic Prophesies Revealing Human Origins*. India, United States: Himalayan Academy Pubns, 1998.

Spencer, John & Anne. *The Encyclopaedia of the World's Greatest Unsolved Mysteries*. London: Headline Book Publishing, 1995.

Stone, Margaret. *Supernatural Hawaii*. Hawaii: Aloha Graphics and Sales, 1979.

Tomas, Andrew. *Atlantis from Legend to Discovery.* London: Sphere Books, 1973.

Wallis Budge, E. A. *The Book of the Dead.* Secaucus, New Jersey: The Citadel Press, 1984 Reprint.

Watson, Lyall. *Supernature.* London: Coronet Books, 1974.

Welfare, Simon and John Fairley. *Arthur C. Clarke's Mysterious World.* London: William Collins Sons & Company Ltd., 1980.

Westervelt, W. D. *Hawaiiam Legends of Ghosts and Ghost-Gods.* Hawaii: Mutual Publishing, 2003.

Whitehead, Ruth Holmes. *Stories From The Six Worlds.* Nova Scotia: Nimbus Publishing Ltd., 1988.

Williams, Neville. *Francis Drake.* London: George Weidenfeld & Nicolson Ltd., 1973.

Wilson, Colin & Damon. *Unsolved Mysteries Past and Present.* London: Headline Book Publishing plc., 1993.

Wilson, Colin and Dr. Christopher Evans, (Eds.). *The Book of Great Mysteries.* London: Robinson Publishing, 1986.

Wilson, Colin. *From Atlantis to the Sphinx.* London: Virgin Books, 1997.

Wilson, Ian. *Worlds Beyond.* London: Weidenfield and Nicolson, 1986.

Young, George. *Ancient Peoples and Modern Ghosts.* Queensland, Nova Scotia: George Young Publications, 1980.